WORLD CLASS
BUYER AGENT

MICHAEL HELLICKSON

with

Ron Anderson, Cheri Benjamin, Misti Bruton,
Brian Curtis, & Jesse Zagorsky

Published by Club Wealth® Coaching & Consulting, Bonney Lake, WA

Cover Design by Damonza.com
Interior Graphic Design by Robin Ludwig Design, Inc.
Formatting by Bob Houston eBook Formatting

ISBN: 978-1-73-108088-2

Acknowledgements

I would like to thank my co-authors, Ron Anderson, Cheri Benjamin, Misti Bruton, Brian Curtis, and Jesse Zagorsky for their dedication and hard work on this book.

Also, a heartfelt thank you to Luigi Caprio and Christine Andreasen for their contributions to the book as well…

Thank you to Traci for her role in making it all happen.

To our Teams, our families, and our spouses a special thank you for putting up with the long hours on nights and weekends putting this together.

Creating World Class content, particularly in book format, is FAR more work than one would think.

Finally, to you, the reader: THANK YOU for purchasing, reading, and implementing what you've learned in this and other Club Wealth Books. We hope you'll feel inspired to give it a 5 Star Review, and to recommend it to others.

Table of Contents

Acknowledgements... 3

Table of Contents... 5

Introduction by Michael Hellickson 7

Chapter 1 The Role of a World Class Buyer Agent 13

Chapter 2 The ISA 39

Chapter 3 The Showing Agent 49

Chapter 4 The Career Path.. 57

Chapter 5 Eagles Don't Flock with Turkeys.........................71

Chapter 6 The Perfect Daily Schedule 77

Chapter 7 CRM 101

Chapter 8 Selling to the DISC Profile 119

Chapter 9 Buyer Lead Generation 131

Chapter 10 Mastering the Massive Open House 151

Chapter 11 Lead Follow Up 171

Chapter 12 Lead Conversion 195

Chapter 13 The Buyer Consultation 219

Chapter 14 How to Create the Ultimate Buyer Experience......... 231

Chapter 15 The VIP Buyer Program 241

Chapter 16 Showing Property 257

Chapter 17 Mastering Key Sales and Negotiating Skills 281

Chapter 18 Writing the Bulletproof Offer 309

Chapter 19 Writing Offers on Short Sales and REO 329

Chapter 20 Working with Luxury Buyers 345

Chapter 21 Safety First 359

Chapter 22 Client Appreciation Program............................. 365

Chapter 23 Building Wealth 379

Chapter 24 Coaching and Training 389

Chapter 25 Scripts and Role Play 403

Chapter 26 Wrap It Up 421

Glossary of Terms..425

About the Authors..431

INTRODUCTION

Introduction by Michael Hellickson

You and/or the Buyer Agents on your Team aren't selling enough homes, you're making just enough to stay in the business, but not enough to be truly excited about it. You need specific systems you can follow that will allow you to attract business instead of chasing business, that will result in more closed transactions and more money in your pocket, and you need, for the love of all that is good and decent in this world, you MUST HAVE some time off and balance in your life!

In this book, we're going to solve all of these problems and more by giving you the specific systems our Buyer Agents use to close over 50-100 homes per year EACH, while working less, dropping fewer leads, and LOVING their Team, what they do, and who they do it with!

We're going to teach you how to get 50-150 people to your next open house; bring in more leads than you can possibly imagine with little effort and little to no money; convert more leads in less time; subtly change what you are saying to compel prospects to do business with you; identify and sell to each of the different DISC personality styles; conduct a buyer consultation that gets clients excited about working with you, and only you; and essentially everything you need to know to sell well over 50 homes a year while taking 2 days a week and 8 weeks a year off!

At Club Wealth® we believe that if you want to climb Mt. Everest, you need a guide who has been to the top of Mt. Everest before.

For that reason, we only consider those who have sold hundreds, even thousands of homes, qualified to teach you how to get to your next level in real estate sales.

As a Team Leader for over 20 years, my Team and I consistently listed and sold over 100 homes per month. My co-authors have each had similarly outrageous results, each having closed hundreds of homes per year as well!

We LOVE helping other agents succeed. We don't have time for BS, and we know you don't either. That's why we've broken down everything in this book to simple, digestible, easy-to-follow steps, and have even given you additional, up-to-the-minute downloadable material you can access quickly and with no additional investment!

By following the systems in this book, you will begin to notice an almost immediate increase in your conversion rates and overall production, resulting in more closings and more cash in your pocket. Your perception of the real estate industry will begin to change quickly as well, as you notice your debt disappearing, your savings increasing, your investments growing, and your lifestyle improving. (We've been told it's pretty good for your relationship and family life as well)

We subscribe to the belief that:

No success in the world can compensate for failure in the home.

We fully expect that you will begin to take far more time off, and have far more disposable income, as you implement what you learn by reading the chapters before you.

That said; don't take my word for it! Jump on Facebook at www.facebook.com/ClubWealth and read our client testimonials. Focus on the many stories, like co-authors Misti Bruton's and Cheri Benjamin's, who each had closed fewer than 40 units in their best year prior to joining Club Wealth®. Within 3 years, they were doing 250 and 430+ units per year, respectively!

Look at the results of Buyer Agents like Eric Eby on the Brian Curtis Team in Bentonville, Arkansas, who, by following the principles taught herein, closed 25 units in his first 9 months in real estate, 38 the next year, and 50 the 3rd year! Oh, and he closed those 50 units taking 1-2 full days off each week, AND he took a full month and a half off to work on the new home he purchased!!

We are SO CONFIDENT that you will sell more homes, make more money, become debt free, have a better life, grow your investments, move closer to an abundant lifestyle, and get to a place where you and your Team LOVE selling real estate and who you do it with, that we will GUARANTEE it, or we'll refund you 100% of the price of this book.

Simply send it back to us (address is on our website at www.ClubWealth.com) with a note that says you've read it in its entirety, and implemented what we've taught you without accomplishing EVERYTHING I mentioned above, and we'll gladly send you your money back!

DON'T DELAY!! You are literally as close as a few hours of reading away from achieving the business and the life you deserve! Get your life back by reading this book cover to cover RIGHT NOW!!

I promise it will be the best decision you've made thus far in your business!

So, start reading it RIGHT NOW. Take notes, highlight important passages, dog ear the pages if you got the paperback, and start shopping for your new [insert dream item here], because your life is about to change FOREVER!

CHAPTER 1

THE ROLE OF A WORLD CLASS BUYER AGENT

Module 1 - Team or Solo?

This may be one of the biggest decisions you make in your real estate career. Should I join a Team or become a solo Agent? Let's take an inside look at the role of a solo Agent first.

As a solo Agent, you will be lead generating every day. Some examples of lead generation include door knocking, hosting open houses, purchasing leads, pursuing online leads, utilizing your sphere of influence, and building referrals.

Other things to consider are knowing how to do lead follow-up and lead conversion. A lot of time will be spent learning how to hone your skills, memorizing scripts and dialogues, and working with role-play partners.

Higher producing solo Agents generally hire a coach, since, according to NAR (The National Association of Realtors), Agents with a coach outperform those who don't have a coach by 8x!

Contract negotiation, marketing, data entry, transaction management, closing attendance, and conflict resolution are some other duties that solo Agents must perform on their own.

And if all that isn't bad enough, you have to fund the entire venture. This means coming out of pocket for expenses such as coaching, training, events, brokerage fees, closing gifts, client events, and marketing. Going to events alone can cost in the thousands of dollars with travel expenses such as airline tickets, gas costs, registration fees, tickets, hotel costs, and your meals.

You also have the cost of lead generation. Realtor.com is about $100 per lead. Zillow is about $300 per month for impressions (not leads). PPC (Pay Per Click) is anywhere from $3.50 to $25 per lead. Facebook is around $1.25 per lead and requires massive nurturing. Sign calls from listings run $950 to upwards of $5000 for marketing the listing properly. Of course, there are hundreds of lead sources available, and it's a good thing, as it can take up to 10+ lead sources to make $100,000 per year.

What about your support staff? One of your first, if not your very first, hires should be an assistant. One of our favorite quotes at Club Wealth® is, "If you don't have an assistant, you are one."

Once you have a decent-sized database, you need somewhere to keep track of all your leads. You will want to investigate purchasing a Contact Relationship Manager (CRM) system, which is a software program (usually online) to input and track all of your clients and leads. Systems can easily run you upwards of $1500 for your CRM. A quality website will likely cost $200 - $1000 per month to maintain.

Let's not forget about your phone system. Your phone system options may include: Call Action, Ring Central, IVR and office phones. This expense alone can easily run up to $1000 per month.

Lead Incubation Systems are another expense. Agentology, Agent Legend, and AVIA can easily add up to another $1000 per month. An in-house ISA can cost upwards of $4000 per month.

You also have to consider office space. Depending on your market area, you're looking at rents in the amount of $900 - $5000 or more per month. That doesn't even include utilities and other expenses like Internet and heat (both nice to have).

What if you have a bad month? What are your options? Cut back? Borrow from family? Run up your credit card debt? Apply for a commission advance? This is a real – and common – issue that a lot of newer real estate Agents face every year. It's also the reason why most end up leaving the business (over 87% in the first 2 years, according to NAR). They didn't financially plan and budget correctly – if at all – for running a real estate business.

The real problem is you have to be a "Jack of all Trades". You can't focus on what you're born to do.

Don't misunderstand; going solo can be a great option for many Agents. That said; it is becoming increasingly more difficult each year to survive, let alone thrive, as a solo Agent. The Team Model has simply taken over the industry, and it's here to stay. In most cases, we recommend newer Agents spend at least two years as a member of a Team before considering going solo.

Module 2 – Why Join a Team?

There are many things an Agent can do to generate income. If you are a brand new Agent, you can't cover them all without the proper training and coaching. Even with coaching and training, there is simply too much for one person to effectively do alone at a high level.

To be successful, and to provide the highest possible customer service, you need to be focused on just a couple of ways to make money. Once you have mastered a few techniques, you can move on to other ways to lead generate.

One great way to cut down the learning curve is to join a Team. What would take you five years to learn solo can be cut down to between six months and a year. Let's take a look at some of the other ways joining a Team can be beneficial to Agents.

Why join a Team?

Agents create Teams for many reasons. The majority of Agents have the same main goal – to sell a lot of properties by building up their client base. Some Agents are just happy to do enough business to keep them busy or to just do it as a hobby. They use only their sphere of influence to achieve this goal. However, if you want to build a career as a successful Agent with massive income – six figures and beyond – you should consider joining a Team first so you can shortcut the learning curve.

The best thing about joining a Team is your Team Leader funds everything so you don't have to! Things like systems for running a real estate business, leads to bring in business, office space in order to conduct business, support staff to help the Team members, events for your clients, education, training, coaching and so much more.

More reasons to join a Team

When you join a Team, your Team Leader will provide:

- Coaching - This can be group coaching or one-on-one coaching.
- Training - Training for the entire Team to cover a variety of

topics.

- Mentorship - Solid mentoring from seasoned professionals.
- Accountability - Accountability in order to maintain and reach your goals.
- Stability - This is the most important thing you'll need from your Team Leader.
- Consistent income – This goes hand in hand with stability. On a Team, you are far less likely to be riding the commission roller coaster, and far more likely to have relatively consistent income month in and month out, while still being in complete control of how much you make based on how much effort you put in.

Being on a Team is a lot like being part of a farmer's co-op. A small wheat farmer needs a combine to compete with the bigger wheat farms. A combine is a machine that can harvest wheat and it costs easily over a million dollars. The really expensive ones have drones that measure the moisture in the air so it can tell the machine where to go using GPS and autonomous driving technology. Of course, the smaller farmers can't afford an expensive piece of machinery like that, so, they get together with several of the other smaller farms and share in the expense of a quality combine. That's working smarter, not harder. Now they can compete with the big boys.

Teams are very similar. Essentially, Agents gather together to share the expense of staff, advertising, lead generation, coaching, training, equipment and more, under the direction support and guidance of a Team Leader.

Career Advancement Opportunities

Generally, the members of the Sales Team start off as an ISA,

World Class Buyer Agent

Showing Agent, or Buyer Agent.

Some Agents figure out early on in their career they like working with sellers rather than buyers, and they make the switch to being a Listing Agent.

Make sure you and your Team Leader are on the same page before making such a transition, however, as Buyer Agents and Listing Agents are two VERY different and distinct personality types, as you will read below.

There are many career advancement opportunities within a Team. As you start growing and you begin getting more and more transactions under your belt, your Team Leader may offer you the position of a Squad Leader.

Seasoned Team Leaders often develop the talent for recognizing who has the qualities of being an ideal leader. The great ones work hard to cultivate talented potential leaders.

Larger Teams generally offer Buyer Agent Squad Leader and Listing Agent Squad Leader positions to their best and most qualified Agents. Each are roles you may strive to grow into. Keep in mind there are MANY factors that determine qualification and selection for leadership positions, including exceeding Team standards at all times, being an example of what positive Team culture is all about, supporting the Team Leader publicly (even when they are clearly wrong), reserving criticism for private conversations, interacting well with others (including staff), displaying a deep understanding and solid implementation of Team and industry standards and expectations, and so on.

Assuming you have extremely strong leadership skills and

capabilities, and you are truly a team player, the sky's the limit for higher positions on the Team. Some may even include Local or Regional Team Leader.

Module 3 - What is the Role of the World Class Buyer Agent

As a Buyer Agent, there are 3 things you will focus on daily:

- Lead Generation - Prospecting for new buyer leads
- Lead Follow-Up - Follow up with Team leads and other leads
- Lead Conversion - Setting appointments

Additionally, other tasks that you are responsible for:

- Facilitating the buyer's consultation
- Getting the buyer agency agreements signed
- Discovering the buyer's wants and needs
- Consulting with the buyer to find which home is right for them
- Find and showing property
- Researching homes in the area
- Scheduling appointments to show the homes
- Writing contracts
- Negotiating with sellers and buyers
- Properly preparing documents for admin staff
- Working with admin staff to ensure a smooth closing process
- Meeting inspectors and appraisers
- Attending final signing at closing

Module 4 - Buyer Agent Additional Duties Part 2

Writing the Offer

Once you find a buyer a home, the next step is to write the offer.

Where is the best place to write an offer? Meet your client in a public place such as:

- Chick-fil-A
- Starbucks
- Office
- Or any public place that has a Wi-Fi (for safety reasons)

How are you going to write up the offer?

- With your laptop or other electronic device
- Use your E-Sign Software
- Bring a Portable Printer
- Use the Club Wealth® Offer Sheet
- Doing a quick CMA before writing an offer will help you and your clients understand the real value of the property, and what it is likely to sell for, thus helping you help them submit an offer that is far more likely to be accepted. The CMA should be:
  - 1 sheet - No pictures – K.I.S.S. (Keep It Simple Stupid)
  - 3 Active, 3 Pending, 3 Sold

Submit and Negotiate Offers

Once you've given the CMA to your buyer, it's time to discuss:

- Offer price
- Contingencies such as financing options (What type of loan are they getting? VA, Conventional, FHA?)

- Lender Recommendations - You should give 3 lender recommendations, and always check to see who is your Team preferred lender. This is a requirement on most Teams, and should be on all. Recommending lenders not approved by your Team Leader is often grounds for termination, as it shows a lack of support and/or understanding of Team goals and objectives.
- Home inspections
  - Recommended inspectors (3 recommendations). Again, only recommend Team approved inspectors. This is a very big deal.
  - Reasonable requests for repairs - Let the buyers know the home inspection report is meant to include a comprehensive look at the home, and many items on the report do not need to be done now, and/or will not likely be done by the seller.
- Submit the offer
  - Present to Listing Agent
  - Present to Seller - if possible
- Negotiate the offer FOR THE WIN!!!

Now What?

After your offer has been accepted, you are just beginning the long road to closing. As a solo Agent, your work has just begun. If you are on a Team, you will hand it off to the Transaction Coordinator.

Each Team differs, but generally, from here forward you would only handle:

- Meeting the appraiser

- Meeting all inspectors
- Negotiating requests for repairs

Some Teams will have a licensed Transaction Coordinator to handle some or all the tasks listed above, depending on Team size.

- Re-commit buyers with remorse. It is possible your buyers may start to get cold feet. It's your job to reassure them.
- Counsel buyers not to make any big credit purchases.
- Attend the closing. This is the best part of your job!
- Follow up with buyers post-closing.
- Host housewarming party.
- Stay in touch and invite to Client Events (Check out our video blog and free checklist on World Class Buyer Events at http://www.clubwealth.com/ClientEvents)

Module 5- The Etiquette of a World Class Buyer Agent

As Real Estate Agents, we must dedicate ourselves to rules of etiquette so we can establish a solid foundation for success. When professional etiquette is followed, all involved are able to feel more comfortable, and things tend to flow more smoothly. When it is not, tensions are high, emotions get out of control, transactions fall apart, and relationships are (often) irrevocably damaged.

Try to remember, you will more than likely bump into Agents over and over again. The Future You will be glad the Today You treated others with respect, thus laying the foundation for a greater opportunity in the years to come.

Communicate Clearly

Poor communications can often lead to increase stress and confusion for all parties. It is essential to place an emphasis on effective communication. One of the easiest ways to do this is to identify the preferred method of communication (phone, text, or email) when working with your real estate clients, your Team members, and all persons involved in real estate transactions. This will ensure clear and consistent communication with all parties throughout every interaction.

Always Be Honest

Creating a circle of trust between you, your clients and colleagues is crucial to your overall success as an Agent. Even if you need to share information that is not necessarily ideal, it's imperative to always tell the truth, and to do so in a timely manner.

Simply put, nobody benefits from dishonesty, and ruining your dependability can be incredibly detrimental to your career as an Agent.

Always Be Polite and Respectful to All Colleagues

We are in a business where we constantly co-op with the same Agents. Answer their questions in a timely manner, return phone calls and emails promptly, and always greet another Agent with a smile. No matter how difficult the transaction or the other Agent is, remember to be polite and professional. You never know when you'll need someone to assist you if the tables are turned. Besides, being courteous isn't just polite; it's good business too.

Don't Prejudge Other Agents

Don't let other Agents' opinions of other Agents influence the way you treat them. Just because another Agent in your office had a bad experience with someone doesn't mean you will have the same bad experience.

Try to get to know the Agents you work with before you pass judgment. If you do have a bad experience with an Agent, don't take it personally. You don't know what's going on in the Agent's personal life that may be affecting their work life.

In essence, always assume the best of intentions in everyone, as you would likely desire them to assume you are well intended also.

Imagine you see a police officer fly by you, lights and sirens blazing. Then, suddenly, the lights and sirens turn off as the officer pulls into a donut shop.

Do you assume they were abusing their power to get their Blueberry Cream Cheese Pillow Donut faster, or do you think to yourself, "The call they were headed to must have been a false alarm"?

In general, striving to be less critical and more tolerant of EVERYONE in our lives is a good policy to live by and will bring greater peace and happiness.

Take Responsibility

Nobody is perfect... we all make mistakes. What will set you apart from everyone else is a willingness to take ownership of these learning opportunities.

If something goes wrong, don't continually try to blame another Agent, the mortgage lender or the title company. Take responsibility for your mistakes, and use them as an opportunity to grow as an Agent and a person.

Don't let the opinions of other Agents influence the way you treat them.
Work out differences before involving offers.

Don't talk trash. Just don't. It doesn't look good on you and you'll gain a reputation you don't want.

Never speak poorly about any Agent, lender, escrow, or anyone else in the business.

That goes for clients too. If people see you are willing to talk about other colleagues behind their back why would they want to do business with you? Won't they assume if you'll talk about others that way, you'll probably talk about them that way behind their back as well?

This type of behavior can easily become a cancer on a Team.

In 2008, we grew from around 400 units a year to over 100 units a month. Things got very busy, very quickly, and soon, my Admin Team was overwhelmed.

The mounting stress was evident, particularly as one Team member began expressing her frustrations with certain clients and Sales Team members, their crazy expectations, and lack of apparent responsibility or accountability.

This attitude spread from her to another Team member, and then to another, and another, until our office was a sea of negativity so tangible it could be felt.

Once I recognized it, and our Team's general lack of appreciation for the people who made our lifestyles possible, I began making gratitude our major theme. We worked hard to fix the problems. Eventually, over a year later, we had finally implemented systems, processes, behaviors, attitudes, and belief systems that enabled us to begin delivering a World Class Customer Experience.

Unfortunately, much damage had been done in the Agent community. Many Agents hated doing business with us. We had earned a terrible reputation, and deservedly so.

It took years to mostly recover from it, and to this day there are still Agents who think ill of us.

Years later, I finally came to understand, the source of the original problem was NOT the Team member with the bad attitude towards some clients and Team members, it was me!

My poor leadership at the time, including but not limited to venting to her and other Team members created the problem.

I had failed to take extreme ownership of the culture I had created.

As a Team member, Squad or Team Leader, make sure you are honest with yourself and take full and complete responsibility for your actions. It is YOUR responsibility to help the Team be the best it can be, regardless of your role on the Team.

Provide Constructive Feedback After Showings

Make sure it is constructive. Remember this is someone's home and while your client may not be interested, you may end up listing the house one day, or eventually doing business with that person or their Agent.

Be respectful; they allowed you into their home. Some Listing Agents provide direct feedback to the seller including Agent information.

Most Agents REALLY appreciate receiving constructive feedback that can help them and their sellers. Due to few Agents providing feedback, they are likely to remember you and your Team as a result of you taking the time to do so.

Make it a habit to ALWAYS take the few seconds to provide feedback on every house you show. When you feel voice-to-voice with the Agent would be a good fit, look for opportunities to see if he or she would be interested in chatting with your Team Leader about possibly joining the Team.

Be punctual! Call if you are running late or if you need to cancel.

Coach's Corner: 5 minutes early is on time, and on time is late.

Encourage your Team to be courteous and update listings right away with accurate information ands status changes. This, again, will foster great relations with area Agents, and will help your Team develop the stellar reputation it deserves!

When Showing Property

When preparing to show property, read the broker's remarks and instructions before scheduling a showing. By doing your research, you won't have problems gaining access to the property, and you can avoid hassling Listing Agents or sellers with dead-on-arrival showing requests.

Getting these relationships off to the right start is critical to the success of any offers you may eventually write on the property.

Don't park in a property's driveway at an open house or during a private showing.

Take off your shoes. This should go without saying, but when you're in other people's homes, take off your shoes.

Leave the home the way you found it. Make sure doors and windows are closed and locked. Double check the lights are all turned off that you turned on (unless there were certain lights left on – the seller may want it that way). Regardless, leave it the way you found it.

Contact Listing Agents about problems with a property. If you uncover an issue with a property, reach out directly to the Listing Agent about it. After all, you would want to know if there was an issue with one of your listings, wouldn't you?

Send complete contracts. If possible, type your contracts so they are presented crisp and clean with no errors.

Give Agents a heads up when sending contracts. Don't just text and email them. Pick up the phone and call them so you can establish a good, working relationship.

Ask them how they would like it written up, and then do your level best to accommodate their requests.

Cancel appointments in a timely manner. Some sellers put in a great amount of time when preparing a home for showing. When you have an appointment to show and need to cancel, please contact the Listing Agent as soon as humanly possible.

If the seller is home during the showing, keep conversation with them light and never discuss terms of potential offers with them. Show respect to their Agent by edifying them and never in any way criticizing or speaking ill of them

Maintain Professionalism

- Answer texts, calls, and emails on time. Don't leave people in the dark. Keeping everyone in the loop even when there's nothing to say will go a long way towards creating your Ultimate Client Experience.
- Make sure you answer the phone in a professional manner.
- Be humble. Anyone involved in real estate understands the industry can be quite tumultuous at times. As a result, it's crucial to stay humble and realistic about the services you can provide.
- Don't boast or over-promise to your clients. If you fail to meet their expectations it can create an unfavorable experience for all involved.
- Use a professional email address. If you are on a Team, use the email address your Team provides for you.
- Keep social media accounts professional. Avoid politics,

religion, and other potentially divisive topics.

- Don't look like a slob. Always dress professionally, no matter where you live. Flip-flops may be okay for your clients to wear in a resort town, but you should still dress professionally. There is much debate about this in the industry, as casual has become trendy. Know this: you are at greater risk of losing opportunity by being underdressed than you ever will be by being overdressed, so why risk tens of thousands of dollars so you can "be your authentic self"? You can be authentic and still look professional, and frankly, the best Teams expect it. Does this mean you need to wear a suit and tie like I do? No, but you should always look the part of a professional who is about to charge their client tens of thousands of dollars.

- If you aren't present for the closing, at the very least, drop off the keys and a closing gift as a thank you to the client.

- Help inexperienced Agents. You were once a new, struggling Agent. Remember to look back and help others as others have helped you.

- Educate buyers. Not only is it your job, but also it's your duty to educate buyers so they are 100% informed and confident in purchasing their property.

At the end of the day, there's no perfect method for ensuring real estate success. However, every Agent should take a moment to step back and reflect on how they can improve. By following a few simple rules of etiquette, you can build a formidable foundation to propel your career forward with fewer bumps in the road along the way.

Module 6 - How Do You Make It Happen?

What is your fastest path to cash as a Buyer Agent?

- Team leads - Some are fresh leads daily. Some leads are follow-up leads. Some are old leads haven't been called in a long time.

Coach's Corner: When I was prospecting, I loved calling the old leads. Why? There is literally no follow-up from other Agents. They just don't do it. No one else is calling those leads, and the leads are just sitting out there.

- Sphere of Influence - Most Teams will send out a *Welcome to the Team* post on social media and maybe even snail mail. Share the post and use it to contact your sphere to let them know about your new role on the Team! Make sure you add your SOI to the Team's CRM, and tag them as your clients. This will enable your Team to help you with marketing to them, and will ensure other Team members don't accidently sell your high school buddies a home!

- Open Houses - This can be a speedy way to cash. Buyers come flocking to open houses if they are marketed correctly. Take advantage of doing open houses so you can meet a plethora of potential clients! We recommend 4-6 open houses per month as a minimum for Buyer Agents not yet hitting 2 closings a month consistently. As a brand new Buyer Agent, consider holding daily open houses using our Massive Open House Strategy.

Getting started can be tough, especially if you are a solo Agent. If you are on a Team or are a new Agent, it can easily be a 6-month process to develop a consistent income. It takes time build a pipeline of solid leads and resources.

It isn't easy, but with hard work, proper systems, the right strategy, and the right Team, it will absolutely be worth it!

Commission Splits

How you are paid can vary from Team to Team, from position to position on a Team, and can be impacted by a number of factors.

Popular Options Include:

- 50/50 split
- Some larger Teams offer 28% – 40% splits (to the Agent)
- Small salary plus commission
- Alternate Tiered Monthly Commission Structure - this is a popular way to pay Agents on a Team as it's dependent on your closed transactions, so the more you close, the more you get paid:
    - 0-2 transactions – 45%
    - 3-4 transactions – 50%
    - 5-6 transactions – 55%
    - 7+ transactions – 60%

- Exclusion list – When you join a Team from another Team or are coming in as solo Agent, most likely any ACTIVE or PENDING clients will apply to the exclusion list. This means you'll need to provide a written list, and discuss with your Team Leader how these will be handled.
- SOI is at same splits as above! It doesn't matter if the leads came from your sphere, you will still be paid the same. That said, providing the Team Leader with a written and/or electronic copy of your SOI list is MISSION CRITICAL so everyone knows who's who.

The Role of a World Class Buyer Agent

Module 7- What am I Responsible for?

There are certain production expectations for a Team member. These may (and generally do) include:

- To close 2 units per month (Team minimum)
  - Set 1-2 appointment/day (NEW client, not existing)
  - Contact (having conversations) 10 NEW people/day
  - 50 not-yet-contacted calls/day
- If you want to be a 60+ unit/year closer:
  - Set 2 appointments per day
  - CONTACT (conversations) 25 people/day
  - 100 not-yet-contacted calls per day (500 per week)
- If you think these numbers sound high, remember: Eagles fly high, Turkeys don't.

Accountability and Motivation

If you want to close 60 units or more with your Team, you must:

- Understand motivation MUST COME FROM WITHIN
- YOU need to hold YOURSELF accountable
- Sharing with your Team will increase level of accountability

> *"When performance is measured and reported, the rate of improvement accelerates!"* – Thomas S. Monson

- Report your numbers to your Team Leader DAILY
- Celebrate the success of Team members

Team Participation Expectations

You will be expected to attend and do the following:

- Morning Team Huddles
  - BE ON TIME
  - Dressed and ready for the day - even if it's over the phone
  - Have numbers ready from yesterday
  - Be positive
  - Uplift others
  - Ask questions
    - Go over your client's wants/needs
    - Policies
    - Contract questions, etc....
  - Complaints can be voiced to the Team Leader privately

- Weekly Call Nights
- Weekly Team Meeting
- Team Activities
- Squad Leader Sessions
- Monthly 1-on-1 with Team or Squad Leader
- Club Wealth® Mastermind Calls
- Club Wealth® Buyer Agent Boot Camp Annually
- Complete ALL Assigned Trainings and Certifications

Coach's Corner: Many of our Coach's Team Huddles are at 7am in the morning. It can be a huge adjustment for most people because it is early. We look for 100% participation. Keep in mind, why you are doing this? Why are you on the Team and whom did you make a commitment to? How will your life change by doing this?

Module 8 - Generalist or Specialist

Where's the money? There is a big difference in being a Generalist and a Specialist.

Let's take for example a Dentist. For a General Dentist, they earn around $153,000 annually. The Oral Surgeon, on the other hand, makes around $1,200,000 year. Which would you rather be?

- The Generalist Agent
  - This is a "Jack of all trades"
  - Does a little bit of everything
  - National Average: 4-6 closings per year

- The Buyer Agent Specialist
  - CAN close 10+ units per month!
  - Usually closes 2-6 units per month
  - CAN make over $500,000/year with NO expenses!
  - VERY common to make $200,000+ with no expenses!
  - GREAT ones get Showing Agents

Deciding between specialties is relatively easy...

Buyer Agents tend to be nurturers, educators, enjoy walking clients through the process, making sure they are having a World Class Experience. They tend to be high I on the DISC Profile, and love loving others and being loved. They are generally warm, caring individuals, and people are often naturally drawn to them.

Listing Agents, on the other hand, tend to be the type who prefers to kick down the front door, punch you in the face, and make you sign. Essentially, they tend to be high D on the DISC Profile, preferring to get down to business, be direct and quick and get it done! Like me, they tend to have to work hard to share their feelings and appreciation towards others, and generally don't very often.

Which do you feel best describes you?

THE DIFFERENCE
– BETWEEN A –
BUYER AGENT & LISTING AGENT

BUYER AGENT:	LISTING AGENT:
• Nurtures	• Kicks Down the Front Door
• Guides	• Punches Them in the Face
• Educates	• Makes Them Sign
• Walks Through the Process	• CLOSER
• Is VERY PATIENT	• NOT Super Patient
	• AGGRESSIVE with the Process

Mastering Your Specialty

To master your specialty, it takes a commitment to professional development. What does this mean? Generally, it takes around 10,000 hours to master any given profession or vocation.

You want to focus on your specialty, not the things a Transaction Coordinator, your Administrative Assistant, or other staff members can assist with.

Final Thoughts on Your Role as a Buyer Agent

One common complaint is Agents don't answer their phone or return phone calls. Don't be that Agent! It's simple: Develop and live by your Perfect Daily Schedule. Done properly, you'll have scheduled time to return calls and check emails. Check out ClubWealth.com/PDS for the video and checklist on how to do it.

Know what speed to lead means and practice it! Once you receive a lead, respond right away! The first person that gets the lead usually gets the sale!

The largest purchaser of Realtor.com leads in the U.S. claims an 18 second speed to lead average on his Team! Clearly their systems and Team are tight and on point!

A simple lead follow-up method that works well and is easy to remember is the Club Wealth® Rule of 3: Essentially, you contact a lead 3 times a day for 3 days. 3 times a week for the next 3 weeks. 3 times a month for the next 3 months, or until you reach them. It's that simple!

Remember, you are here to provide a World Class Customer Experience. It's not just a service. A World Class Customer Experience gives you more referrals. When you provide it, you are able to work less because you get more referrals!

Your Team provides much of this for you. Don't bog yourself down with transactional and administrative work. Don't just chase listings instead of focusing on what you should be doing. Focus on giving your client a World Class customer experience. Focus on what you were born to do.

Focus on becoming a World Class Buyer Agent!

CHAPTER 2
THE ISA

Module 1 - What is an ISA, and WHY does it matter to you?

ISA stands for Inside Sales Agent. An ISA should never leave the office. Inside Sales, by definition, is done INSIDE the office. This means they stay inside ALL day. Often, the career path to becoming a Buyer Agent begins with becoming an ISA. As a Buyer Agent, the ISA can make a major difference for you on the Team, so you need to fully understand their role, and how it impacts you.

What does an ISA do? From the confines of their office, they provide leverage for the Buyer Agent. They are dedicated to lead generation, lead follow-up, and lead conversion (converting leads to appointments). Think of them as a safety net for missed calls and leads. That said; they are an augmentation to Agent activity, but not a replacement for the Agent's own prospecting and follow-ups. ISAs are like an injection of steroids to an Agent's already established lead-generating strength.

ISA WHAT THEY ARE:

- A safety net for missed calls and leads
- An augmentation to Agent activity
- A valued and beneficial member of the Team

40

ISA WHAT THEY AREN'T:

- A replacement for Agent prospecting and/or follow-up
- They are as skilled or knowledgeable in Real Estate as Agents
- An Agent's personal assistant
- Licensed in most states

Module 2 - What are the 3 Types of ISA?

There are three types of ISAs. In your quest to find the right Team, you may run across Teams that offer one, two, all three, or none of these.

Some ISAs take on a mix of multiple roles. The ISA is not one-size-fits-all, and you may find different variations depending on your Team's needs and budget. That said, let's go over the 3 basic types of ISA:

Buyer-Focused ISA

These ISAs take inbound lead calls such as Internet leads, sign call leads, and more, in an effort to set an appointment for a Buyer Agent. Whether it's a newlywed couple who saw your Team's billboard, or a hotshot investor scouring the Internet and probing Agents for opportunities in your market, this person handles their inquiries and expertly converts them into appointments for the Buyer Agents.

Seller Focused ISA

These ISAs make outbound calls like FSBO, Expireds, Circle Prospecting, Probate leads and more. Where a buyer-focused ISA handles the clients coming in, the seller-focused ISA utilizes these tools to go create clients, and they do it all from their corner of the office (generally a stand up desk!).

Recruiting Focused ISA

An ISA can also recruit Agents for the Team. This ISA can be licensed or non-licensed, depending upon your state requirements. More Agents mean more leads for the entire Team, which means more money for everyone. This makes the recruiting-focused ISA an important, and often underrated, part of the most successful Teams.

Other duties for an ISA:

- Putting leads into the Team CRM. The ISA should verify all the information is accurate. Every member on the Team should know the value is in the database, and all information should be as up-to-date and accurate as possible. Every minute spent writing emails to no one and making cold calls to dial tones is money lost for everyone.
- Setting up the next follow-up call. The ISA should follow up with leads, nurture those leads, schedule appointments for Buyer Agents, and refer clients to Buyer Agents and Team Lenders.
- Warm transfer, or taking a buyer's call and immediately transferring to an available Buyer Agent on the Team, along with sending any hot leads to Buyer Agents or Team Lenders.
- Keeping their skills sharp by practicing their scripts regularly and participating in role-play. Working from the office, an ISA has to rely heavily on their phone presence. In order to keep their scripts and improv abilities sharp as knife, they need regular honing.
- Attending Team meetings call nights, and daily huddles is a must. ISAs can't help their Team if they don't show up. The

Team can't help them if they don't participate fully. Showing up is simple, yet crucial.

- Participating in Club Wealth® trainings and events is expected, as is taking part in all other activities needed to become indoctrinated in Club Wealth® and into the Team.

Module 3 - Should All Teams Have ISAs?

The answer is: not necessarily. In order to understand how a potentially important role can go unneeded or unfilled, let's ask ourselves this: What does it take for a Team to have an ISA?

Generally, a Team will start with at least 10 Agents before they hire their first ISA. Most of these Agents should be selling a minimum of two houses a month. Why is that? You have to lead with revenue. Its important Team Leaders not lose money as they are growing the Team.

You'll want to make sure you have the Agents in place, and those Agents are creating the revenue necessary to pay the ISA. The ISA helps stimulate growth for a Team already approaching high volumes.

Basically, a successful Team doesn't utilize an ISA before it is necessary, much like a farmer wouldn't buy a combine harvester for the first garden in his backyard.

Should you expect leads and appointments from your Team as a Buyer Agent?

No, you shouldn't.

First of all, you have to understand the leads that come from the ISA are a benefit and a reward for the Agents who are already producing. These leads and appointments are for the Agents who are already making their calls, who are already scheduling their own appointments, and who are already closing two or more homes a month, and sometimes a minimum of four closings a month. Again, the ISA helps keep the Team from plateauing. They stimulate growth, but they don't kick start it. You need to be producing on your own, and at a high level, before you'll likely be eligible for ISA leads and appointments.

Module 4 - What are Qualities of an ISA?

There are certain qualities Team Leaders should look for when hiring an ISA. The ISA position is not for everyone and requires these specific qualities, talents, and skills:

- Action-oriented and high achiever
- Innate sales talent
- Thick skin – handles rejection frequently and moves on because they'll get told "NO!" a lot, and MUCH worse! Can they handle being sworn at, cursed at, being called a jerk by prospects? Are they okay with being screamed at and threatened? It's all part of the job and as an ISA, and can NOT be taken personally.
- Tenacious – Follows up on leads consistently and doesn't drop the ball
- Organized and manages time well
- Articulate and well spoken (strong phone voice)
- Team player – enjoys working in a Team environment
- Communicates effectively with peers, customers, and vendors in written and verbal form

- Focused – Has the ability to block out distractions and listen intently to conversations
- Knows how to create a sense of comfort and familiarity with leads/clients and is able to build instant rapport
- Career-development and training focused

Module 5 - Compensation Plan for ISA

There are several different ways an ISA can be compensated:

Salary plus commission model - A small salary (often minimum wage) is offered to take the edge off as the ISA builds their pipeline. A nice commission is also paid because you want the ISA to be motivated to set a lot of high quality appointments, which result in contracts and closings.

Straight commission model - Again, commission is a great motivator to set a lot of appointments. However, there's not a salary on top of this. The downside is sometimes a person doesn't have enough money set aside while they are building up their pipeline of leads and appointments. That's oftentimes why a salary plus commission is more appealing to potential ISAs.

Generally, compensation is tied to appointments and closings. As an ISA you want to get the most closings per lead.

Let's dive deeper into the mechanics of the ISA's compensation: The ISA only gets X amount of leads per month and they want to make sure they convert the highest percentage of those leads into closings. Guess what they're going to do? They are going to work really hard to cultivate those leads and nurture them properly, and they're probably going to want to have a say on which Agents get those leads. If you're that Agent who is a hard worker - who turns appointments into closings (an Eagle) - the ISA is going to know what will happen to a lead that's given to you.

If you're that Agent who doesn't close well (a Turkey), the ISA will not likely get paid for their efforts. If the ISA gives a hot lead to an Eagle, they will know with confidence it will close and they will get paid. What would you do?

An ISA will be picky about whom they give leads to and they will be in the Team Leader's ears. Be aware of that because it's just not the Team Leader who is going to want to see a Buyer Agent closing at a high rate. Smart Team Leaders listen to their ISAs when it comes to passing along leads.

An ISA will likely have oversight on Agent conversion ratios, meaning they are going to know exactly how many leads and appointments you/they create, how many of those leads you write contracts on, and how many of those contracts you close. Of course, no Agent will be batting a thousand on all of their leads, but if the final number - percentage of leads closed - gets too small, the ISA will be one of the first to know. And he or she will starve you for leads if they know they aren't going to be making commissions by feeding you before the other Agents.

See, ISA compensation comes from the Agent's side. The Team has to fund this in advance. That means the Agent contribution must be more than the actual cost to cover the ISA for the Team. That compensates for the risk, overhead, and profit.

Is it okay for the Team Leader to profit? Absolutely! You need your Team Leaders to be profitable. If they are not profitable, you won't have a Golden Goose for much longer, because they'll go out of business. If they're not profitable then you don't have an environment in which you can achieve your goals and the money you need. The Team Leaders need to make a profit so they can provide resources to make the whole Team successful. Success begets success, and failure begets failure. A winning Leader makes a winning Team and vice versa.

Module 6 - Career Path of an ISA

The career path of an ISA often starts as the entry point. If you are just beginning your career in real estate, you can choose to start off as an ISA. Eventually, you may become a Showing Agent once you're licensed, or you may become a Buyer Agent on the Team. From there you can advance to a Squad Leader, where you have multiple Buyer Agents working under you.

Another career path opportunity is to advance on to a Listing Agent and then a Listing Squad Leader. The natural progression from Squad Leader is on to the Director of Sales. Next is a Local Team Leader, then an Expansion Team Leader, and then on to a Regional Team Leader. From there you can travel on the path to the King or Queen of the Real Estate World. You never know!

All in all, you can be assured there is a career path and it doesn't just begin and end as an ISA. There are a lot of opportunities on Club Wealth® Teams. There are a lot of advancements through our model that allow you to grow as far and big as you'd like to grow assuming you are on a Club Wealth® Team or a Team that subscribes to the Club Wealth® model.

The question is will you engage and capitalize on this opportunity?

CHAPTER 3
THE SHOWING AGENT

CLUBWEALTH

Module 1 - What is a Showing Agent?

Showing Agents are a great addition to Teams that are ready for them. They provide leverage to every Buyer Agent on the Team; they assist in the home buying process, and showing homes is their bread and butter - just like it sounds. But they can also do so much more.

What is the role of a Showing Agent?

The Showing Agent's primary job is to perform the most time-consuming task for any Agent: showing homes. This enables the Buyer Agent to sell more homes in less time. (There are Buyer Agents, with Showing Agents, who close as many as 100 homes per year!)

It is not uncommon for future Buyer Agents to start off as Showing Agents. In order to grow in and beyond the Showing Agent position, consider shadowing a Buyer Agent while he or she performs tasks like conducting the buyer consultation, writing offers, and negotiating contracts. Other developmental tasks that can be performed in order to grow in and beyond the position are:

- Identify homes to show.
- Schedule showings.
- Show the house.
- Answer buyer questions.

50

- Provide buyer information on the area.
- Schedule and attend inspections.
- Provide buyers access to the home throughout the home buying process so the Agent can focus on what they need to do.
- Promptly return buyers' calls.
- Always promote Team concept.
- Consistently talk (even rave) about how great the Team is - that everyone on their Team is focused on certain responsibilities so the buyer gets the best service they possibly can - a World Class Customer Experience.
- Participate in Team meetings and trainings.
- Run any Team errands for the Team.
- --When a Showing Agent is picking up laundry, taking cars to get cleaned, or running errands for the Team, it allows the Team members to focus on their higher paying, dollar producing activities.

As you can see, starting off as a Showing Agent can be a wonderful option for an inexperienced Buyer Agent or for an Agent that is not getting any traction as a solo Agent.

Module 2 - Showing Agent Qualities

- Highly gregarious and sociable
- Optimistic and upbeat
- Comfortable spending copious amounts of time with a client (and possibly their family/kids) in the car and while showing homes
- Analytical ability in order to match clients' needs to homes
- Oriented toward growth and development

- Willing to learn and utilize scripts and dialogues
- Good at handling objections
- Dress and conduct themselves in a highly professional, but friendly manner
- Willing to do anything - no job is too small for the showing assistant
- Outgoing
- Strong desire to serve
- Ideal DISC profile: High IC or CI

As a World Class Buyer Agent, you'll provide leverage to the rainmaking Lead Agent, Squad Leader, or Team Leader by assisting buyers in their home buying process. Having a Showing Agent on your Team is providing the same leverage to you by increasing your capacity to handle more clients. In turn, this will increase your commission, as well as your time off!

Additionally, a Buyer Agent that utilizes a Showing Agent can develop into a leadership role on the real estate Team by grooming the Showing Agent to virtually build a Team within a Team, and to manage the buyers' side of the Team's business. Buyer Agents can also use multiple Showing Agents simultaneously, which unlocks the potential for increased income and leadership growth.

Module 3 - Showing Agent Compensation

Following the Team organizational model, a Showing Agent enables Buyer Agents to close more transactions and increase commission income by servicing more clients. Simply put: the more clients you can show houses to at once, the more potential closings you have on the books.

Think about this: on a given Saturday, you could easily be showing homes to 5, 10, or even more families **at the same time** if you had enough Showing Agents! Imagine if all you had to do that day was to write and negotiate contracts!

That said; how do we compensate these valuable assets to our Team?

There are several ways you can compensate a Showing Agent. These are the most popular:

1. **Share your split with the Showing Agent**. For example: A Buyer Agent is on 50/50 split with the Team, and shares half of that split (25%) with a Showing Agent. If the Buyer Agent normally closes 50 transactions annually at 50% commission split, and then uses a Showing Agent to close an additional 25 transactions at 25%, that Agent has increased his or her overall ability to earn. Assuming you use the Showing Agent on all of your transactions, you should be able to increase by even more closings, and you will have likely create more free time as well!

Coach Kase Knockenhauer suggests: "On the Shared Split Model, for each property [Buyer Agents sell] using a Showing Agent, the Buyer Agents save approximately 50-80% of their time while retaining 80% of their commission." Not bad!

2. **Pay your Showing Agent a flat fee - by the hour**. A flat fee of $25 per hour with a 2 hour minimum is the Club Wealth® preferred compensation model. It's clean, it's simple, it's fair, and it allows both the Buyer Agent and the Showing Agent the predictability they need to forecast and reach their income goals.

You can also pay a bonus for each buyer transaction that closes (from a property the Showing Agent showed). Should you choose to bonus (which we don't recommend), we suggest keeping it to a reasonable and immediate bonus, rather than a large bonus at closing. Showing Agents will likely prefer the instant gratification of a bonus at offer submission rather than a larger one only on those transactions that close.

Club Wealth® prefers the hourly pay route, paid by the Buyer Agent to the Team, who then pays the Showing Agent. For example: A Buyer Agent pays $25/hour (with a 2 hour minimum) for the service. The Showing Agent gets $20/hour of that. Why the disparity? The $5 difference goes to handle Team expenditures: e.g., offset paying the payroll taxes on the Showing Agent, making sure the book keeping is done properly, overseeing the Showing Agent Program etc.*

*Check with your state licensing board on how Showing Agent can be paid.

Coach's Corner: Ensure the Showing Agents are paid on a W2, it is tracked properly, and that taxes are paid appropriately.

Module 4 - Showing Agent Growth & Development

Team Leaders want a Showing Agent to grow within and beyond the position that they are in. At Club Wealth®, we recommend that a Showing Agent shadow one or (preferably) more Buyer Agents on a regular basis. Here are some steps to take in order to assure your own personal growth as a Showing Agent. If you are a Buyer Agent looking to turn your Showing Agent into a heavy-hitter like you, have them do these things as well. Keep in mind, as you do so, you may be able to build a Team within the Team, so helping your Showing

Agents grow is definitely in your best interest:

- Learn how to conduct a Buyer Consultation with a Buyer Agent present.
- Write offers with the help of a Transaction Coordinator or Buyer Agent.
- Negotiate contracts with supervision of Buyer Agent or Transaction Coordinator.
- Set S.M.A.R.T. goals - weekly, monthly and yearly.
- Develop your Perfect Daily Schedule (see www.ClubWealth.com/pds)
- Attend trainings as often as possible - be a sponge and soak up the knowledge.
- Establish role-play and dialogue practice. Get with other Showing Agent and/or Buyer Agents on the Team, and/or other Club Wealth® Teams for regular role-play.
- Participate fully and religiously in the Team meetings and daily huddles.
- Attend the Club Wealth® Annual Buyer Agent Boot Camp at Business Strategy Mastermind Conference (www.ClubWealth.com/bsm) and the monthly Buyer Agent Mastermind Calls included with your Team Leaders Club Wealth® Coaching.

A Showing Agent can be one of the most useful members to a Team looking to take on more buyers without sacrificing time in other areas. If you are a Buyer Agent who wants a Showing Agent on your Team, you have to earn it. Make sure your production is where it's expected to be, and go to your Team Leader and request one.

Remember that YOU ARE World Class, and act as if you are ready for that Showing Agent!

CHAPTER 4
THE CAREER PATH

CLUBWEALTH

Even if you're new to real estate, it's never too early to think about your career path. As a licensed Agent, you have exciting options for your future, including growing your career from an Inside Sales Agent to a Showing Agent and on to a Buyer Agent. From there you can go into management, be a Squad Leader, and follow the path all the way to National Team Leader, in charge of Expansion Markets. As you see, there are numerous career choices, each of which offer new and exciting opportunities and compensation possibilities!

Module 1 - Basic Team Structure

What does a Team look like? Well, that depends on a number of factors, but primarily on the Team Leader's vision, expertise, motivation, and relative success in building the Team.

There is no ONE RIGHT WAY to build a Team, there are many.

Let's begin by discussing the typical growth patterns of Club Wealth® Teams, understanding that these are fluid and will vary slightly from Team to Team.

Tier 1 Teams:

0-24 units per year usually comprised of a Team Leader and an outsourced Transaction Coordinator at best. Occasionally, they may have an assistant, but generally not until they reach Tier 2, unless they are in a higher price point market like Southern California.

Tier 2 Teams:

This is where Team Building **really** begins. Closing 25-74 units per year, the Team usually consists of: Team Leader, 1 Administrative Assistant (who also fills the role of the Transaction Coordinator), and as many as 2-4 Buyer Agents. In Tier 2, Team Leaders usually take a few steps backwards in time and earnings, to focus on the bigger vision of building a sustainable Team.

Would-be Club Wealth® Coaches MUST be in at least Tier 2, and can only coach Tier 1 Agents.

Tier 3 Teams:

75-149 closed units per year. This is where Teams really begin to take shape. Usually consisting of 4-15 Buyer Agents, 1-2 Administrative Assistants, the Team Leader, and possibly even a Listing Agent or two. It is here that Showing Agents begin to become an attractive option, although some Team Leaders hire them as early at Tier 1. Tara and I hired our first Showing Agent in Tier 2. In Tier 3, the Team Leader begins to reach a level of consistency, but often struggles to move out of production so they can focus on working "ON" the business rather than "IN" the business.

Approved, vetted, and trained Tier 3 Coaching Clients who become CW Coaches may coach Tier 2.

Tier 4 Teams:

150-249 Units/year. Team size grows to 15-35 Buyer Agents,

multiple Admin, and Team leadership in the form of Buyer and Listing Agent Squad Leaders begins to take shape. Here, the Team Leader usually exits production and begins really dialing in systems and recruiting at a very deep level. FINALLY, the Team Leader begins to earn a decent living, which by now is on par with what other Agents on the Team make, and occasionally slightly higher.

Approved, vetted, and trained Tier 4 Coaching Clients who become CW Coaches may coach Tier 3.

Tier 5 Teams:

250-499 closings per year... Almost always 25-45 Agents on the Team (unless they do a ton of new construction or REO properties), these Teams are well-oiled machines and have high expectations of their Team members. Lead gen, follow-up, conversion and the majority of Team systems are dialed in. Tier 5 Teams frequently implement ISA positions, and often make them a required starting point for advancement to Buyer Agent roles.

Typical Buyer Agents on Tier 5 Teams sell upwards of 35-40 homes per year, with some closing far more. Team Culture is a top priority, and Teams at this level and above generally have little to no patience for knuckleheads on the Team causing negative culture disruption.

Approved, vetted, and trained Tier 5 Coaching Clients who become CW Coaches may coach Tier 4.

Tier 6 Teams:

500-1,000 units. As they have now begun to master not only real estate sales systems, but recruiting systems as well, Tier 6 Teams often begin to branch out and expand into other markets within the same state. This provides even more leadership, and corresponding income opportunities, to existing Team members. Think about it: the bigger the Team grows, the more leaders it will need, and it will have to pay for those leaders. Want to create more opportunity for yourself? Help your Team grow, and your opportunity and income will grow with it (assuming you are on the right Team).

Tier 6 Teams often add Director of Operations, Lead Coordinator, and Director of Expansion positions.

Approved, vetted, and trained Tier 6 Coaching Clients who become CW Coaches may coach Tier 5.

Tier 7 Teams:

1,000+ units per year... These are the big boys and girls. Very frequently operating in multiple states, Tier 7 Teams are business machines! They are no-nonsense, aren't caught up in the drama that often plagues the industry, and they have no time for slackers. Opportunities for advancement abound on these highly successful and organized Teams.

You guessed it: approved, vetted, and trained Tier 7 Coaching Clients who become CW Coaches may coach Tier 6.

The first hire for most Team Leaders is either an outsourced Transaction Coordinator they pay by the transaction, or an in-house Administrative Assistant. That said we strongly encourage the addition of Buyer Agents as soon as possible, as their production can help offset the expense of the Assistant(s). Once a Team leader is comfortable growing even further, they should be looking to hire more Buyer Agents, and eventually Showing Assistants and ISA's.

In each of these positions, I generally recommend having more than one pig at the trough... what does that mean?

Years ago, Tara and I decided to help our kids learn responsibility on our small quasi-farm. Don't ask me why, but our decision was to have them raise pigs, something we knew NOTHING about!

So, I did exactly what you have done: I found a great book on the topic of raising pigs, and went to school.

In a matter of days, I felt equipped with enough knowledge to help Austin and Madison raise pigs for the first (and last) time.

One of the lessons learned from the book was that you never want to have just one pig at the trough. You see, the object of raising pigs is to feed them, get them fat, and harvest bacon (I mean, who doesn't like bacon, right?!).

It went on to share the importance of having more than one pig at the trough because they would each then compete for the food, eat more, and get fatter faster. This of course meant more bacon, faster!

Well, not only did it make sense to me at the time, but it also made me think of sales Teams and the synergistic dynamic that only seems to exist on Teams with the right culture who work at the same location together.

There is just no substitute for sitting or standing next to a Teammate who shares the same job role as you. Each of you motivates, encourages, teaches, and learns from one another. Each of you gets better, faster.

We've seen this in the Club Wealth® ISA role as well. My son, Austin, who had been with us for 2 years (since he was 14 years old), was our top salesperson. We had many adults in that role as well, most of who worked from home in other states, and none of them could seem to consistently beat Austin's numbers.

As our Team grew, we added in-house ISAs, who worked in the same location as Austin.

They were able to learn from him in real time, hear all of his calls, and he could hear their calls as well. They were able to motivate and encourage one another and create a level of friendly competition that became a noticeable synergy in the office.

They had fun together. And guess what, they ALL out-performed the remote Team members on a regular basis, which meant more money for them AND for the company!

You ALWAYS want more than one pig at the trough, ESPECIALLY if you're one of the pigs! Don't take that personally. Embrace it. You'll make more money and have more fun doing it!

Module 2 - Matching Your Strengths to the Path You Choose

If you want to become a successful Buyer Agent, you need to discover your strengths and leverage them each day. It goes without saying that you need to be darn good at what you do.

Taking the time to discover your strengths and actively playing to them is key to succeeding in the real estate world. In fact, your strengths may have been the spark that drove you to want to give real estate a shot in the first place. That's why you need to focus on building the best strengths for being a Buyer Agent.

There are certain traits and natural skills and talents that are woven into the DNA of successful Buyer Agents. They are nurturing, educating (heart of a teacher), outgoing, likeable, gregarious, patient, compassionate, and sociable. Connecting with people should be almost as easy as breathing. Top Agents are talented at making others feel comfortable, safe, secure and supported.

Many Team Leaders use the DISC profile or similar testing to determine who will make a successful Buyer Agent.

The deciding factor in how successful you'll become is directly influenced by how quickly and effectively you can identify your strengths, build them into valuable assets, and focus relentlessly on only doing activities (like setting buyer appointments) that utilize your strengths.

Coach's Corner: You have a greater chance of success if you stick with your core strengths and natural talents. If you were born to be a Listing Agent, focus on that, if you were put here to be a Buyer Agent, then make that your mission in your professional life!

Part of figuring out what your strengths are as a Buyer Agent is taking a look into the past and thinking about what you have always been good at. What have your friends, family, teachers, and past colleagues told you you're a natural at? Knowing your strengths and exercising them daily may propel you into the right career path.

Module 3 - Going from BA to Squad Leader and Beyond

- Start as an ISA
- Become a Showing Agent
- Become a Buyer Agent
- Advance to Buyer Squad Leader
- Become a Listing Agent
- Advance to Listing Squad Leader
- Advance to Local Team Leader
- On to Expansion Team Leader
- On to Regional Leader
- Eventually Become a National Team Leader

Start as an ISA

Some Teams will require that you start your career with them as an ISA. Whether it's a general ISA or an Outbound (cold calling sellers to set listing appointments) or Inbound (handling incoming leads) focused ISA, you will learn how to prospect for leads, nurture and follow up with leads, convert leads, and properly receive incoming leads.

Once again, you must develop thick skin in order to deal with a lot "No's" and hang up calls. Also, being a Team player is a must. An ISA has to develop strong communication skills, as their job requires a majority of their time on the phone with prospects.

Become a Showing Agent

If you are not ready to become a Buyer Agent, you can become a Showing Agent. This is an opportunity to work your way to becoming a Buyer Agent. As a Showing Agent, you'll get your feet wet showing houses. You will also learn how to work with buyers, overcome buyer objections, utilize scripts and dialogue, and become a master at closing for the offer.

Running Team errands may also be a task you'll have to do for your Team. This teaches humility, brings you into the Team family, and helps the Team become far more efficient with their time. Starting at the bottom leads to the top!

Buyer Agent

See Chapter 1 - The Role of a Buyer Agent

Buyer Team Squad Leader

One of the best positions on the Team for a nurturer who wants to help others and make more money, the Buyer Squad Leader can literally build a Team within the Team, without the overhead, staffing headaches, risk or many other challenges that come with building a Team from scratch!

As a Buyer Squad Leader, you'll have up to 10 Buyer Agents reporting to you, and you'll likely be receiving an override on every commission dollar each of them earns.

Make no mistake, it will be work... hard work, but it will also be extremely rewarding.
Generally speaking, your Team Leader will add, and occasionally remove, Agents from your Squad. They may even mix the Squads up from time to time.

Usually, you will also have the ability to recruit outside Agents to your Squad. As you do so, and as you approach your cap of 10 Agents on your Squad, you'll want to "top grade" your Squad. Essentially, this means you'll release lower producers to join other Squads within the Team, thus making room for new recruits, and giving other (often newer) Squad Leaders opportunities to earn some income and experience by adding them to their Squad.

Over time, you'll build a World Class Squad of Eagles, and together with them, you'll make a ton of money and help a ton of people improve their lives!

Listing Agent

You DO NOT have to be a Listing Agent to advance to Local Team Leader. That said, if you have some serious "D" in your DISC, and generally like to kick the front door down, punch them in the face, and make them sigh (so-to-speak...clearly figuratively, not literally!), then you may have what it takes to be a Listing Agent.

On many top Teams, despite the generally lower per-transaction commission splits, Listing Agent is almost always the most sought after position. Why? Because World Class Listing Agents:

- Do 100+ transactions per year.
- Don't work weekends
- Don't take calls after hours (usually)

Listing Squad Leader

For serious ballers: structured exactly like Buyer Squad Leader positions, the Listing Squad Leaders can build Teams within the Team, keeping in mind, of course, that if you leave the Team, you will be contractually prohibited from taking those Squad members with you.

The Career Path

Local Team Leader

Your Team Leader provides their experience to the entire Team. With their leadership skills, you'll find they also provide accountability and stability to new Agents as well as veteran Agents. A Team Leader will provide all the leads and systems as discussed in Chapter 1 The Role of a Buyer Agent. The Team Leader always eats last, and sometimes not at all.

In the beginning, they generally lose money because they pay for everything. It takes years to make a solid profit before a Team Leader can get "out of production". Taking over the Local Team Leader role will allow you to shortcut this process and go right into profitability, instead of starting your own Team.

As the Team Leader, it is your responsibility to lead the Team meetings and huddles, and to recruit new Agents and Team members. A Team Leader lives on a schedule. Great Team Leaders take responsibility for the Team failures and give credit to the Team for their successes.

Team Leaders will generally be responsible for 4-6 Squads. There may eventually be more than one Team Leader in the same market, as the Team grows large enough.

Expansion Team Leader

Once a Team is established, expansion will likely take place. It's not uncommon for Teams to expand into several cities and states. It's even possible to have a Team out of the country. You can think of an Expansion Team as a "Team within the current Team located in different market". The Expansion Team Leader has the same duties as a Team Leader, just in the new market. They are also referred to as Local Team Leaders.

Regional Leader

Much like Squad Leaders have 5-10 members on their Squads, and Team Leaders have 4-6 Squad Leaders, the Regional Team Leader may have 4-10 Teams reporting to them. Essentially, the Regional Leader leads the Expansion Teams in more than one market. They are focused on growth and development of Expansion Team Leaders and their members. They get paid on EVERYONE below them.

National Team Leader

They have all the duties that a Regional Team Leader has, but lead the entire Team nationally.

You may or may not decide to pursue advancement opportunities within your Team. That's okay. Whichever role you decide is right for you, be the best you can at it, and you'll likely enjoy years of success and the financial and lifestyle from that come with it!

At the end of the day, there's no perfect method for ensuring real estate success. However, if you take a moment to step back and reflect on how you can improve, you can create a formidable foundation on which to build your career.

CHAPTER 5:

EAGLES DON'T FLOCK WITH TURKEYS

CLUBWEALTH

Module 1 - Are You An Eagle or a Turkey?

Why would we call it the *Club Wealth® World Class Buyer Agent* book instead of the *Club Wealth® Buyer Agent* book? Because we aren't here to be average and neither are you.

On a sunny winter morning in Salt Lake City, Utah, in the Grand Hotel, I caught a glimpse of a small book leaning against the inner wall of the elevator as I entered. The book was written by Steve Siebold, and was entitled *"Secrets of the World Class"*. I picked it up without hesitation, glanced at the table of contents, and immediately walked over to the front desk. I told the clerk about my discovery, and asked her to contact me should its owner come looking for the book.

I found a comfortable seat in the lobby, and read the work cover to cover.
In it, Siebold artfully draws comparisons between the "World Class" and the "Middle Class"; clearly understanding the reader will gravitate towards a desire to become World Class.

It is my sincere hope that you too, will envision yourself, not as you are today, but as you were meant to become…World Class. It is my prayer that you will strive towards that goal, and that this book will, in some small way, help you in your quest to become such.

The wording "World Class" is very important.

World Class Buyer Agent

What's the difference between a "World Class" Agent and a "Middle Class" Agent? A Middle Class Agent does about 4.5 transactions per year, not even remotely the Club Wealth® standard.

Also, a Middle Class Agent works 24/7, doesn't take vacations, or have time for their family.

For World Class Agents, it doesn't matter if you are a Listing Agent or Buyer Agent; you understand "No success in the world can compensate for failure in the home." And they don't just talk about it – they live it.

World Class means that you aren't satisfied with 4 transactions a year. You want to be hitting 4 transactions a month and more.

Think about the Animal Kingdom for a moment. Eagles don't flock with Turkeys.

Ask yourself: Are you an Eagle, or are you a Turkey? If you're a Turkey, the Eagles will simply eat you eventually.

You are World Class.

You may not feel like it right now, or at least not every day, but know this: inside you is a World Class BEAST just dying to get out! Only YOU can unleash that beast. You must consciously decide to do it, and you must be willing to pay the price.

As you remain truly willing, and continue to work hard to get to that level, you'll grow into an Eagle and never have to worry about being eaten. You will become World Class.

Eagles Don't Flock with Turkeys

I remember a time when we lived on Lake Tapps in Washington State. There was a rather large Canadian goose wading in the shallows in our backyard. I watched an eagle of approximately the same size as this goose literally swooped down and carried that goose about 40 yards away. You could hear this ravenous experience as the eagle devoured that goose in just a matter of a few minutes, as the goose cried out for its life.

Let me ask you this question – do you want to be devoured, like that helpless goose? Or do you want to be fed like the eagle?

You want to be an Eagle! That means you have to push yourself harder. You have to push yourself further.

You have to embrace the suck, get into the grind, and give up FOREVER the excuses that have held you back until now.

You'll have to dig deep, not just at times, but often.

You'll need to discover your "why", and draw a line in the proverbial sand saying, "I'm a turkey no more!"

Remember, excuses are like noses: everyone's got one.

Now, it's time to take responsibility for your success, not because your family wants you to, not because your friends want you to, not even because your Team Leader insists on it, but simply because you are tired of making just enough to stay in this business, but not enough to be excited about it.

Because you know that you are destined for something better... a greatness you can't yet fully define, but know is there, waiting for you to step up and take it!

Only you can truly motivate yourself.

If you look to outside sources for motivation, you'll become a Turkey. An Eagle's motivation comes within.

Accountability? Yeah, that's something you'll provide for yourself as well. You will, from this day forward, hold yourself to a higher standard than those around you. You KNOW you are capable beyond measure. You don't need others to tell you that. Eagles don't require someone to tell them they can fly high. It's part of their DNA, just as the World Class Beast within you is part of yours!

What are the steps to becoming an Eagle?

1.   Get motivated. Find your motivation from within. You have to decide you are going to be successful no matter what. It doesn't matter who your Team leader is, who your Teammates are, what brokerage you're with, what family you come from, what kind of car you drive, or what leads you have. All that matters is that you are going to be successful because you have decided that you will be.

2.   Get educated. This is what you're doing right now. Get and read the right books, take the right courses, attend the right events, and hire the right coach.

3. Take MASSIVE action. Knowledge without implementation is like rowing with one oar in the water. All you do is spin around in circles. So you have to implement. You must take massive action on a daily basis.

What do you implement? We will teach you, with the Club Wealth® books, courses, and Club Wealth® Coaching events. We'll teach you exactly what to implement, step by step. If you are doing the Club Wealth® World Class Buyer Agent course online, that's fantastic. That's a great way to do it. Do the entire certification course and get certified. You are going to learn more at a deeper level than you can even imagine.

For those simply reading this book, go through the entire book. Don't just read the e-book version. Get the paperback version, dog-ear the pages, and make notes in the margin. Underline words and highlight the passages that resonate with you. Use it like a reference library.

You need to make sure you are using the Club Wealth® tools and materials to their fullest. Get everything you can out of them. Everything you need to know is right here and all you have to do is take advantage of it.

So if you want to be an eagle and go from 4 houses a year to 4 or more a month, we are going to show you how to exactly do that. We're not here to breed mediocrity; we don't do "Middle Class". We are here to develop Eagles and build World Class Teams.

Don't be a Turkey.

Be an Eagle!

Don't join an easy crowd. You won't grow. Go where the expectations and the demands to perform are high. –Jim Rohn

CHAPTER 6
THE PERFECT DAILY SCHEDULE

CLUBWEALTH

Why do some Agents make more money than others when we all have the same number of hours in each day? It's because many of those Agents are living by the Perfect Daily Schedule (PDS). As a World Class Buyer Agent, you'll want to spend your day performing dollar-productive activities (DPAs) - while most Agents spend their time doing "tasks" that they have determined are important, but make them no money.

Fill your day with Dollar-Productive Activities and you can't help but be successful. Tasks that qualify as DPAs are lead generating in nature: making phone calls, hosting open houses, showing property, and holding buyer consultations. Essentially, anything that leads directly to a sale or a listing. Implementing the PDS makes it easy to develop the right habits, and the right habits will practically guarantee your success! Let's dig in and learn how to do that!

Module 1 - Time Management is a Myth

Time management is a myth. You hear about this idea of time management over and over again. Here's the reality. Each one of us gets the same twenty-four hours in a day. And you can't manage that. You can't make that time go quicker and you can't make the time go slower. The question is what are you going to do during that time? And how are you going to manage your activities within that time? How are you going to lead yourself? Instead of focusing on managing our time, let's start focusing on our goals and habits.

Coach's Corner: You can't manage time so focus on your goals and habits!

Module 2 - Multitasking and Task Switching

The University of Utah did a study on multitasking and discovered that it's estimated that only 2% of the population is actually proficient at multitasking*. And ironically, these people are the least likely to actually multitask.

Yes, it has become this popular idea that we should be multitaskers. You're about to learn that multitasking is the most inefficient thing you can do as a real estate Agent. If you are currently a multitasker, it's time you started to change your time management strategies, or better yet, your habits.

Did you know that a recent article in Psychology Today tells us that task switching decreases your efficiency and productivity by 40%*?

Something that people do that is inefficient and ineffective throughout their day is task switching. Here is an example of task switching that most Agents do and don't even realize: The Agent is lead generating and has a great conversation with a potential client, so they stop lead generation at this point and set up listing alerts or send that person information. What they should do is hang up, call the next person, and then send all emails at the end of their lead generation time-block.

Task switching crushes our ability to be efficient. By doing so, you will have cut your productive work time in half. Our goal is not to teach you to work harder and work longer. Our goal is to teach you to work more efficiently and more effectively. Eliminating task switching is one of the simplest things you can do to achieve greater productivity with the time you are already working.

What's the opposite of task switching? It's called batching.

Module 3 - Batching and Blocking are the Best Time Savers

Efficiency and effectiveness are two different things. Efficiency essentially means getting more done in less time.

Google defines it as: *the ratio of the useful work performed by a machine or in a process to the total energy expended.*

Effectiveness means getting the RIGHT things done.

So, it is possible to be highly efficient (get a lot done), and at the same time be completely ineffective (fail to get THE RIGHT things done)?

Likewise, you can be highly effective (get all the right things done) but be completely bloody inefficient (take WAY too long to do them).

The goal is to become BOTH efficient AND effective.

Two of the most important things you can do to become simultaneously more efficient and more effective with your time are Batching and Blocking.

Batching is essentially doing the same thing over and over and over again. A popular, yet simple, saying is that "Success is boring." For successful people, the idea rings true. We want to do one thing and master it. Then we want to go do the next thing and master it. Over and over and over again.

Blocking is setting aside specific periods of time (blocks), within which each batch of tasks must be completed. For example, working out from 4-5 a.m. or prospecting from 8-noon, or, even better, calling new leads from 8-9 a.m. and making follow up calls from 9-10 a.m., etc.

What are some examples of things that you can do better by batching and blocking? Let's take a look at reading and sending emails. You could start off your day by sending out an email at 8 o'clock. Then send another at 9 o'clock. Then another at 10 o'clock. Then another email at 11 o'clock. Does that save you any time? Not really.

What if, instead, you sent off all those emails at once? And then you went to the next block on your schedule? You can accomplish twice the amount of work if you simply just knock out a task all at once. Batch them into one task within a specific time block. Batching and blocking is the most efficient AND effective way to spend your time.

Module 4 - Spend Your Days Doing Things That Make You Money

Most of time we hear Agents talk about how hard they work. Are we working in an efficient and effective way? That is the question. What are some things that make you money? Phone calls, door knocking, and holding open houses are examples of things that can and will make you money. These are DPAs, or Dollar Producing Activities.

Here's an interesting quote about open houses: 82% of people that walk into an open house do not have an Agent. So, theoretically, if you hold an open house this weekend and meet 10 new people, you have the potential to obtain approximately 8 new clients.

If you follow the Club Wealth® MASSIVE Open House System (see www.clubwealth.com/openhouse for the video and checklist), and you get 50-150 people to the Open House, you could get as many as 40-120 potential clients! Now, realistically, your numbers will likely be more conservative than that, but here's the truth: don't do the open house and you won't get any of those potential clients!

Another DPA that can generate income is showing property. Showing property is arguably the best use of your time, unless, of course, you have a Showing Agent. Showing property is a golden opportunity to meet with clients and establish solid relationships.

Six Things That Must Be On Your Daily Schedule

1. Lead Generation: phone calls, open houses, door knocking
2. Lead Follow Up
3. Lead Conversion
4. Showing Property
5. Checking Email
6. Self-Development

Module 5 - Great Start to the Day

Let's talk about the beginning of the day. You have complete control of the first hour of your day. You can get up as early as you want and no one is going to call you at that hour. You don't have to look at your phone, email, or social media. It's your time to dedicate to whatever you want.

Coach Brian Curtis says: "For me, I start my day by reviewing my goals. Why? Because my goals tell me where I want to go and give me a point of reference for what I have accomplished."

Nothing will provide you more focus than goals. This is a great way to make decisions. Every single decision that you make either points you toward your goal or points you away from your goal. If you can look at the choices that you make during your day and ask yourself, "Am I moving toward my goals or away from my goals?" It really helps us to make better decisions.

What does the morning routine look like for a World Class Buyer Agent? A fantastic book to read on morning routines is Hal Elrod's *Miracle Morning*. Get up and set aside time for the four or five things that you'd like to do that morning. For instance, you could begin your day with reading, journal writing, exercise, and meditation. The key is to start your day the exact same way every single day. That may sound boring to some people, and maybe it is. Success is often boring. Starting the day the same way every time will put you in a state of mind to be ready to go out there and be successful.

Module 6 - Six Things That Should Be On Every PDS

There are two hours in a day that you have complete control of. The first hour of the day, if you're like most successful people, starts at five in the morning. The reality is, no one's calling you at four in the morning. Your phone probably doesn't start ringing until at least eight or nine o'clock. So you have complete control over that time. No one is interrupting you. You can choose not to check your email or browse Facebook. Remember, you control the first hour of your day.

Here's what a lot of people don't think about: you can also control the last hour of your day. It is the last opportunity of the day to set you up for success. Let's look at what happens before you go to sleep at night.

We've all heard about Netflix binging. Let's say you binge watch your show for five or six hours at a time. When it's time to go to bed, all night long you dream about that show. Is that something you want programmed into your brain? Instead of binge watching at night before you go to sleep, what if you took that last hour of the day and fed your brain something positive?

A solution I've found that works great is to write down your goals. Write down things you want to accomplish the next day. Get your focus on things that can move your life forward in a positive direction. Of course, we aren't suggesting that you work another eight hours in your sleep! Just focus on something that will benefit and help you start your mornings off in the right direction.

This is a terrific opportunity to think about something you've struggled to solve, such as a problem or opportunity that remains unresolved. You see, by going over it as you fall asleep, while you sleep your subconscious mind will actually continue working on the problem. Often, you will awake to new insights into appropriate solutions, almost like magic!

Now, it is critical that you keep pen and paper next to the bed, so when you awake, you can immediately write your newfound knowledge down before you forget it!

Coach Scott Gregory advises, "There's a concept called the Pareto Principle, which states that 20 percent of your activities produce 80 percent of your results. Most agents spend their time the other way around, which limits their growth and their incomes."

Here are five things that you want to have on every Perfect Daily Schedule (PDS):

Number 1 - Lead Generation, Particularly Prospecting. There is nothing more important than following a consistent, habitual process for ensuring that you will have business in the future. If you lead generate every day, you CONTROL your income. Control your income, and you control your life. The Agent who has too many clients can decide which ones they choose to work with, they can decide what is worth their time, and they decide who, what, where, when, and why they will do things. The only thing that ensures this will happen is generating leads consistently. For example, you could have a client who won't write a reasonable offer and who takes up all your time. Most Agents will continue to work with these people to their own detriment, whereas the professional Agent who consistently lead generates can fire that client without a doubt or concern because they have many others who will take their place.

Coach's Corner: Although it occasionally feels great to fire a client, you should always check with your Team Leader before doing so, especially if they are a lead provided to you by the Team.

Number 2 - Follow Up. "The fortune is in the follow-up" is a favorite saying at Club Wealth®. Why is that true? Because prospective buyers will call an Agent one time and tell them they are looking to buy a house in six months. The Middle Agent will wait about 5 ½ months and call the prospective buyer again. "Hey Mr. Buyer," they'll say, "are you still interested in going to look at a house?" Guess what happens nine times out of ten? Mr. Buyer bought a new house a week ago. Sorry, Middle Agent, you missed out on a commission, and the lifetime value of what could have been a client who would refer you often.

What should you have done instead? Follow up! Follow up! Follow up!

> **Coach's Corner: When Coach Michael Hellickson was listing 50-75 homes a month, not counting his Team or REO; he did so making 115-125 follow-up calls per day. Numbers don't lie. More follow-up calls = more transactions. Get your follow-up call numbers up!**

Follow-ups allow you to build relationships. It's an opportunity for you to get to know people. Don't just search for the low-hanging fruit - the person that has to go see a house this afternoon. We all want those people, too, but that's not how you build a business. You build the business by religiously following step one: lead generation, and habitually implementing step two: follow-up!

Think about it: by the time you've followed up with someone for 3-4 months, you've not only built a relationship, you've also eliminated the competition who quit following up almost immediately! Now converting that lead to an appointment is easy!

Number 3 - Showing property. Showing property - this is the goal of all the lead generation, lead follow-up and lead conversion. This is where the rubber meets the road and you go from prospect to client. It is so important that we dedicated an entire chapter to it.

Number 4 - Email. There's a lot of great communication that can happen in an email. There is also a problem that we have as Real Estate Agents when it comes to emails. We believe as a group that the contents of an email are urgent and important. There definitely are important things in your inbox, but let me also say there's almost nothing that is urgent and important in an email.

No one is going to send you an email saying that they need something done in an hour. If by some chance they do, they will follow up with a text message or a phone call.

Stop treating email like it's mission critical to your life. Set aside two times a day to check your email. Once after your prospecting is done, and a final time later in the afternoon. That's it. No more. The same goes for social media accounts like Facebook that have direct message options. A good solution is to assign this task to your assistant - whether it's your personal or Team assistant.

Turn off all notifications on your phone and PC. They serve only one purpose: to distract you from the more important task at hand.

When you allow notifications to interrupt your day, you have allowed others to control you. This puts you out of control. Clearly, being in control is better.

Coach's Corner: Never check your email before you lead generate. Nothing can derail your day faster than reading email!

Number 5 - Take a break. All too often we work straight through the day without a break. By the end of the day our productivity and focus begin to falter, and we become less efficient and less effective. This is why taking a break is so important. It doesn't matter what you do during your break. Take a nap. Meditate. Just relax. Have something to eat. What you do is not important, so long as you give yourself a chance to recharge your batteries. So add "Take A Break" to your daily schedule.

Number 6 - Self Development. In life, we are either moving forwards or backwards... we are rarely ever standing still. Investing your time back in yourself is arguably the best investment you can make. This is not an item that needs to be on your schedule every single day, but definitely one that belongs on it every single week.

The Perfect Daily Schedule

The beauty of today is you can also create NET time around self-development. What is NET? NET stands for No Extra Time. Examples of how to incorporate NET time are driving and listening to books on audible, driving and listening to people on YouTube, carrying on phone conversations with prospects or clients in the car, and working out and watching or listening to inspirational or motivational content. Today there are tons of free podcasts, YouTube recordings, and many others sources of free or inexpensive ways to get great content that can change your life. Remember your schedule is a reflection of who you are. Does your schedule show you are stagnating, or does it reflect the growth you really want?

Access the Club Wealth® Podcast
https://clubwealth.com/tv/

Subscribe to the Club Wealth® YouTube Channel
https://www.youtube.com/clubwealth

Coach's Corner: Sitting is the new smoking. Make sure you are being active throughout the day.

Module 7 - Questions to Ask Yourself That Lead to Successful Habits

As you build your schedule, you have to take a look at the questions that you ask yourself. The quality of your life is determined by the quality of the questions that you ask. Let's take a look at some of the questions that people typically ask and then give you some questions that might be better.

Here are examples of questions people commonly ask themselves:

"What do I have to get done today?" or "What should I do today?" One of my favorites is "How can I get all of this done?"

Those questions are not great questions. Why? Because they're negative. They focus on those things like "should". If you are using the word "should" in your questions that is a good indication that you need to be asking a better question. Let's instead focus on some potential positive questions that you could ask.

Instead of asking negative questions:
What should I get done today?
What do I need to do?
How am I going to get this all done?
What should I do?

Focus on asking positive questions:
What's the best use of my time?
What's the one thing that I can do today that will move me toward my goals?
What's one thing that will set me apart in my market?
What's one thing that people will remember me for?
What's the one thing that I can do better than anyone else is doing?
What is one thing that I can accomplish today?

Asking Great Questions

What is the best use of my time? Imagine if you started every single day with the question: What is the best use of my time?

We talk about the "Twenty Two-Hundreds". This is when a task makes you either $20 an hour or $200 an hour. Those are non-exact numbers and they vary from Agent to Agent, but the concept is the same. Do you want to be doing a task that makes you $20 an hour or a task that makes you $200 an hour? Am I doing something that is making me a lot of money, or am I wasting my time for a little bit of money? Who can I give the $20 tasks to accomplish, and free up my time for the $200 tasks?

What's the one thing that I can do consistently that will move me toward my goals? What is the one thing that, if I did it every single day, would get me closer to where I want to be?

Another great line of thinking is: What is one thing that will set me apart in my market? What is one thing that people will remember me for? How about this: What is one thing that I can do better than everybody else?

Remember, by the time you actually speak with a potential client, they may have already spoken to five or six Agents. What are you going to do to set yourself apart?

"What is one thing that I can accomplish today?" The truth of the matter is that when you go out and accomplish one great thing every day that pushes you toward your goals, you'll be ahead of 95% of the world.

Module 8 - How Do We Build a Schedule – RPM?

The first step in designing your PDS is to fully understand and be able to articulate your real "Why". This is much harder than it sounds. So much so, that we recommend seeking the help of your Club Wealth® Coach or your Team Leader. Working together with someone who has been through, and fully understands, the process of discovering your true WHY will enable you to cut through the reasons on the surface, and get to the real core of what makes you tick.

Once you've done that, you're ready to dive into designing the actual PDS itself.

Start by setting an alarm for every hour, on the hour, in your calendar. When it goes off, write down everything you did the previous hour.

Do this for one week.

Then, review the week. You will likely come to the stark realization that you, like most of us, waste a lot of time.

Next, you can begin implementing RPM.

RPM is a process that many believe was developed by Tony Robbins, but some suggest it predates him. RPM is one way to maximize the results in your life and give you a sense of fulfillment.

R stands for Results. It has to question what you want. What **are** your goals? What are you trying to accomplish? What is the end result you want to achieve?

Napoleon Hill is frequently quoted as suggesting that we "begin with the end in mind."

The second question is: **What is the Purpose**? We don't understand the purpose behind things in most cases. If you have a purpose behind things when they get hard, you can push forward. If you don't have anything behind your purpose, it just doesn't give you the strength to push forward when you are getting those 95 "No's" from your prospective clients or leads.

This is why it is so important to really understand your 'Why'.

Finally, **what is your MAP**? MAP is actually an acronym. It stands for **M**assive **A**ction **P**lan. If you want to be extremely successful in life and you know what you want and why you want it, you have to take massive action or you won't accomplish it.

Module 9 - What Do You Want? (R) Results

The first letter in our acronym RPM stands for Results. What do you want? Asking a general question like that almost never works. For example, Coach Brian Curtis says that people tell him all the time that they want more money or that they want to lose weight. But they aren't specific about their goals.

He contends that he needs to start carrying around a pocket full of pennies, so the next time someone tells him that they want more money, he can hand them a penny and say, "Congratulations, you have more money." Being specific in your wants and needs helps paint a clearer picture for success.

When setting our goals, we focus on S.M.A.R.T. Goals:

Specific
Measurable
Attainable
Relevant
Time Sensitive

Instead of saying, "I want to close more transactions", find a way to ask better questions. For instance: "I want to make fifty thousand dollars in six months." Or "I want to lose 50 pounds this year." Those goals are tangible things you can see in your mind and use as a measure to see how you're doing.

They fit the S.M.A.R.T. model.

Great goals have 5 characteristics:

1. They are specific in nature, not vague.
2. They are measurable. For example, 'more transactions' is not measurable, but a goal of 100 transactions is.
3. They are attainable (I can set a goal to pick up a loaded semi truck with my bare hands by next week, but it's not possible or attainable.)
4. They should be relevant to your purpose and values, and in harmony with your "why".
5. They have a time-sensitive deadline.

The next step is focusing on results. Your brain is programmed to be very task-oriented, and for good reason. If you want to be successful, focusing on results is incredibly important. It's easy to make a list of 27 things to go through the day to accomplish and check off all those things. If I were to ask 100 people how many of them liked to accomplish tasks, they would all raise their hands, because knocking out a task list makes them feel good. If I make a list of 20 things and I accomplish 19 of them, it feels like my day has been extremely successful.

The problem is, you look at that list of 20 things and the 19 that you accomplish are probably the simplest tasks. The 20th task is the one that most people skip because that's the hardest one. That's the task that takes focus. That's also the task that gives results. We want you to focus on making sure that you are doing the things throughout your day that are moving you toward your goals. The things that are getting you the results that you need, and more. We want to focus on achievement. Not activity.

Module 10 - Think Outcome First

You want to think of your outcome first - every time. We want you to think of outcomes before you go on every appointment. Before you go and shake someone's hand and talk to him or her, ask yourself, "Am I ready for this appointment?" Before you pick up the phone to make an appointment or lead generate, did you just have a fight with somebody? Did you look at something that was negative? Did you just watch the news? Where is your mindset before you make that phone call or meet that new client? Before you take action, we'd like you to think about what the outcome will be. If you treat each conversation and each appointment like it is important, you will come prepared and you will make the most out of every opportunity, and that's how you become World Class.

Coach's Corner: If you ALWAYS focused on your outcome before you acted, how would that change your life?

Module 11 - 2nd Question RPM - (P)urpose

The second letter in RPM stands for Purpose. What is your purpose? Your purpose is your "Why".

People say they don't know what they want. They don't know why they're doing the things they do. Purpose is the thing that drives us. Purpose is what pushes us when life gets hard. Everybody wants to make more money and I can appreciate that. But **why** do you want to make more money?

Everybody wants to close more transactions, but **why** do you want to close transactions? Find that purpose. That purpose propels you forward, reaching out constantly for success.

It's easy to say "I'm doing this for my family", but we've found that, more often than not, the **real** purpose behind our motivation to succeed is much deeper than that.

Your purpose has to be personal, too. It is not someone else's purpose. If you're appropriating somebody else's purpose, I promise you that when life starts to take a turn for the worse, you're not going to be able to push through. Make sure you own your purpose and that it makes sense to you.

You'll know you've found it when the mere mention of it evokes strong emotion from you. You may cry or get excited. You may even get angry or agitated. One way or another, though, you will feel raw emotion.

For instance, maybe I want to be a millionaire. Maybe I want to take care of my family. I want my kids to go to college. I want to give away $100,000 a year to a cause that is important to me.

Those are all great things, but you have to dig even deeper than that. WHY do you want those things? Were you deprived of those things in your youth? Are you afraid of what might happen to your kids if they DON'T go to college?

Make your purpose meaningful, powerful, and impactful. If you can do that, I can assure you that when a buyer disappears on you or your transaction starts to fall apart, or it's just a bad day all together...it will be okay. Because you will think hard about why you're here, get back on your feet, and fight twice as hard tomorrow.

Module 12 - 3rd Question - RPM (M) stands for MAP

The third question is what is your MAP? MAP stands for Massive Action Plan. This is ultimately a reflection of your identity and what you are going to do. One of my favorite things to say is, "If it's not on your schedule, it doesn't exist." So we're going to put together a plan that ultimately approaches action in a systematic way.

Things we would like to see on your schedule are really simple. How do you start your day? What if the first item on your schedule is how you get up in the morning? That sounds crazy, right? But you should have a time that you are typically going to get up every morning. You should also put on your schedule what time you exercise. Why? Because exercising gives you momentum, which pushes you throughout your day. It helps build energy.

Set a time to get dressed in the morning. I know that sounds silly, too, but I've seen so many people's schedules that say, "Workout, Breakfast, Go to Work." Well, guess what? You'll probably need to shower at some point. Don't forget to add the little things in the morning to your daily schedule. Set up a time for your Team's morning huddle. If you're on a Team, it will be required that you attend a daily huddle call. It's a way to get the Team together and jumpstart everyone's day. It's also one of the many great benefits of being on a Team.

Next, you'll need to set some time aside for prospecting, and the next point of business is follow-up. Follow-up is vital. Emailing is something else we talked about. Some people forget to put that on their schedule. Put lunch on your schedule. Show property.

If you do not have to show property in the afternoon, it is not an opportunity to slack off or watch television. That's an opportunity to work on something else. For me, the most logical and easy thing to do, if you do not have an appointment during your show property time, is to actually prospect more.

At some point in your schedule, build in a break. Building some time to just unwind and give your brain a few minutes to relax is important. Recharge yourself and get ready to move forward. And let's not forget that we need to put some time in for YOU, your family, and your friends.

Because here's the thing, no matter how successful you are in real estate and no matter how successful you are in life, if you do not set aside some time for your family and put your family first, then at the end of the day you could end up very lonely. There are so many opportunities out there. Build a schedule that reflects what your goals are and what you need.

Remember the Club Wealth® Core Value:

No Success in the World can Compensate for Failure in the Home!

The Perfect Daily Schedule

6:00 AM	Work Out
6:30 AM	
7:00 AM	Get Ready for Day
7:30 AM	Morning Huddle
8:00 AM	Prospecting
8:30 AM	
9:00 AM	
9:30 AM	
10:00 AM	
10:30 AM	Follow up
11:00 AM	
11:30 AM	Email
12:00 PM	
12:30 PM	Lunch

1:00 PM	
1:30 PM	Show Property/Prospect
2:00 PM	
2:30 PM	
3:00 PM	
3:30 PM	Break
4:00 PM	Transaction Cleanup
4:30 PM	
5:00 PM	Show Property
5:30 PM	
6:00 PM	
6:30 PM	Family Time
7:00 PM	
7:30 PM	
8:00 PM	
8:30 PM	
9:00 PM	
9:30 PM	
10:00 PM	BED

Having a daily schedule may sound restrictive to you, but it's actually the most liberating thing you can implement. This is not the type of job where you have to punch a clock. However, having no schedule at all is a recipe for chaos. As a World Class Buyer Agent, it's important to implement your Perfect Daily Schedule right away so you can achieve the success you want, in the time you want, while maintaining the quality of life you deserve!

*Sources:

https://mic.com/articles/185040/life-hack-your-brain-the-best-way-to-multitask-and-improve-productivity-according-to-science#.M67ih8To3

https://www.psychologytoday.com/us/blog/brain-wise/201209/the-true-cost-multi-tasking

CHAPTER 7
CRM

CRM

Module 1 - What is a CRM?

A CRM is a software program that is typically used to organize and manage customers for a business. The acronym CRM stands for Customer Relationship Management.

The backbone of an Agents' business is their database. It's where they keep everyone they know and have done business with, and all of their leads for future business. Since this database is so critical to success, many companies provide a computer and database software platform for their new Agents. For you to build a solid long-term business, you must be able to use your Team's CRM well.

> **Coach's Corner: Money does not grow on trees— it grows in databases. Your database is what you sell if you ever decide to sell your business. More importantly, it is the lifeblood of the business you have today, and DEMANDS that you keep it up to date and accurate.**

Module 2 - Why Use It?

Your database is the most valuable part of your business. It is the relationships we develop over time that will determine our financial outcome. Your CRM will allow you to effectively leverage yourself, and those relationships, in lead generation and other ways. Everyone

102

with whom you interact should be in your database, even the ones who say they don't want to work with you.

Once upon a time, 61% of most Agents' business came from repeat and referral clients.

Just 5 years later that number dropped to 44%.

WHY is that?

92% of homebuyers start their search ONLINE.

72% of those buyers work with the first Agent they connect with (face-to-face).

Your job is to increase the number of referrals/repeat business, while simultaneously increasing the amount of business coming from other sources. Ultimately, the percentage of referral transactions as compared to your overall closed transaction count will decrease, even though the number of total referral closings will increase.

How is that possible? Because the rate of growth of your non-referral based business will be faster than the referral based business at some point, even though both will be growing rapidly.

Your CRM is a necessary component in BOTH your referral and non-referral based business.

Coach's Corner: The size of your real estate business will be in direct proportion to the size and quality of your database.

CRM

Cost of Non-Completion

Why is it important to you to have, and fully utilize, the right CRM? What happens if you don't get this done? This is called the cost of non-completion.

If you don't utilize the CRM you will:

- Drop the ball on follow-up.
- Fail to stay in front of the people you need to.
- Lose business.
- Have far less referral and repeat business than you deserve.

This exact situation happened to Coach Misti Bruton. She had a friend who bought a house from someone else because she wasn't "top of mind". She shares that this was a painful and hard lesson to learn. After losing that business, Coach Misti resolved to add all of her friends and family (her SOI) to her database, use it, and market to it properly. That way she knew everyone would remember her when they were ready to buy or sell.

Module 3 - How to Use It?

Every time a prospect or client completes a transaction or finishes a marketing campaign, be sure that:

1. Their contact information is updated. (i.e., bought a new home, FSBO turned Listing, etc.)
2. They are in the correct database category and group. (i.e., If an Expired moves into a Just Listed category)
3. They are on the correct database plan. (i.e., No longer a seller

or buyer?)
4. The notes are current and accurate. (i.e., Client recently got married, Buyer moved to new address).

The 4 Rules of a Successful CRM:

1. **Build a powerful database.**
2. **Feed it daily.**
3. **Communicate with it daily.**
4. **Service all the leads.**

The Importance of Complete and Accurate Data

When entering contacts into your database, be sure to include all relevant information. The more specific you are with the data, the more you can target your marketing dollars to those groups. Your database is only as good as the information in it.

That being said; try not to write a book in the notes. Develop your own kind of shorthand: DNC for Do Not Call, FU for Follow-Up etc.... This will save time and ensure you have what you need.

Why Add Your Own SOI to CRM?

If you are on a Team, be sure you are adding your SOI to the Team's database.

By adding your own contacts and leads to your Team's CRM:

- You are showing goodwill to the Team Leader.
- The leads will be tagged as yours, so you own them.... forever.

- You'll be able to properly "work" your database and close way more business.
- Your Team will help you market to your SOI so YOU get more business with little or no effort!
- Adding your SOI will ensure turning your database into a referral gold mine.
- Don't be afraid to add them. Be afraid not to! :)

The Most Important Thing – The Next Call Date

The most important piece of information you can put in the database is when you will call the contact again. The fortune is in the follow-up, and if you don't consistently use the database to follow up on your leads, you will lose opportunities and money. Every contact you want to work with in the future should have a "next follow-up date" in your CRM.

When I was listing 50-75 homes a month (not counting my Team or REO properties), it was a direct result of making 115-125 follow-up calls per day, 4 days a week, from my car, in between my 6-8 appointments per day.

The single most important thing you can do in this business on a daily basis is follow-up with your leads!

Module 4 - Which is the Best CRM?

The one you use is the best answer. Is that true?

I know there is a lot of controversy around this, but here's the truth. If you have a leading edge CRM and you don't use it, it's worthless. If you have a basic CRM, but use it consistently, you will see results. If you're on a Team, the best CRM is the one your Team provides. If you're a solo Agent, the real question should be: What CRM is the best for me? What capabilities does the CRM have that integrates with other technology, especially other tech I am currently using, as well as for future growth and for automation? Does the CRM have automatic lead routing as an option, in case I begin building a Team in the future?

However, you MUST choose and you MUST use one immediately.

What Features Should a CRM Have?

A CRM can't convert a lead for you. Only YOU can convert a lead.

Here are some features your CRM should have:

- Texting capabilities
- Email integration
- Tagging of leads
- Custom fields
- Anniversary and birthday reminders
- Call recording
- Drip campaigns
- Customizable Action Plans
- Ability to find leads with no Action Plan
- Lead stage tracking
- Lead source tracking
- IDX integration

These are some of the must haves. We need to leverage as much as we can so we can focus on running our business. After all, we are all running small businesses. Let technology do what it does best, embrace that, and allow yourself to leverage it so you can grow.

In addition to the basic features of a good CRM, here are few features a cutting edge CRM can provide as well:

- Video emails
- Auto-responders
- Email and phone number verification
- Behavior detection
- AI (as it improves)
- Some can even send behaviorally based texts or emails on your behalf, like Ylopo (one of our favorites)
- Transaction tracking and coordination
- Lead triggers to help keep leads engaged
- Email newsletter features
- Lead routing for Team
- Whisper Coaching - one of the best features EVER... see www.clubwealth.com/crm for the CRM's that have it! :)

To recap which CRM is best? The one you will consistently use is the best answer.

When it comes to databases, size and frequency of use is what sets apart the World Class Agent and a "Middle Class Agent".

Should I Change My CRM?

CRMs change all the time, but that doesn't mean you need to constantly change CRMs.

Remember, change is disruptive. It's hard on you, your staff, and on your Agents. Just because it has some new latest and greatest features does not mean moving to it will be good for you or your Team.

CRM Brands

There are many CRMs to choose from and far too many CRMs to list here. Things like options, features, who's best, and functionality change so rapidly, we recommend visiting www.ClubWealth.com/CRM for the most up-to-the-minute information on all things CRM, including special Club Wealth® discounts on the most popular CRMs.

When it comes to CRMs and the databases they house, size and frequency of use is what sets apart the World Class Agent and a Middle Class Agent.

Module 5 - The Process of Creating a Valuable Database

Your job is to fill your database with as many clients as you possibly can. Make a list of everyone who knows you. Take out a piece of paper and do this now. A name is all you need for this step. You will get more specific later.

Visit our CRM page for a memory jogger that will help you think of more people you should include... This is important. We don't want you to forget anyone, because EVERYONE could potentially send you your next closing!

Put everyone you know and who knows you into your CRM.

Collect the following information in order:

Name

Email

Phone (prefer cell)

Address

Connect to the people in your CRM on social media, specifically and especially Facebook. For example, "Friend" everyone on your list.

Building, Sorting, and Qualifying Your Database

You must build, sort, and qualify your database to get the most out of it.

Building Your Database

The key to building your database is to set a specific and measurable (S.M.A.R.T.) goal for how many people you will add to it each and every workday. For example, if you can commit to purposefully adding the contact information of 5 new people you meet to your database, 5 days per week, you will grow your databases by 1300 people **in just one year**. Before you know it, you'll have a powerful database full of contacts.

To take it a step further, if you systematically stay in touch with these people, these 1300 contacts should bring you approximately 40 new transactions a year! This way you'll have a powerful database full of contacts.

Done right, you should close 1 transaction each year per 10 people in your database who are classified as "B" or higher (SOI, see Qualifying Your Database Section below)… do the math!

Sort Your Database

Your database should be sorted into the following categories:

- Buyer
- Seller
- Vendor
- Next Follow-Up Date

- Sub Categories
    - Lender
    - Referrer
    - Influencer
    - Asset Manager
    - Escrow Officer

Qualify Your Database

- A+ = Have done multiple transactions and/or referrals
- A = Have done 1 transaction or referral
- B = Would work with or refer you if they were taught how and consistently reminded
- C = Everyone Else (all your cold leads go here)
- D = Knuckleheads- People you don't want to work with – Ding Dongs, Jerks, Knuckleheads*.

*Note: These are people you would normally have deleted, but you want to remember who they are so you don't accidentally allow them back into your life. Knuckleheads will end up back in your CRM, make sure you tag them a "D", but keep them in your database, so you remember them!

CRM

Feed It Daily

Once your CRM is completely set up, you'll need to put your system in place to maintain and utilize it. How will you feed your database?

All Team Members should enter new contacts into the CRM when:

1. A lead calls looking to buy or sell.
2. Any time a Team Member meets a potential client, resource, advocate, referring Agent, etc.
3. You make a new friend.

Once set up with all the correct fields, the CRM should automatically generate a list of contacts that must be followed up with by you and your Team, and should tell you how, when, and why you are contacting them.

Module 6 - Follow Up Schedule

A+= Call 1x month (and lunch once a quarter to once every 6 months)
A – Call 1x quarter
B – Call 1x every 6 months
C – Call 1x year if time allows, or Next Follow Up Date and email only

Stop by with SWAG = Same frequency as above – A and A+ only, and only if you are in Tier 1.

Staying Consistent

Your CRM should have systematic marketing and prospecting plans, which ensure constant contact with all of the prospects, referrals, advocates, business contacts, and past clients in your database. By following up in a consistent manner, it cements your relationship with the contacts in your database and maintains ongoing communication.

Remember: NEXT FOLLOW-UP DATE! (Under "Add Activity" in Contact Record)

Coach's Corner: A simple script to use to when following up with leads is: **"I just want to make sure I'm not dropping the ball on my end."**

Unresponsive Buyers

If you have an unresponsive buyer that just won't answer or return your calls, should they be trashed? The answer is 'NO!', especially if you're on a Team.

Remember, those leads belong to the Team Leader.

If the buyer isn't returning your call, they just aren't ready to talk to you.

What do you do?

Send them the following text, and if they are still unresponsive, put them on a long-term nurture program in your CRM. Drip campaigns are essential with most of these.

Video Text for Unresponsive Buyers: Video a new countertop with the following voiceover: "I'm so excited the new countertops got put in!! Shoot that addendum back to me right away so we can get this closed tomorrow and get your family moved in!"

You'll be surprised how many people will respond: "I think you sent this to the wrong person".

PERFECT!! At least they responded! Now, you can engage with them and determine whether or not there is even a reason to follow up with them going forward!

Module 7 - How to Use a Drip Campaign

Drip campaigns are a series of emails, texts, and other forms of communication, which go out automatically to clients over a long period of time. These can span years, and even a decade.

The goal of a drip campaign for inbound leads is to stay top of mind with the potential client.

Think of it like when you go to the store to buy new shoes. You walk in, and a salesperson immediately greets you and says, "May I help you?"

You, of course, respond with "No thanks, I'm just looking..." and he walks away...

After a few minutes of looking, you find it! That PERFECT pair of Louboutins! But, alas, the salesperson is all the way on the other side of the store by now...

Do you walk all the way over there to get him, or do you simply grab the nearest salesperson and ask for that shoe in your size?

I'm sure you'd agree that you'd likely do the latter, as would most normal human beings.

In real estate, we are like the first salesperson, but we need to do a better job of being the second. People will grab the closest, most convenient person or option. Our job is to be THAT person.

We need to be top of mind and easily available when THEY are ready to buy.

Automated drips CAN be helpful in staying top of mind.

Most Agents use a drip campaign to blast listings to everyone on their CRM as well.

If you are on a Team, your Team Leader will likely already have these in place.

If you are a solo Agent, make sure you have 3 year+ drips for buyers and sellers at a minimum.

Always offer something of value when you send out these messages on your drip campaign. They MUST be in the habit of **wanting** to open your messages, because they know there will always be something good in them, like a gift under the Christmas tree or a birthday card from a valued friend.

Here is a list of value added drip campaign ideas for buyer leads:

- Send them a copy of your vendor list - from your favorite home inspector to your favorite handyman.
- Event lists - invite them to community events in your area. Don't forget to invite them to your Team's client events.
- Housing market updates. Mortgage rates, recent property sales, and relevant real estate news are a great update for your

buyers.
- Any and all real estate listings in their area.
- How to tips for homeowners.
- Blog posts

When dealing with non-responsive leads, still keep them on a drip campaign. You can send blog posts about the market, more homeowner resources such as tips on home maintenance, and housing price updates. If they want to buy in the future, then you still will have "top of mind" presence for that buyer. So don't ever take non-responsive prospects off your list unless they specifically ask for you to do so.

Finally, it's a good idea to occasionally sprinkle in (lightly) some "evidence of success" messages. Telling success stories about your clients is a great example here.

Module 8 - Using a Dialer

What is a dialer? A dialer will help you phone more leads in less time. As a matter of fact, sales phone dialers increase your prospecting efficiency by more than 183%!

Here's another shocking fact: 80% of all sales are made on the 5th to 12th contact - and 45% of leads are not contacted again after the initial first touch!

If you are doing your daily lead generation, but not getting any traction, take a long look at your follow-up process.

The "Middle Class Agent" can call around 30 leads per hour. With a dialer, you can call up to 85 leads per hour. That's a lot more opportunities to convert a prospect into a client!

If you use a dialer, you can easily leave recorded voicemails at the click of a button, integrate with your CRM, avoid burnout from "regular" phone dialing, and save time. This all results in you making more money in less time.

What you want to find is a set of tools that can integrate with each other. For example, your CRM and your dialer should communicate so you can keep track of your emails and phone calls in one place.

Some CRMs come with built-in dialers, others you'll need an add-on:

- Sales Dialers (While we don't recommend it for your SOI, we use Sales Dialers for cold leads in house and **love** it. We love it so much that we've negotiated a discount for everyone who reads this book. Visit www.clubwealth.com/SalesDialers to get our special price.)
- Vulcan 7 (Great data for expireds, we get a discount here also, which is good, because it's on the expensive side, but well worth the expense for serious prospectors)... www.ClubWealth.com/Vulcan7).

For a complete list of Club Wealth® CRM reviews, recommendations and discounts, visit www.ClubWealth.com/CRM.

In order to be a World Class Buyer Agent, you will need to fully utilize your Teams CRM. Add all your friends and family (SOI), and always remember, "*The fortune really is in the follow up!*"

CHAPTER 8
SELLING TO THE DISC PROFILE

Module 1 - Intro to the DISC

As Real Estate Agents, we are trained in sales techniques such as prospecting, negotiating, and closing a deal. No matter how successful you are you should always strive to develop skills that improve your client interactions. One way is to focus on selling to the DISC profile.

What is a DISC profile?

The DISC profile is a behavior assessment tool based on the theory of psychologist William Marston. It focuses on four different personality traits, which are:

Dominance (D), Influence (I), Steadiness (S), and Compliant (C).

Take It One Step Further

"Dominant" (D) people prioritize results over everything else. They are most concerned about their bottom line and are very direct in their communication.

"Influential" (I) people care most about influencing or persuading others. They put a lot of weight on their relationships. They like people, and like to be liked.

"Steady" (S) people emphasize security. They look for sincerity and dependability over anything else. They tend to have the heart of selfless service.

"Compliant" (C) people want as much information as possible about your product or service. They value quality and accuracy and are afraid of making the wrong move.

Why Use The DISC?

If the DISC can help you better understand the preferred way to interact with others, how can you apply the DISC profile to selling real estate?

You need skills that help build rapport, and help you quickly understand and communicate with your clients and prospects at a level that they are engaged and comfortable with. In other words, communicate the way they communicate.

You can use the DISC tool to enhance your skills so your clients are more likely to trust you and feel comfortable with you, listen to you, and close the deal.

Module 2 - Simple Steps to Identifying Buyers' DISC

Look at what they do for living

D- Leaders, CEOs, owners of companies

I- Salespeople, office receptionists

S- Health workers, administrative assistants

C- IT workers, program writers, technology field

Sometime it's easier to determine what they are not rather than what they are.

Here are some behavioral and body language clues you can use to quickly figure out the personality of your customers:

How to Identify a D Personality Style

- "D" people typically move fast and are always on the go.
- They'll talk with their hands, using big gestures, and are direct when they talk to you.
- They're not enthusiastic about small talk.
- Sometimes, they can give the impression that they're rude or hard to deal with.

What Should One Remember to Do When Working with a D Personality?

- Be direct, to the point, and brief
- Focus on tangible points and talk about "What" instead of "How"
- Be confident
- Don't focus too much on the problems
- They don't want to hear the small details. They are big picture thinkers and may perceive you as negative
- Speak with confidence
- Avoid repeating yourself or rambling, they want you to get right to the point

What is the Greatest Fear of D Personality Types?

- Not being in control
- The fear of being taken advantage of

How to Identify an "I" Personality

- High "I" people are typically trusting and optimistic.
- They use lots of facial expressions and hand gestures while they talk.

What Motivates the "I" Personality?

- Approval
- Flattery
- Praise
- Popularity
- Acceptance by others.

What Should One Remember to Do When Working With an "I" Personality?

- They are not good with detail
- Build rapport and be friendly with them
- Approach them in a favorable and friendly environment
- Give them plenty of opportunity to verbalize their ideas
- Write details down for them
- Don't eliminate being social
- Don't do all the talking or strictly tell them what to do
- Don't react to them in a way that makes them feel rejected

What is the Greatest Fear of an "I" Personality?

- Since acceptance and approval by others is the main desire of "I" personality types, rejection is their biggest fear.

How to Identify an "S" Personality

High "S" people tend to keep "poker" faces and don't display much emotion. They will observe a conversation before they join in.

They'll talk and walk with a steady, easy pace.
They are the ones who are always making sure everyone is happy

What Motivates the "S" Personality?

- Motivated by safety and security
- They want to avoid conflict
- Peaceful environments
- Appreciate recognition for their loyalty and dependability

What Should One Remember to Do When Working with an "S" Personality?

- Be personable and build rapport
- Show sincere interest in them as a person
- Be kind and patient

What Should One Remember NOT to Do When Working with an "S" Personality Type?

- Avoid being confrontational
- Avoid using strong tone or body language
- Don't be unkind or impatient
- Avoid being overly aggressive, pushy or demanding

What is the Greatest Fear of "S" Personality Types?

- Because the "S" strives for stability and a feeling of peace and safety, they fear the loss of security through change.

How to Identify a "C" Personality

- High "C" People will ask direct, detailed questions.
- Their classic body language is having their arms folded with a hand on their chin.

What Should One Remember to Do When Working with "C" Personality Types?

- Be prepared and do your research
- When disagreeing with them, work with facts instead of people examples
- Be patient, persistent and diplomatic

What Should One Remember NOT to DO When Working with "C" Personality Types?

- Don't speak in broad generalizations with no specifics
- Don't answer questions too vaguely or casually
- Do not criticize
- Avoid being confrontational as they will not respond well to this and will close off

What Motivates the "C" Personality?

- Information and logic
- High standards of quality
- Researching before deciding
- Clear parameters and instructions

What is the Greatest Fear of "C" Styles?

- They fear criticism
- Not being well informed
- Being Wrong

12 Different DISC Combinations

- DI/ID - I Lead/I Sell
- SC/CS - I Execute
- SI/IS - I Participate
- DC/CD - I Build/Create
- DS/SD - I Plan
- IC/CI - I Explain

Module 3 - Why This is Important to Your Career

The DISC Behavioral Styles can provide you with the insights and skills necessary to enhance your career status. By understanding your own DISC Behavioral Style, and the style of others, it gives you powerful social interaction tools. This also will enable you to tailor your social interactions to bridge potential conflicts that sometimes occur between different DISC Profiles.

Steps to Success Using DISC

In order to master the DISC and use it successfully in your sales career, you have to ask yourself these 3 important questions:

Do you understand personality traits?

Do you know how to effectively communicate with each of them?

Can you confidently build rapport and trust with each of the different personality styles?

If you can do these 3 things, you should be able to get more people to know, like, and trust you, and to do business with you.

What Will Knowing the DISC Do for You?

In both personal and professional relationships, DISC gives us a simple way to understand one another. The more you understand the DISC, the more you will get into rapport, which means the more people will trust you, and in turn, the more people will do business with you.

Module 4 - Using the DISC in Sales Process

For the World Class Buyer Agent, you should keep your client's DISC style present throughout the ENTIRE sales process, and where the entire Team can see it so all will know how to properly communicate with the client. Keep it in mind throughout the entire transaction - not just when building rapport.

As an example, keep DISC in mind when it comes down to

negotiating the contract, moving a buyer forward, dealing with inspections, and making the final decision on a property.

Coach's Corner: You can put the client's DISC identifier in their contact sheet and/or in your CRM. You'll always know how to handle any situation when it comes to your client, no matter what their DISC profile is.

Tips for using the DISC Profile:

- Don't interrupt when someone is giving you an objection, as they would feel you are discrediting their objection.
- Realize objections are sales opportunities. Objections are a reason to close. Objections reveal your client's prime concern.
- Remember the importance of observing your client to determine what style they are.
- Recognizing your client's personality style is one of the most important skills for you as a salesperson to assess and build a relationship with your client.
- Have you ever worked with a client and it seemed like you didn't connect? It's probably because you didn't analyze your client's style, or worse, you didn't try.

Sample Objection Handlers for each DISC Profile:

1. I want to wait until _____rates come down_____(or fill in blank for whatever reason for waiting).

D - I fully understand you want to wait. Yet, you know interest rates are rising. Don't you want to buy now so you don't risk out on a great property?

I - I understand that you want to wait. You know, I had one client that wanted to wait because they thought they couldn't afford it at this price. However, prices could come down, but interest rates will continue to rise. So do you really want to wait?

S - I understand that you want to wait. However, I'm sure you want to get your family in the house, right? I had a client that wanted to wait, they couldn't buy it and they had to lose out on the house. So do you really want to wait?

C - I totally understand that you want to wait. I'm sure you've read the Feds are raising interest rates, so do you really want to take that chance?

2. I want to work with more than one Agent.

D - I know you realize that a lot of Agents will not tell you what to do to get your offer accepted? You know I don't work that way. I'm going to get the best deal on the house and I will do that for you. You don't want to be taken advantage of?

I - You realize my mission is to do the best for you? Why would you want to work with other Agents after all the work I've put in for you? I will get the best deal for you. Isn't that what you want?

S - Don't you feel that I will do the best for you? My main concern is doing a good job for you and your family. Don't you want the best home for you and your family?

C - You know, that having me as your Agent, I will make sure that you are going to have all the facts and details to make an informed decision. Isn't that what you want?

Do you know what your DISC profile is? Go to our website and find out for free! Take the test or simply learn more about the DISC at https://www.clubwealth.com/disc/

CHAPTER 9
BUYER LEAD GENERATION

The 3 most important things an Agent, whether on a Team or working solo, must do every single day are:

1. Lead Generation
2. Lead Follow-Up
3. Lead Conversion

Your lead generation should be focused on setting appointments. Stop being picky about appointments.

At Club Wealth®, we affectionately refer to Agents that require leads to get "Pre-Qualified" by a lender prior to showing them homes as 'The Sales Prevention Team'.

TEAM LEADER: **It is mission critical that you teach your Team this principle. They need to experience not only the appointments themselves, but also the habit of consistently SETTING and attending at least one appointment EVERY DAY.**

We'll share scripting for this AND for getting the prospect to WANT to talk with your lender in the chapter on Lead Conversion.

For now, get your Team setting appointments with EVERY possible prospect, regardless of qualification.

If you're doing less than 4 transactions a month, you need the practice. Each appointment, qualified or not, provides you with an opportunity to hone your skills.

It's like crack… first one's free, and then you've got to pay!

In other words, EVERYONE gets to see the first home, WITHOUT having to jump through ANY hoops!

Lead generation is not just about cold calling, it also includes your SOI and other lead sources.

You'll know you're on the right track with lead generation if you're scheduling at least 1 appointment per day!

Find ways to be passionate about Lead Generation, and you'll have found the secret to a SOLID 6 or even 7-figure income!

Join networking groups that interest you:

- Church groups
- Book club
- Cooking
- Hobbies & other interests that you have

Be authentic to whom you are and build relationships with people who are like-minded; don't join a book club if you don't like to read!

Coach's Corner: Your lead generation must never stop! When your lead generation stops, your business stops 3 months later!

The biggest challenge most Agents have is to maintain focus and consistent effort on lead generation, even when they become incredibly busy, successful, and at times overwhelmed. Once a high number of leads are being generated, there is a tendency to settle for that number and devote more time to servicing that business. Don't take your eye off the ball - don't neglect your lead generation program.

You MUST consistently lead generate on a DAILY basis, no matter how successful you think you are in the moment.

Your goal is to build a MASSIVE PIPELINE of leads that you will nurture long term. Some will buy now, some in 90 days, 6 months, a year, or even 18 months down the road. By nurturing all of them, AND generating new leads on a daily basis, you will have a consistent river of business flowing to you month in and month out!

Module 1- What is Lead Generation? And How Can I Be Intentional With It?

Lead generation is simply the act of searching for AND FINDING potential clients who need or want your service. It centers on cultivating and nurturing prospective clients. Very simply, we want to consistently generate leads, bring value to them, and nurture them, all in an effort to get them to do business with us now or in the future.

Did you know there are over 2,000 ways to lead generate?

While that provides a lot of options, ultimately you only need two or three ways that you are willing to lead generate daily. Be very deliberate and consistent with your effort. Once you have mastered each lead generation method you are using, you need to add one new lead source every quarter.

Lead generation opportunities are all around us. You can find lead opportunities in most of the places you go every day. The playground, parties, grocery stores, PTA meetings, and so forth, or interacting with business owners, friends, family, etc. No matter where you find opportunities, you must make lead generation a scheduled and intentional daily task.

In fact, lead generation is the #1 most important aspect of your business. You must find prospects to work with so that you can get people into contracts and ultimately get paid for your service.

Some of the most common places real estate Agents generate leads are:

- SOI (Sphere of Influence)
- Sign Calls
- Facebook
- Pay Per Click (PPC) leads
- Phone duty (also known as "Floor Time")
- Open houses
- Geo farming
- Craigslist
- Networking
- Prospecting

Really, anywhere you can meet new people and have conversations is a good source.

One of the quickest ways to find leads is by prospecting. Prospecting is best used when you need to find leads to fill your pipeline *right now*. Maybe your pipeline is thin and you need to replenish it. Or maybe you're a few deals short of your quarterly goal and you need to quickly identify, engage and close new customers.

Prospecting is all about urgency and aggression. That said we are always aggressive with the process, never with the people.

There many different ways to prospect, but the most effective way is by picking up the phone & dialing. The difference between prospecting on the phone versus door knocking or other methods ultimately comes down to the time required.

For example, dialing 200 people and having 20 conversations on a dialer can likely be done in less than 4-5 hours. Yet, going out and finding 20 face-to-face conversations could likely take eight hours or more.

Module 2 - Who Can You Prospect?

- Team leads or leads in CRM are #1
- Any current or past clients
- SOI (MAKE SURE you call them at least quarterly to invite to client events)
- Current/Past open house attendees
- Circle prospecting around an open house

What is Circle Prospecting?

Circle prospecting is simply calling the neighbors around a just listed, just sold, or open house to inform them about what's going on, invite them to see the home, and see if they are at all interested or open to selling. It is a way to target and interact with homeowners in geographical areas where you want to grow your business.

Circle Prospecting Scripts

Agent: Hi, this is Misti with ABC Realty. I'm calling because your neighbor just listed their house and personally requested that I reach out to let you know we're holding an Open House on Saturday. We'll have a private hour between 9am-10am. It is exclusive to neighbors, like yourself, and any friends that you choose to invite. Can I add you to the list for attending? **PAUSE.** Perfect. Real quick, one last thing. I'm not sure if you are aware but your neighbor's property being listed MAY have changed the value of your property. Would you be interested in finding out how your home is worth in the current market?

"I'm working with..." Circle Prospecting Script

Agent: Hi, this is Michael with Hellickson Real Estate. I'm working with John and Suzy Smith (Make sure you have an agency agreement). They've been looking for a home in the neighborhood for some time now, with no success.

I was wondering... If they were to pay you whatever price you wanted, pay for all repairs, closing costs, commissions and expenses, had no contingencies, paid cash, and were willing to close whenever you want and even be flexible on your move date, would you even consider entertaining an offer from them to buy your home?

You would?! FANTASTIC! Would Tuesday or Thursday at 5 be better for you for me to come by and see if the floor plan and finishes will fit their needs?

Don't be a secret Agent.

With the technology available at our fingertips today, some leads will search you out on social media. Don't be a secret Agent. Make sure your profiles are open to the pubic, and that your credentials and contact information are visible.

To those who have a profile for personal use/friends, and a separate profile for business use, we say: STOP IT!!

Your potential clients don't care about your privacy. They want to get to know you.

When you chose to go into real estate, you consciously or unconsciously made the choice to be transparent and authentic with the world. Embracing this will serve you well in your career.

You'll need ONE Personal Profile, and Business Page. Note: a Profile and a Page are two different things.

You may often notice on some other Agent's profiles that it's hard to tell they are even an Agent. Although you don't need to flood your personal page with all business, it shouldn't be hard to see what you do for a living. Your personal FB profile/posts should be 80% personal in nature, and 20% business related.

Credibility is key. Prospects are looking for reasons to trust you and believe that you are a trusted advisor. Show them what they're looking for. You must be positioned as having high-level expertise. People need to know, like, and trust you to work with you.

Coach's Corner: Be careful about what you post on social media: no politics, no religion, and avoid unprofessional pictures and posts. You and your

friends might enjoy hard partying in sketchy attire, but posting pics of that will NOT get you the volume of business you'd like!

Market authority and credibility is key! You must give them the perception that you are in authority in your market.

Nothing shows market authority and dominance like consistently posting your clients success stories.

Make it about them, not you.

Example of what NOT to post: I just sold another house!

Example of what TO post: Help me congratulate SSgt and Mrs. Smith on the purchase of their first home! Upon returning from defending our country in Iraq, SSgt Smith was able to get a ZERO DOWN loan using his VA benefit, and after 3 months of searching for the perfect home, they found it! Now he and Suzy and their 3 children have a wonderful backyard in which they can play with their dog Bubba and their hedgehog Speedy.

You get the point...tell THEIR story.

Time Block for Lead Generation

Commit to at least 3 hours a day for lead generation. Be consistent and disciplined with your lead generation time.

You'll need to specifically set appointments in your Google or Outlook Calendar for "Prospecting for ___" for example.

This should be a regular, recurring appointment in your calendar, with notifications that remind you on your phone and PC that "It's time to prospect".

Treat these with respect, like any other appointment in your calendar, and FIGHT HARD to make sure you adhere to this schedule.

You must elevate these appointments to habits, for as you do, success will surely follow.

Take a look at Chapter 6 on Perfect Daily Schedule for Buyer Agents, and also watch the video and download the free checklist at http://www.ClubWealth.com/PDS

Remember! Consistency is key!

Find an Accountability Partner

As a member of a Team, you already have this covered, as your Team Leader is your accountability partner. As a solo Agent, this will be a critical factor in your success.

It is MISSION CRITICAL that you report your performance on a daily basis.

*When performance is **measured**, performance improves. When performance is **measured** and reported, the rate of improvement accelerates* - Thomas S. Monson

This means you MUST track, record, and report your calls, contacts, appointments and contracts each weekday. Ideally these will be shared during the Daily Team Huddle (http://clubwealth.com/real-estate-daily-team-huddle/), which we recommend take place as early in the morning as possible, ideally 7:30am.

Participation in the Daily Huddle is a critical component in your success, Team culture, and your overall development as a World Class Buyer Agent. On most Mega Teams, daily participation in the Huddle is also a prerequisite for obtaining leads from the Team.

Always come from a place of contribution.

When we come from a place of contribution, all things are possible.

The late great Zig Ziglar said often, "You will get all you want in life, if you help enough other people get what they want."

Separate yourself from the commission. As the old saying goes, "Avoid commission breath." Take it step by step, and realize these people have no reason to trust you… YET!

Their trust has to be earned. Commissions won't come if trust isn't earned. But they surely will when it is!

So what does it mean to TRULY "Come from Contribution"? It means earnestly striving to find ways to help others, whether there is financial or other gain in it for you or not.

Ask yourself, "How can I be of service to others?"

Only AFTER you have delivered truly selfless value can you then begin answering the following:

What do I REALLY bring to the table?

What differentiates me from my competitors?

141

How do I articulate the value I bring?

How do I make my value visible?

Don't chase shiny objects

We tend to chase shiny objects: the newest technology solution, the newest lead source, the newest "Guru" with the magic beans, etc. As we do that we begin to ignore the old school ways that have always worked and still do.

As advanced as the industry is with new and improved technology you will often see Agents ignoring the most basic and fundamental ideas. Find mundane things that make you great, and be prepared to roll up your sleeves and do the work.

Things like time blocking, prospecting, open houses, clients events, call nights, door knocking, farming, simple CRM's, and many other "Old School" techniques and technologies are still powerful tools in your arsenal today!

If you don't master the foundational items and meet as many people as you can for FREE, you won't have the experience or the money to move on to bigger and better lead generation tools, technology, and lead sources, many of which cost money.

Module 3 - Mindset for Lead Generation

Remember: Eagles don't flock with Turkeys…

Turkeys say "My Team does the lead generation for me"

Eagles say: "No matter how many leads my Team does/does not provide me, I make lead generation a daily habit."

Turkeys say: "I'll get around to lead generation when I can"

Eagles say: "I LOVE that lead generation is my daily habit!"

Our minds are incredibly powerful, particularly our subconscious mind, and when properly trained, it can accomplish unbelievable things!

With that power we can generate enormous wealth in all 5 Key Areas in our lives. Feeding your mind daily with affirmations can and will change your subconscious mind's belief of what reality really is. This, in turn, will literally become your reality.

If we keep telling ourselves the same story, we are doomed to repeat the same patterns.

Change the story you're telling yourself, and you'll change your life!

Your subconscious mind is FAR more powerful than your conscious mind, and can't tell the difference between reality and what you tell it to believe.

This is why you can LITERALLY change your reality by simply reprogramming your subconscious mind!

Here are some tips for creating a Mindset for Lead Generation:

Expect each lead to genuinely be interested and ready to communicate.

Start priming your mind each day with affirmations like:

"I will call until I find someone TODAY who is ready willing, able and excited to do business with me TODAY!"

"I love prospecting because it helps me reach my goals!"

Module 4- Team Generated Leads vs. Agent Generated Leads

It's important to understand the difference between Team-generated leads and personally generated leads: Team generated leads are leads that you get directly from your Team leader OR leads generated from Team efforts. Your personal leads will include those from your SOI, and may or may not be compensated differently than Team generated leads.

Coach's Corner: Remember, what you make at year-end is far more important than what you make on a particular transaction. Try to focus on the big picture and not on squabbling over nickels and dimes with your Team. You and your Team will be happier, and you'll make more money in the end anyway!

Don't forget to leverage client events and open house events as touch points and opportunities to call your SOI.

Examples of Team Generated Leads are:

- Sign calls & leads coming from flyers
- Portal & internet Leads
- Client events
- Referrals from Team leads
- Open houses
- Any leads that come through social media
- Any leads that come in through Facebook and Instagram ads

144

Listings to Leads

Virtually every vendor in the industry would LOVE an endorsement from Club Wealth®. That said; few receive it. One of the vendors we especially like, for all Tier Levels is the extremely affordable Listings to Leads Platform, which, with the discount we have arranged for our readers, provides more tools for less money than any platform we have seen...ever!

To get the Club Wealth® discount on L2L, visit: ClubWealth.com/L2L

As a Buyer Agent, you can advertise listings in an effort to generate buyer leads. Check with your Team Leader to be sure you're not duplicating efforts.

L2L offers:

- Gorgeous single property websites
- E-flyers
- Syndicate to social media
- Print Flyers
- Upload virtual tours
- Text IVR features
- and much more

So, what do you do if your Team doesn't have listings for you to market?

- Ask Agents in your office
- Ask outside Agents
- Approach FSBO's
- Check with the HUD Homes LLB in your area (They are

required to let you market HUD Homes)
- Check with local builders about marketing their listings (check with their Agent if they are listed)

When you ask another brokerage to advertise their listings, it is usually best to get their permission in writing. Check with your broker for language that should be included in the written permission.

A good email script to use when asking other brokers to market their listings is:

"Hi ____, per our conversation, please respond to this email with 'YES' to confirm that it is okay for me to market your listings. Thank you so much, and I'm looking forward to working with you on some transactions soon!"

Other ways to generate buyer leads:

Craigslist

In addition to marketing through L2L, you can market listings on Craigslist and through Open Houses.

Some Tips to Remember when posting to Craigslist:

- Renew the ad every 3 days
- Repost the ad every 30 days
- Utilize ONLY a single call capture#, ideally through http://www.ClubWealth.com/IVR

If your goal is to get the highest possible volume of leads, avoid the "Fatal Four" in your marketing:

- Bedrooms
- Bathrooms

- Square Footage
- Price

It is also wise to omit the address

Facebook

Join groups and community pages near you and be involved in them! Engage with their followers with non-business related posts as well. It's important to present yourself as an interested and interesting person, instead of simply a real estate Agent. Network within these groups, and for goodness sake, COME FROM CONTRIBUTION, and you will get traction on your listings and pages.

- Swap Sell Pages
- Local Area Pages

When posting listings to Facebook or other Social Media Sites, remember:

- Use lots of emojis
- Omit the fatal 4 - Bedrooms, Bathrooms, Square Footage and Price
- Have a link to an external "find out more" landing page, like L2L
- Use call capture number

The Price is Right

Running a contest on your business page works well... Challenge people to guess the correct listing and/or sales price of the home, and give the winner an Amazon gift card ($10-25 is sufficient).

- Run a contest on your business page

- Share on your personal page
- Share on swap pages and other sites
- Engage with comments, tag friends etc.
- Always have a link to more information on a landing page, like L2L

Instagram

Use Hashtags! Having 9-11 hashtags on each post gets you more traction and gets your photos in front of more people. Search hashtags near your area, or ones that you will be using, and start commenting and liking on photos with those hashtags. Post relevant and interesting content; don't consistently post ads and listings.

For deeper discussion and strategies on Instagram, check out the video and free checklist at ClubWealth.com/Instagram

Module 5 - Lead Generation for the Buyer Agent

Remember, lead generation is one of the most important tasks as an Agent.

Without lead generation, we can't build and nurture a consistent pipeline, and without a consistent pipeline, our incomes become sporadic, unpredictable, and weak at best.

To be a World Class Buyer Agent:

- Be consistent!
- Time block daily for lead generation activities.
- Make lead generation a non-negotiable task on a daily basis and protect it fiercely.

TEAM LEADER: Lead Generation must be a daily habit for EVERY member of the Sales Team. Furthermore, you must consistently "Inspect what you expect", meaning you will need to check in on a daily basis with each Team member, asking them how many calls, contacts, appointments and contracts they had the previous day.

This is best accomplished using the "Daily Huddle" as described in video and with the free checklist at http://www.ClubWealth.com/Huddle.

Participation should be mandatory to receive Team leads.

We recommend the following minimum KPI's per Agent per day:

- 100 Calls
- 25 Contacts
- 1 Appointment Set
- 2 closings per month

Remember: Eagles don't flock with Turkeys. You aren't doing anyone any favors by being soft on KPI's. Do yourself, your clients, and most of all your Team members a favor and hold them accountable!

CHAPTER 10
MASTERING THE MASSIVE OPEN HOUSE

Module 1- Why Hold an Open House?

As a Buyer Agent, why would you want to hold an open house?

I mean, most Agents spend 3+ hours at an open house and only get 3-4 buyers coming through, right?

Well, that may be true, but when you follow the Club Wealth® MASSIVE Open House Formula, you'll likely get closer to 50-150 people out to your open house, AND make a ton of money over time as you nurture the leads that come from it!

The biggest reason is to find interested buyers. It goes without saying that if you don't have buyers, you don't have business. It is also a great opportunity to build rapport with prospective clients, get known as the World Class Agent in your marketplace, and build your business.

You should be hosting 4-6 open houses a month if you aren't closing 2 or more transactions per month, or if you have less than 6 active buyers.

Frankly, holding 4-6 open houses a month is a great habit to be in no matter what your production or workload is, as it will ensure that you are ALWAYS building your pipeline. This will allow you to effectively avoid the "Real Estate Income Roller Coaster", and have consistent income all the time.

Hour for hour, holding open houses (when you follow the Club Wealth® MASSIVE Open House Formula) can be one of the most productive lead generation activities you do, and one of the most enjoyable!

How do you get people to come to your open house? Door knocking, circle prospecting, and personal invitations to open houses are good ways to add people to your database, and can really be magnified with paid and organic social media traffic.

Key points to follow for hosting Open Houses:

- Follow the Massive Open House checklist (Download the latest version of the checklist for free at www.ClubWealth.com/openhouse)
- DO NOT reinvent the wheel. Too often, we as humans (especially driven ones) like to tweak everything to "make it ours". Trust this: The Club Wealth® Systems have been designed, implemented, tested, vetted, and perfected by some of the brightest minds and most successful Agents in the business... DON'T MESS WITH WHAT WE KNOW WORKS, until you have done it over and over again (at least 30 times). Then, and only then, once you have really made an effort to do it EXACTLY like we teach it, should you begin testing tweaks (one at a time) to see where you can make improvements that resonate with you and your bank account!
- Sellers often search social media to see who's killing it! It's more than just ads... showing consistent evidence of success and lots of activity can give the perception of Uber Success!
- Many of the people who come through your open house will be neighboring homeowners, and even FSBOs. In fact, you should go out of your way to invite neighboring FSBOs to your opens! The vast majority of FSBOs will eventually list

153

with an Agent. Most will list with an Agent within 21 days of initially going FSBO! Remember: EVERY visitor to your open house is a potential client and/or referral source!

- Don't forget about cancelleds, expireds, and withdrawns. Each of these are potential clients as well… Invite them out! Call, text, email and snail mail them an invite.
- If the home sells before the open house, you still hold it open!
- Open houses are NOT about selling THIS house; they are about lead generation. You can use the leads you get from that ONE open house to sell MANY houses!
- Run a contest for a $100 drawing and promote it. Get your lender and/or other vendor partners to come up with the prize money. Then, use big starburst add-ons to your signs that say "$100 giveaway"… If you were driving through the neighborhood, and saw 12 different open house signs, ONE of which was giving away $100, which would you stop by FIRST? Exactly…
- Use free and inexpensive websites to edit advertising pictures:
  - Canva
  - PicMonkey
  - Picisto

Make It Look Like a Circus!

I don't know about you, but if I'm going to take 3+ hours of my life away from my family to hold an open house, I'm going to make it worth my time. I'm going to expect to get 50-150 unique visitors, thus maximizing my chances of doing a ton of business for my time.

When planning an open house, the goal is to literally make it look like the circus came to town! You want to attract LOTS of attention (beware, some of it may not be positive), so it will help to have every tool at your disposal. That includes (among other things):

You'll need several flags, BIG ONES, in front of the house. Two at a minimum, but aim for four. Even better, add one of those fan-inflated air tube guys that flop all over the place and dance around...

Banners that say "Open House" or "The Big Event" are GREAT, and attract lots of attention.

A-Boards (aka "Sandwich Boards")... this is where it gets REALLY interesting... we recommend 50+ signs per open house! That's right, 50+!

When I was 26 years old, I ran for office in a town called Federal Way, Washington. I ran against a professional lobbyist and a woman who admittedly deserved the Mother Teresa Volunteer of the Year Award in the City.

No one believed I had a chance in you-know-where to win.

But win I did, handily, and signs were the key!

You see, I learned early on while door knocking that I could say 10 things someone agreed with, but if I said just ONE thing that they disagreed with, they'd vote for the other candidate. They might not be sure about my opponents, but at least knew they didn't disagree with them!

Enter my sign domination strategy... In just over 3 months, I put up over 3,500 campaign signs in this little town of 80,000 people. You could practically walk across town on my signs without touching the ground!

People thought I was nuts. Expert campaign chairs said I was foolish to spend literally 98% of my campaign budget on signs alone.

Here was my theory: sure, there are people who ONLY vote party lines, but the majority of people are in the middle. Can you guess how those people vote? When unsure or indifferent in any way, they vote name recognition.

It's also how sellers often think. They may have NO IDEA how many transactions you close, but if they're used to seeing your name all over town and on the Internet, they'll ASSUME you are successful.

I even upped the ante by creating multiple versions of my signs throughout the campaign, and by being the first to implement my last name.com on them. They literally said "Hellickson.com for City Council". I figured they didn't need to know my first name to get it right on the ballot, so why clutter the signs with it?

So, how can you apply this principle to dominate and win YOUR campaign to sell more houses? Easy. Put out more signs than you think reasonable. Lots more. By putting out 50-75 signs for each open house, often 4-8 at a single intersection, you will attract more attention, get more people to your open house, and have EVERYONE who sees your signs thinking, "That Susie is one aggressive Agent!" (that is a good thing, by the way!)

Now, be sure to check your local governmental sign restrictions. That said; even if they fine you for putting out too many signs, it might be worth it.

I remember a particularly AWESOME location at a major intersection as you came into Federal Way, right next to McDonalds. I used to put a sign up in the center island there on a Friday, and by Monday afternoon, it was gone.

Knowing the value of that high traffic location, I'd replace it with another sign as soon as I realized it was gone. This happened at least 10 or so times, before I received a phone call from Betty, the cities sign Nazi.

Her job was to ensure all signs met the city code, and apparently she was the one removing my signs at this, and other, locations.

"Mr. Hellickson, are you aware that there is a sign code in Federal Way?"

"I suppose there is..." I replied.

"Mr. Hellickson, I'm going to send you a copy of it so you can read it. You see, I have been picking up a lot of your signs lately, so I assume you don't understand the code."

I didn't say this to Betty, but I knew, and understood, most of the code. More importantly, though, I understood marketing.

"Well, thank you Betty! I really appreciate that!"

"My pleasure, Mr. Hellickson. Now, about those signs. I have about 50-75 of them here in my office, and I'd like you to come pick them up."

"Absolutely! I'd be happy to pick them up!"

"I need to tell you, Mr. Hellickson, that there is a fine of $3.50 for each sign that must be paid before you can retrieve them."

Ok, at this point, my mind went immediately to math. You see, the signs and the stakes combined cost me $2.50, so it was cheaper to simply buy new signs.

I explained this to the clearly dismayed Code Enforcement Officer, who, as politely as possible given her agitated state, hung up the phone.

I received a call two weeks later: "Are you going to come pick these signs up or not, Mr. Hellickson?"

"Well no, Betty. As I explained before, it's cheaper for me to simply buy new ones."

"Okay then, Mr. Hellickson. May I have your permission to throw them in our dumpster since they are cluttering up my cubicle?"

I thought about this for a moment, and enthusiastically replied with a simple, yet deliberate "YES."

Get this: what I knew, that she may have forgotten, is that as soon as trash hits the curb (or the dumpster behind City Hall) it becomes public property. So, armed with that knowledge, I simply waited until 6 p.m. when I knew she would have left for home, and yet before the garbage company could empty the dumpster, and I took a drive by City Hall.

Sure enough, there, stacked neatly beside the dumpster, were over 175 "Hellickson.com for City Council" signs.

Being the ecologically minded, responsible citizen I am, I promptly gathered up the wayward signs, loaded them into my car, and quickly recycled them into their proper positions all over town.

I cannot confirm nor deny whether or not I may have taken special care to have written nice notes to Betty on the back of the signs that were, and continued to be, placed in the busiest of all intersections in Federal Way, WA.

Always obey the law and City Ordinances. That said, in remembering to do so, ask yourself "Is the juice worth the squeeze?"

In the words of J. Lennox Scott (then owner of John L. Scott Real Estate): "A problem you can write a check for isn't a problem, it's an expense."

Think about it… if they confiscate 20 of your signs, then charge you $10 each to get them back, your net expense is $200.

If you got ONE buyer that closed from putting up those 20 signs, was the juice worth the squeeze?

Next, you'll want some helium balloons. I heard one extremely disrespectful Agent say, "Only old blue-haired Agents with no clue hold open houses, and only the dumbest of those have balloons swinging from their signs."

Wow, just wow. Seriously, not only was that disrespectful, he was dead wrong!

Balloons swinging from your signs create motion. Motion creates emotion. Emotion causes people to act, and who knows, maybe that action will be to visit your open house. At the very least, they will see your sign, get another impression of your name and/or Team name, and become that much more familiar with and trusting of your brand. Balloons work, don't let anyone tell you otherwise!

One of my favorite tools are arrow signs, or "directional arrows". Another great branding tool, they also direct people to your open house. These little 24/7 warriors are GREAT at extending the reach of your open house and your for sale signs.

Put tons of them up, and replace them as often as Betty takes them down.

Have you ever thought of hiring sign spinners or buying mannequins that can hold and spin signs? Aggressive Agents are doing just that! For as little as minimum wage, you can hire people to stand on the street corner holding and ´ spinning your open house signs, thus attracting a TON of needed attention to your MASSIVE Open House!

The mannequins are even cooler, and, at under $1,000 each, will provide you and passersby with a ton of engaging entertainment as people struggle to determine if they are real people or robot aliens from another planet!

One Agent even had a camel mannequin (true story). People were so interested in it that it nearly caused several accidents from rubbernecking enthusiasts before he was sadly run over and placed forever on the injured reserve list.

Things to Remember:

- Contests and special themes draw people in. Get with the local antique or muscle car clubs in town and do a car-show open house. Hire a taco truck and do a Mexican fiesta. Do a derby day at a local mansion you get to hold open. There's a ton of great ideas at www.ClubWealth.com/openhouse. In the end, be creative, have fun, and people will want to have fun with you!
- Gift cards to local businesses are great because you can usually get them donated by the business since they do that business a favor by advertising for them, and people love them! The local coffee house, donut shop, bakery, hardware store, diner, heck even Home Depot or other big box retailers may be willing to donate a gift card or two. Oh, and guess who often buys and sells nice houses? You guessed it: business owners and big box retail store managers!

- Get vendors like lenders, inspectors, insurance Agents, movers, and anyone else who could benefit from an introduction to a potential client, to donate or match your contributions to the event.

- Craigslist really works! Seriously, we see a ton of Agents doing very well with Craigslist, both for general marketing and for attracting people to open houses. Best of all, IT'S FREE!!

- Door knock like a champion! You've heard of the old 10/10/20 model, where you knock on the 10 doors on either side of your listing, and the 20 doors across the street. And yes, that good, but you don't want to be "good" do you? HECK NO! You want to be World Class!!! Well, here's how you do that: knock on EVERY door in the neighborhood, before the open house, and after it sells. This is especially helpful if you are farming the neighborhood.

- Circle Prospecting – Call the 300-500 closest neighbors and invite them to the open. Offer a special "Neighbors only pre-screening" of the home to make it feel more exclusive.

- Do not get stuck in analysis paralysis. Like Nike said, JUST DO IT!

- Video text invites to everyone relevant is a must. Keep it simple, and feel free to reuse the video on social media to invite people. That said; Facebook Live bets out recorded video every time.

- Speaking of social media and Internet, advertising there is a must. It's not enough to simply boost a post or two. Make sure you are running specifically targeted ads to custom and geo-targeted audiences. Make sure you run ads and, where necessary, boosted posts on Facebook, Instagram, Zillow, Trulia, and Realtor.com.

- Choose homes in a large neighborhood, near busy

intersections, in front of shopping centers, etc. Ideally, no more than 1 mile from a busy shopping center, from which you will place TONS of signs all the way to your open house!

- What do you do if you have no listings and want to hold an open house? Borrow someone else's listing! This can be easy, but often takes a little work. Start by asking your Broker if there are company listings you can market. Then, ask local Agents if they would be interested in doing some "co-marketing"... Still need more listings to hold open? Check you local HUD broker. They are required to let you market the HUD homes. Next (and one of my favorites) is to ask FSBOs to let you hold their homes open. This is easier than you think, and VERY effective, not only because you get the open house traffic, but you'll also often get the listing, too! Here's the script for the seller:

  - "I'd love to bring 50-150 potential buyers to an open house at your home. You don't even have to pay me on the one that buys it. I just want the 49-149 who will end up buying something else. I'll pay for all the marketing, make sure the house is monitored the entire time, and ensure it is left spotless when the open house is complete. I'll even give you the contact information for all the attendees, and have my lender reach out to each of them to ensure they are qualified."

- You can also use this same strategy with expired and cancelled listings

Module 2 - Countdown to the Open House

There is a simple yet effective system for marketing the MASSIVE Open House. Now, keep in mind, you do NOT have to do EVERYTHING in this system. That said, the more you do, the more people you'll get to your open house.

This system counts down from 2 weeks prior to the open house, and walks you through each step along the way. If you are a Buyer Agent on a Team, MANY of these steps will likely be done for you by your Team, ASSUMING, of course, that you are following through on you parts of this system and getting traction in the way of active buyers and closings.

2 Weeks Prior to the Open House

Select your target home. There are a couple of things to keep in mind when selecting a home to host an open house:

What price range do you want to target? If you want to have buyers that are in the 500k ranges you should choose houses listed at between $450,000 and $600,000. If you want to work with luxury buyers, choose homes that are considered "luxury" in your market.

Traffic is key. Make sure you select homes in areas within 1 mile of a busy shopping center, in neighborhoods that preferably adjoin additional neighborhoods that have slightly lower price points (from which people would likely move up into your neighborhood), without gates or strict sign restrictions, and with at least 500+ homes in them.

Turnover matters, depending on your goal. As you select the neighborhood, look for those with low turnover rates as compared to other nearby neighborhoods. This is the opposite of what we suggest when farming a neighborhood. Why? Because low turnover neighborhoods are usually high demand, and will attract lots of buyers and even Lookie-Lou's (which is ok, because even Lookie-Lou's buy and sell houses occasionally, or send a referral now and then). High turnover neighborhoods are great if you're farming, because every time you hold an open house there, you are exposed to many potential near-future sellers.

Take video of yourself at the home and post it to YouTube and Facebook - but just enough to pique their interest. You want them to come see it for themselves so you can meet them!

*Tell the Who, What, Where, When & Why for the Open House! Remember to omit the "Fatal Four" - bedrooms, baths, square footage and price. This will elicit engagement on social media.

*Introduce yourself. Give the home address. Give the day and time of the open house, and why they should come see it. Be high energy and smile.

Promote on Facebook ($25 - $40 ad spend)

Neighbor Only Preview – Do this for neighbors that you invited prior to open house. Have the neighbors come during the first hour of the open.

Get lender or business partner support

Plan a special theme (with seller's permission)

- o   Wine and Cheese Night
- o   Ladies Night Out with Vendor Shopping
- o   Ice Cream Social

Door knock the entire neighborhood and hand out invitations.

Every day before the Open House, advertise on Zillow, Trulia, Realtor.com, MLS, and Craigslist.

Do NOT share the Fatal Four (bedrooms, baths, square footage and price) on any ads!

Countdown to Open House - One Week Before

- Make the home sound AMAZING so people will want to come and see it! Talk about the neighborhood, community, kitchen, backyard, nearby parks and schools etc.
- Door Knock the neighborhood again a night or two before the open house.
- Include LISTED homes in handouts to and conversations with neighbors
  - "We are holding an open house for your neighbor at 123 Main Street on Saturday from 1-4pm. We usually have excess buyers for whom the house we hold open is not the right fit. Would it be okay to show your home that day to anyone who might be interested in yours?"

Countdown to Open House - 3 days to go

- Run Facebook Ads ($25 boost / ad spend)
- Listing to Leads is a GREAT tool to use for marketing opens, among other things. Dollar for dollar, this is one of our favorite tech tools at any Tier! Get the Club Wealth® discount at www.ClubWealth.com/l2l
- Target the neighborhood on Facebook using Ads Managers
- Video yourself in front of the house and use the video for the targeted post.

Circle Prospecting – Remind Neighbors of Open House & Neighbor Preview

- View the home and introduce yourself to the seller
  - Dress professionally!
  - On time is late. Be 10 minutes early!

  o Greet with last name and firm handshake.

  o Remind sellers to be out of the home 1 hour prior to the start of the Open House.

- Prepare your Open House Kit

Open House Kit Items

- Plug-ins/Air Freshener
- Small table and chair
- Flowers
- Shoe covers
- Table cloth
- Refreshments
- Toilet paper
- Laptop/pad
- WIFI (always use your own)
- Flyers
- Nearby listing MLS printouts
- Business cards
- Mat for front door (inside & branded)
- Name tag
- Buyers Consult forms and presentation
- Sign-in sheet (always have a paper sign-in handy, even if you use an electronic one)
- BRB sign
- Glass cleaner
- Paper towels
- Napkins (for refreshments)
- Small trash bag (never leave your/attendee's trash in the house)

- Sign-in policy (in clear stand for the welcome table and placed on the front door)
- Thank you card for the seller

Countdown of Open House - Today's the Day!

Dress for Success – Remember, this is a job interview. Dress like it.

Bring your lender with you, as well as additional Team members if you expect a large turnout.

Blanket the area with signs – 50+

- including all major intersections
  - 50% of the signs should have street address and be placed near stores near the home.
  - 50% of the Signs should be directional with arrows pointing in the direction of the open house.
- Place large flags / balloons on the road by the house.
- Make sure Agents in the area are ready for showing requests.

- Arrive at the home 45 minutes early to prepare the home.
- Using online registration? Have a backup of paper registrations just in case. Using paper? Fill out first 3 names with "dummy names", or better yet, use an existing sign in sheet with names on it. NO one likes being the first to sign in.
- Do NOT bring flyers about the home. Everyone registers, and you can email this and other information.
- Know your USPs and be ready to discuss with buyers/sellers

- Provide something to slow the pace – cookies, cupcakes, refreshments, prize drawing

- Place a sign on the front door that notifies visitors of registration policy.

- Welcome Script: "For the sellers safety, and mine, we require photo ID and sign in for everyone who enters the home. We'll also need your phone number & email to be eligible for the drawing."

- Alternate Script for Objections – "This is by sellers request, I just want to show them I am doing a good job, and I want to make sure I'm safe while I'm here. I will be going over all registrations with them after the open house."

- Let buyers explore the home, stay within earshot, but don't follow them around.
- Use the F.O.R.D. (ask open ended questions about their Family, Occupation, Recreation and Dreams) technique to B.R.O.T. (Build Relationships on Trust)
- Take notes about each attendee to use in your follow-up, and set next appointment now.
- Conduct drawings on video after the open house. Remind people of next open house. POST, POST, POST, POST!

Countdown to the Open House - After the Open House

- Leave the house better than you found it.

- Make sure all lights are turned off.

- If home has an alarm, be sure to set it on the way out.

- Lock doors that were locked, if seller leaves doors unlocked (garage to home), do the same.

- THE FORTUNE IS IN THE FOLLOW-UP

- Make sure raffle winners get their prizes!
- Send a Facebook friend request to attendees with whom you've made a connection.
- Post a photo on Facebook / Instagram of them picking up/receiving their item.
- Send a video text to each attendee, thanking them for attending, before you leave the open house

- Set up an MLS/IDX search for all attendees. Even if you don't know what they are looking for, put them on a drip campaign.

- Call everyone within 24 hours of sending MLS/IDX search.
- For your listing – Email/Text seller immediately after open house with feedback

Module 3 - Open House Etiquette

If you held open for another Agent, always email the Agent and text the Agent immediately after the Open House and share:

- How many Agents came through (include numbers of with/without clients)

- How many potential buyers
- Feedback from Agents
- Feedback from buyers
- Your feedback for the seller
- Send the Agent a Thank You card within 24 hours of open house

Congratulations! You've held a MASSIVE Open House! Now what? Rinse and repeat!

Remember, to be a successful World Class Buyer Agent, you will need to hold 4-6 open houses this month, and every month thereafter. Use the checklists in this chapter each and every time you schedule an open house.

CHAPTER 11
LEAD FOLLOW UP

Module 1 - Lead Follow Up

One of the Greatest Service Organizations in Business...
In Seattle, we have a department store called Nordstrom, which is named after the Nordstrom Family, who built this well-respected empire.

Ever since I was a kid, I remember the name "Nordstrom" being synonymous with "Customer Service".

Ask anyone who has shopped there, and they'll tell you about both the World Class Customer Service, as well as their ULTRA-Liberal return policy, wherewith literally ANYTHING purchased there could be returned at ANY time for a full refund.

Did some take advantage of this, wear a pair of shoes, and bring them back for a new pair of shoes years later after they had worn them out? Yes. But that didn't deter, nor hinder, Nordstrom. In fact, they wore it like a badge of honor, which brought customers in droves!

Who wouldn't want to shop where there was absolutely no risk?!

That said, their shoe department was arguably the most popular section of the store, and it wasn't cheap! You could easily spend hundreds of dollars, even over $1,000, on a pair of shoes there.

Their shoe salespeople routinely made over $100,000/year, and enjoyed the fruits of working in the most highly sought after position arguably in all of retail-America!

We can learn much from salespeople in all Nordstrom departments, but for the moment, let's focus on the customer experience in shoe sales.

When you walk in, you are almost always immediately and pleasantly greeted by a very non-salesy shoe sales person.

For the vast majority of customers, the response is a simple yet polite "I'm just looking for now..." to which the salesperson replies "No problem, let me know if I can get you anything in your size."

At this point, you proceed with your search, and the salesperson casually walks around the store to see who needs help.

As you browse various shoes, you see them... the ones you didn't know you were looking for, but absolutely MUST HAVE... there they are, the perfect, one of a kind, can't believe they even exist pair of Louboutins!

Excited, you realize life simply cannot go on until and unless you have tried them on, in your size, of course!

So, now, excited to see them in your size, you are faced with a question, a conundrum, if you will...

Do you walk all the way across the Nordstrom shoe department to grab the first salesperson you spoke with, who so politely and kindly greeted you upon your arrival to the Mecca of World Class Footwear?

Do you interrupt his current conversation with what appears to be a wealthy would-be buyer of well-made moccasins?

Or, do you simply follow in the footsteps of the millions of loafer-loving land crawlers who simply grab the closest salesperson and say "Could you please get this in my size?"

EXACTLY!

Does this mean you didn't like the pump-pimping person who initially greeted you? Of course not!

Does it indicate that the would-be sultan of slippers did something wrong? Not in the slightest!

It simply means you, like Bruce Lee and water, took the path of least resistance to get what you want, in the time you want.

Well, guess what. Your prospects are no different!
They too will travel the path of least resistance to get to their goal quickly, and without drama.

The key for you is to be that resistance free path! This means you need to be available and top of mind, as well as easy and convenient to reach when they are ready to make their move!

Enter Pleasantly Persistent Follow Up!

What is the REAL problem in Real Estate Today?

Often, Agents believe that lead generation is their biggest challenge. Our experience shows us that lead generation for most Agents is relatively simple, and even consistently well performed. Lead follow-up, however, is consistently NOT performed at a high level by most real estate Agents, and sometimes not at all!

You'll hear the saying throughout the book, "The FORTUNE is in the follow-up!" It's true - if you aren't constantly following up with your clients, you'll still do some business, but not nearly as much as those who have mastered lead follow-up.

How you are going to follow up? Coach Misti Bruton says that she often gets buyers who feel like they already have a relationship with her even though she's never met them. Coach Misti's follow-up is based on the Club Wealth® "Pleasantly Persistent" Method.

To her, this means being pleasant and persistent, extremely consistent, and focusing on always keeping her team top of mind. She consistently blocks time for follow-up activities daily, and she knows that, while lead generation is necessary, follow-up is where you make your money. Remember: don't give up... the last man standing wins!

Think of it this way: when you have followed up with a lead 27 times over 4 months, there are likely few, if any, other Agents still following up with them. This makes you the natural, logical choice for the consumer, assuming you have been pleasantly persistent throughout your follow-up process.

What Follow-Up Methods Should I Employ?

We recommend the Land, Air, and Sea approach. Think of it this way: if you were going to battle against an evil dictator with millions of minions at their disposal, you wouldn't roll in with a Humvee and a couple of privates who had never seen action... You would ensure you had control of the land, air, and sea, overwhelming the enemy with SHOCK AND AWE!

This is exactly how you should approach lead follow-up.

There are many ways to follow up: calling, texting, emailing, sending a video text and/or video email, handwritten personal notes, automated direct-to-voicemail blasts, automated voice broadcasts, and Facebook Messenger. (Check local and national laws before using automated blasts of any kind)

So which do you use?

The answer is simple... ALL OF THEM and more!

Truth be told, you can't possibly follow up too much. Unless you are frequently hearing "You're contacting me way too much", you're not there yet!

How Often Should I Call?

At Club Wealth®, we believe in being aggressive with the process, but never with people. In an effort to create an easy to remember system for this, we created the Rule of 3.

The rule of 3 allows you to be very aggressive in the beginning of the follow-up process, moderately aggressive in the middle, and only slightly aggressive towards the end of the manual follow-up process (you'll still continue with automated follow-up systems, but upon completion of the Rule of 3, you'll likely discontinue calling, and doing other manual follow-up steps).

Following the Rule of 3 will help you keep track of how often you should be following up with you client, and ensure you are doing so in a consistent manner.

Put Simply, The Rule of 3 says:

- You should be following up 3 times a day, for the first 3 days.
- Then 3 times a week for the next 3 weeks.
- Then 3 times a month for the next 3 months.
- Once you have completed this, you should keep them in your email list, continuing your drip campaigns, automated texting, and continues to include them in your listing alerts and broadcast voice, email, and text messaging.
- You should also continue to reach out by phone at times when they are extremely active on your site searching homes.

It is important to note, that if you reach them in call number 1 on day 1, that you will need to adjust your follow-up, as there would be no need to continue calling them 2 more times that day, and 3 times a day for the next two days.

Likewise, if, when you speak with them, they indicate they will be moving in the next 12 months, you need not be so aggressive with follow-up.

Simply cut the time in half, and call them in 6 months.

Initial Lead Follow-Up - Connecting with the Lead 85% of the Time

One of the biggest challenges in selling real estate is simply getting voice-to-voice with your leads. Too often in this day and age, people "cocoon-up" in their homes and hide behind text messaging, Facebook Messenger, SnapChat and other technology roadblocks to communicating voice-to-voice and face-to-face.

Furthermore, it really sucks when you follow up with someone for several months, only to have them FINALLY tell you "No". I'd MUCH rather get that "No" in the first week.

So, how do we get to more people voice-to-voice in the first few days? Simple... Follow the CWGRLS, created with help from Gabe Cordova (800+ units his best year as an Agent/broker, and President of Firepoint CRM).

The Club Wealth® Guaranteed Responsive Lead System (CWGRLS):

Leads are like cows; they graze the fields of the Internet, roaming from site to site, chewing on what they can easily reach, and then they move on to greener pastures.

Wrangling them takes talent. I've long believed that if you want something done right, have a woman do it.

That said; fear not men. We still have a chance, but for now, think about the benefits of skilled CoWGiRLS wrangling these cows and bringing them safely home!

This is the heart of the CoWGiRLS Follow-Up Method:

When a lead comes in, call it BEFORE looking it up. As the phone is ringing, you can look it up. This enables you to get to 20 seconds or less, speed to lead.

If they don't answer, DO NOT leave a message. Simply hang up the phone and call back again immediately. (This is called "Double Dialing")

If they still do not answer, DO NOT leave a message.

It is at this point that you'll send the Gabe Cordova Magic 3 Word Text (Guaranteed to get a response up to 85% of the time!): Is this [first name they registered with]...

Now think about this for a moment... especially you parents out there...

If you get a call from a number you don't recognize, you don't answer, and they hang up without leaving a message. Then, it happens again. You ignore the call; they hang up without leaving a message.

Could it be the kids, or someone calling about them?

The school perhaps, or worse, the authorities, or a hospital?

Then you receive the mysterious "Is this ____..." text!

What in the world could be wrong with the kids?

What do you do?

If you're like 85% of the leads we get, you respond with "Yes. Who is this?"

Mission accomplished!

Now the lead is calling you instead of you chasing them. You are now "Attracting" the lead instead of "Chasing" the lead!

Now, before you freak out and start crying foul... "That's so misleading", understand this: all you did was call them and send them a text asking if they are who they said they were. What is misleading about that??

The fact that they may assume the call is of great importance because of the sequence of calls/text is not only **not** misleading, it is extremely understandable and not at all out of the ordinary.

Remember, THEY contacted YOU via the Internet somehow, NOT the other way around!

Module 2 - How Do I Make Follow-Up Simple, Efficient, and Still Effective?

One of the first things you want to do is make sure you have a CRM. And not just any CRM - you want a GREAT CRM. You need one that can funnel all of your leads into one place, and help make follow-up as simple, efficient, and effective as possible.

Read thoroughly the chapter on CRMs, and visit www.ClubWealth.com/CRM for more information on which CRMs we recommend, which we recommend avoiding, and why.

That said, a CRM is only as good as those who use it, and how well and consistently it is used. It's GIGO (Garbage In, Garbage Out).

If you want follow up to be simple, efficient and effective, you have to make sure you put good information into your CRM, including notes and, especially, the Next Follow-Up Date (NFUD) for each lead.

GREAT CRMs will be able to automate this by automatically assigning a NFUD for each lead, unless you change it.

The Most Efficient and Effective Agent EVER!

As a young Agent, I noticed that another Agent in my market, John

Schlanbusch, was CRUSHING IT by taking 25+ listings a month **regularly**!

All I could think about was beating him!

So much so, that it consumed me...

I worked harder, longer, and strove to work smarter than John. I had hit a plateau in my business. My current coach was a one-trick pony (all prospecting, all the time), and I knew I would need to add another tool to my toolbox or I'd never break the barrier that was holding me back.

So, I hired a new coach.

At the same time, and only after much introspection, prayer, and discussion with my incredible wife, Tara, I began to realize that I had to STOP competing with John, and begin focusing on being the very best version of ME I could be.

These things combined helped me to refocus, and rekindle the fire inside me.

I knew I had the skill set necessary. I knew I had stacked the odds as much in my favor as possible by being prepared, showing up to appointments a few minutes early, memorizing key scripts and dialogues, getting "In State" prior to appointments, and more. But some things were missing.

I began to realize that the most important things I needed to do to break the 25 listing a month barrier were to change my daily habits and to gradually improve my Listing Appointment Checklist.

I also came to learn that I had to take my career more seriously, stop wearing khakis and a nice polo and start wearing a suit and tie (I figured if it worked for John, maybe it would work for me).

As I began to implement these things, things changed. Quickly. Almost magically. And I started to list. I mean REALLY list WAY more homes.

Within a few months, I was listing over 50 homes a month, and doing it consistently!

Want to know what the habits I changed were?

I looked at my schedule, and realized I was doing a ton of lead generation manually.

What I failed to notice until this point is that I had been adding lead sources consistently for some time. I now had so many new leads coming in, and so many in the pipeline, that I could really begin focusing 100% of my time on just TWO THINGS: Lead Follow-Up and Lead Conversion.

These were a MUCH better use of my time, and so I immediately changed my habits. I gave all the lead generation to other members of the team, and I began making 115-125 follow up calls... per day... from my car... in between what was soon to become my 6-8 appointments per day!

As you can imagine, by limiting the scope of my responsibilities, I became VERY GOOD at following up with sellers and going on listing appointments. Some would say I was the best... I suppose the numbers support that, but honestly, there are far better salespeople than me out there.

I simply got really good at being the best version of ME I could be, and the results followed.

I eliminated ALL distractions. I stopped taking calls from family and friends during work hours, I got hyper-focused on the task at hand, and I systemized EVERYTHING in my life (this also helped me compensate for my off-the-charts ADHD).

I had made the decision to become the most efficient and effective Agent ever, and if I wasn't there yet, I was darn close!

Here's how focused I became:

A well known Coach, and longtime friend of mine, Verl Workman called me one day and asked if it was true that I was listing 50-75 homes a month, NOT counting my team and NOT counting REO.

I acknowledged that it was in fact true, and if he wanted to see for himself, I'd gladly bring him along for a couple days.

He quickly accepted the offer, and hopped on a plane for Seattle.

I picked him up from the airport, and, as I dropped him off at his hotel, explained what was to happen in the next two days.

"I'll pick you up at 7. Please eat beforehand, as we won't have time to stop for food. You'll also want to bring something to eat with you, as I drink protein shakes throughout the day, and don't stop for lunch or dinner. I'll have you back to your hotel by 10-10:30 tonight, and will pick you up again tomorrow at 7:00am.

During the day, I'll need you to sit in the back seat of the car, as my stuff sits in the front seat so I can work while I drive.

(This is the point at which I think he called home to make sure his life insurance premium had been paid! lol)

I'll be making 115-125 follow-up calls in between the 14 appointments I have set for us during these 2 days.

I have my printed week-at-a-glance calendar for 2 weeks, as well as the days follow-up calls printed out from my CRM.

My goal is to set 8 appointments each of the 2 days, and take all 14 listings.

When we go into the listing appointments, it is important that you not say anything. In fact, it's probably best if you don't say anything at all today, including to others on the phone, as I need to be 100% focused all day to accomplish our goals.

At the appointments themselves, it's okay for you to say hi, but after that, please don't say anything at all.

If the sellers look at you as if to say, "Save me from this crazy person", simply sit there and smile.

If the house catches on fire during the listing appointment, quietly, without saying a word, walk outside, call the fire department, quietly come back inside, and watch me close them before the house burns to the ground!

We will debrief when we arrive at your hotel each night, which is when it makes sense for you to talk and ask any and all questions you may have."

He was surprised, stunned, and maybe even a little offended, but by the end of day one, he understood, was no longer offended, and couldn't possibly get enough of this experience!

We had every situation you can imagine:

- Divorced sellers who were yelling at me about each other, as I stood between them, but would not address one another
- Young would-be flippers (investors who buy, fix up, and resell homes for an immediate profit) who got in way over their heads on a burnt out house in South Tacoma
- A luxury home in a neighborhood controlled primarily by the Queen of Real Estate, as it were
- Several short sales where homeowners had no idea they were upside down in their equity positions until I broke the news to them that day
- Homes with no furniture and even one with no counters, so we had to do the paperwork on the hood of my car
- An estate sale where the other heir had to be called in at the last minute to sign the listing
- Sellers getting cold feet minutes after signing

You name it we encountered it!

Most of the homes were at least an hour from my home, and several were over 2 hours from my home (distance is only an objection if you allow it to be!)

To his surprise, we listed all 14 of the 14 appointments we went on. And we did it all in my 1998 Toyota 4Runner with over 200,000 miles on it (DO NOT tell me you have to drive a fancy car to be successful in real estate, no matter what price point you serve! Clean, yes, fancy, no. If you can't pay cash for it, you shouldn't be driving it! It's an unpopular opinion, true, but so is spending less than you make, and all my Millionaire buddies believe in that, so maybe we can all learn from them?)

I finished out the 2 days with 14 new listings, 17 new appointments, and a friend with a GIGANTIC SMILE on his face having experienced something most people in the real estate industry would never even dream is possible.

ALL of this was made possible because:

1. I switched my Lead Generation time out for Lead Follow-Up
2. I decided being rich and reaching my goals was worth the price of being focused.
3. I put habits in place that forced me to succeed
4. I defended my habits FIERCELY and allowed NO ONE to come between me and what I knew I had to do EVERY DAY to reach my goals.

Eventually, the team and I amassed literally over 750 listings in active/pending status.

Was it worth it?

You bet your sweet potatoes it was! :)

Module 3 - Automation - Touch Methods

One of the best ways you can avoid dropping the ball is having automated touch points. These are what are called "Set it and forget it" type touches. Again, you do these touches by: email, text, voicemail, video text, video email, snail mail or postcards, and Facebook targeting or retargeting ads and messages.

There are many different automated services that will do these things and more for you. Be sure to check with your Team Leader or coach and ask what they prefer to use. Some automated services offer:

- Video Emails
- Video Text Messages (Drip and/or Bulk)
- Drip Campaigns
- Automated Home Searches (IMPERATIVE for Buyer Agents)
- Direct to Voicemail Broadcast Messages
- Market Reports
- Home Value Reports
- PostCard Campaigns
- Artificial Intelligence Text and Facebook Bots
- Low Tech High Response Text -On-Demand Autoresponders
- and so much more!

Once you have determined how motivated the lead is, you can categorize them accordingly in your CRM. Here is an easy guide to follow:

- If a buyer likely to purchase in the next 30 days - you contact them every other day.

- If a buyer likely to purchase in the next 30-60 days - you contact them 1-2 times/week, or more.
- If a buyer likely to purchase in the next 60-90 days - you contact them weekly, or more.
- If a buyer likely to purchase in the next 90-120 days - you contact them bi-weekly, or more.
- If a buyer likely to purchase in the next 120+ days - you contact them 1 times/month, or more.

When in doubt, always cut their time frame in half, and remember, "Contact" means primarily voice to voice, with other forms of communication being ancillary.

So what if they don't respond after repeated attempts?

If, after repeated attempts, over a period of weeks, you can and should employ one or more "Nudge Texts" designed to get unresponsive leads to engage in SOME way.

There are LOTS of great Nudge Texts; here are some of our favorites (in no particular order):

1. Is this _____
2. I just want to make sure I'm not dropping the ball on my end...
3. Did you see the house that just popped up in _____?
4. Let me know...
5. [first name]? example: Misti?
6. Did you just call me?
7. Are there any homes you want to see this weekend?
8. Are we okay?
9. Are you still thinking of buying?
10. Hey, saw a house that is perfect for you but just a tiny bit out

of your price range... want me to send it to you?

11. A house like you've been looking for is coming on the market... no one even knows I know about it... want to see it before it hits the market?

Video text can be especially great for nudging people to respond.

For a complete list of nudge texts we recommend (a list of ones we DON'T recommend), and some examples of great Video Nudge Texts, visit www.clubwealth.com/nudge

World's Greatest Follow Up Script

All too often, Agents use self-serving scripts like: I just wanted to see if you're ready to buy (or sell) yet?

Wouldn't it be nice if instead of being perceived as a sleazy, self-serving (how our industry is perceived by many), you could be viewed as a valued, professional servant who cares?

Well, using this one tiny sentence in your follow up calls and text messages, you can be!

When you get in contact with the lead, and when leaving a voicemail or text message for the 300th time, the number one thing you should say is:

"I just want to make sure I am not dropping the ball on my end".

Seriously, it's that simple. Watch what happens next...

What is their response to that script?

Their response is typically...

"Oh no, no, no it's not you, it's me!" (like that girl in high school, right guys?)

You have now invoked what is known as "The law of reciprocity." (Coach Ron Anderson is an especially rabid fan of this technique!)

They feel guilty for not responding to your many calls, texts, emails etc.... PERFECT! That's right where you want them. Now they feel like they **have** to work with you because they "owe you"!

Lead Follow Up and Your Wallet

Your income will be a direct result of, and in direct correlation with the number of leads you follow up with on a daily basis. If you make more follow up calls, you'll make more money!! When I was listing 25 homes a month, I was making around 50 follow up calls per day. When I began making 115-125 follow up calls per day, I almost immediately began listing 50-75 homes a month!

It's not rocket science; it's simple math. Heck, even a caveman could do it... if cavemen had phones, I suppose.

How quickly should I be following up?

Well that depends on how much money you want to make.

For a long time, Agents felt same day was soon enough to respond to leads.

Then, they began stepping it up to "within the hour".

Soon, the Harvard Business Review came out with a study that suggested that the difference between following up within the first 5 minutes versus the first 10 minutes is a 900% INCREASE in contact rate. In other words, your chances of connecting with a lead DROPPED by 900% if you wait longer than 5 minutes to contact them.

In 2018, we did an informal test with the Inside Sales Agent (ISA) of one of our clients, Jesse Zagorsky.

We'll call him Joe.

I called Joe one day, and asked him to try something new. I wanted him to hit "send" on his phone the very instant a new lead came in, and wait to look up the lead until the phone was already ringing.

The goal was simple: see if we could get the majority of the leads on the phone within 30 seconds of them submitting their information online.

Joe did as I asked for the next two weeks, and the results were not only informative, they were STAGGERING!

He made contact with the VAST majority of the leads, and ended up setting a ton of appointments.

Interestingly, and not surprisingly, the number one buyer of Realtor.com (RDC) leads nationally buys approximately $2mil RDC leads annually for his 200 Agent team. Their average speed to lead = 18 seconds!

What was extremely interesting to me about the test with Joe, however, was the number of Agents who contacted the lead WHILE Joe was on the phone with them...

On average, in the first 5 minutes of the call, the client received no less than 4-5 calls from other Agents! (If you don't think real estate is a competitive industry, I've got news for you!)

Armed with this new knowledge, I instructed Joe to keep the lead on the phone for at least 5 minutes each time. Why? Because we know all to well that 48% (nearly half) of all the Agents out there will NEVER make a 2nd call to that lead, so, by keeping them on the phone for 5 minutes, the other Agents go to voicemail. Neither the lead, not the Agent are likely to call each other ever again, so we have effectively eliminated 48%+ of our competition by simply staying on the phone with the lead for 5 minutes!

Here are the actual statistics:

- 48% of Agents don't even make 1 follow-up call.
- 25% of Agents make 2 follow-up calls, and then stop.
- 12% of Agents make 3 calls and then stop.
- Less than 10% of Agents make 4 or more follow up calls before stopping.

Here's what's REALLY crazy about that:

- Only 2% of all sales happen on the first contact.
- 3% of sales happen on the second contact.
- 5% of sales happen on the third contact.
- 10% of sales happen on the fourth contact.
- 80% of sales are made on the fifth or subsequent contact.

That's not calls; it's contacts! So if you call 100 people, and on average get 25 to answer (that's a generous number) it would take an average of 4 calls to get the lead to answer the phone.

Thus, according to the stats above, the average Agent misses out on 80% or more of the sales opportunities, and more than 90% of the

Agents will never even make 4 or more calls, thus, they are unlikely to ever even speak to the lead!

Essentially, by making 4 or more calls to the lead, you have a FAR better chance of contacting, and subsequently doing business with each lead.

We actually recommend 27 calls with no response before relegating the lead to automated follow-up alone.

Lead follow-up is a unique animal. It is both a marathon AND a sprint! Initially, you must sprint to get to the lead first and fastest. Then you must run a marathon of lead follow up and nurture to ensure you eventually get the client!

Module 4 - Long Term Nurture and Rapport Building

Building rapport ultimately builds loyalty. Remember that people have to know you, like you, and trust you to do business with you. If you are always coming from a place of contribution (giving selflessly for the benefit of others without expectation of anything in return), you'll help others WANT to get to know you. They will be attracted to you because of whom you are, and will naturally begin to like and even eventually trust you.

Long-term follow-up can make up for lack of skill. You can be a complete moron and yet, if you follow up consistently over a long period of time, they'll still think you're a rockstar!

Remember to always schedule a follow-up task after every activity you complete.

There are only 3 acceptable outcomes from an appointment:

1. You write a contract.
2. You schedule a next appointment.
3. You decide you don't want to work with this person going forward.

Final Thoughts on Follow Up

- Get a great CRM and use it properly.
- Follow a systematic approach and use multiple methods of communication.
- Follow the Rule of Three.
- Always ensure a "Next Call Date" is set.
- Use the CoWGiRLS system to engage leads!
- Always work to take the online, offline and always go for the face-to-face appointment.
- Don't overthink complicated drip campaigns or rigid set schedules. Just set the next follow up appointment and schedule time to complete your follow up tasks daily.

CHAPTER 12
LEAD CONVERSION

Module 1 - What is Lead Conversion?

Simply put, lead conversion is the process of converting a lead into an appointment, an appointment into a contract written, and a contract written into a closing. But to get there, we move through the stages of conversion.

- Step 1: Get them into voice-to-voice conversation: In other words, once you have a lead, contact it IMMEDIATELY (within 20 seconds of receiving the lead). If they don't answer, follow the CoWGiRLS System. If they still don't respond, follow the Rule of 3.
- Step 2: Take the conversation to a face-to-face: This is done by focusing entirely on SETTING THE APPOINTMENT, and not worrying about silly things like getting them pre-approved (more on this later).
- Step 3: Take that face-to face-conversation to a contract: To do this, you'll need to learn and consistently use some great closing scripts, master some World Class NLP (Neuro-Linguistic Programming) techniques, and become unafraid to ask for the business EVERY TIME and as often as necessary to get them to sign on the line that is dotted!
- Step 4: Close the transaction: This will ultimately be done by your team, an assistant, or an outside fee-based transaction coordinator if you don't yet have a team. Once the purchase and sale agreement is fully executed by both buyer and seller

and you have handed it off to the appropriate team member, your continued involvement in the transaction should be limited, specifically to reclosing the client if need be. On a well built out team, every other detail can and should be handled by the administrative staff, up to and including ongoing negotiations regarding inspections, appraisals and more. (Yes, this likely means you'll have to have some licensed administrative staff members, which is not only okay, it's a big benefit.)

Leads are nothing but an expense if you can't convert them to transactions AND get those transactions closed. Furthermore, your return on investment (ROI) or that of your Team's (which you should be equally if not more concerned about) will be GREATLY increased as you not only close the leads you have, but also earn referrals from them in the coming days, weeks, months and years. Over a decade ago, I once calculated the lifetime value of a client in my business; based on the transactions they and their referrals were likely to do with our team and me over their lifetime.

It was to my pleasant surprise to find out that the Lifetime Value of a Hellickson Real Estate Client was well over One MILLION Dollars ($1,000,000)!!

Think of it this way: If Sgt. John and Susie Smith move just 3 times with me as their Agent (buy first home, sell it and buy another, sell that and buy another), that's actually 5 transactions!

If the average sales price were just $250,000, and my average commission just 3% (which mine was significantly higher, at 3.5% as a Buyer Agent, and listings at 7%+$695, which was weighted heavily towards the listing office...more on that in the World Class Listing Agent Book!), I'd make $37,500 on transactions with them.

Assume they refer 5 people to me, and I likewise do 5 transactions with them. That's EASILY another $187,500 in commissions.

Now, let's say those 5 each refer me to 5 more people who each close 5 sides with me... those alone are a WHOPPING $937,500 + $187,500 (the first 5 people) + $37,500 (Sgt. and Mrs. Smith) put us now at a cool $1,162,500 in gross commission income, NOT counting all the sign calls we'll get from all those listings, NOT counting the additional income in other fees, higher commissions, ancillary businesses (mortgage, title, escrow, etc.) that will contribute, and so on and so on! (and yes, we'll teach you or your Team Leader how to access ALL of these various sources and streams of income and more!)

Voice-to-Voice Conversations Lead to Closings.

Voice-to-voice conversations create connections; connections create opportunities to meet face-to-face. Meeting face-to-face allows the consumer to begin to know, like, and trust you. When they know, like, and trust you, AND you get good at lead conversion, you'll begin to write and close transactions.

The problem is, most Agents don't even know what to say on the phone to get the appointment set.

Their focus is getting the lead to agree to speak with a lender to get "Pre-Qualified" (speak to the lender and answer a bunch of personal and often uncomfortable questions about their income, debt, credit and finances as a whole). I like to affectionately refer to these Agents collectively as the "Sales Prevention Team".

Why? Because they are more concerned with making the lead or prospect jump through the Agents hoops than they are with actually

"SERVING" the potential clients.

How would you feel if you went to a used car lot looking for the perfect [insert favorite car here], and before they would even let you look at the cars on the lot, the salesperson forced you to get "Pre-Qualified" with their Finance and Insurance (F&I) guy?!

You wouldn't like it at all, and would likely leave the car dealership upset and committed to never returning or referring anyone else to that dealership in the future! In fact, if you're like me, you'd probably share your less-than-stellar experience with everyone you know who is thinking of buying a car!

It's no wonder why consumers rate real estate Agents somewhere BELOW attorneys and used car salespeople! At least the used car salespeople are smart enough to show you the cars before asking you to talk to their lender!

So why, then, do so many Agents on the Sales Prevention Team push to get prospects "Pre-Qualified" from the beginning? Is it because they don't want to "waste their time" with unqualified prospects?

Perhaps they don't want to waste the prospects' time (I doubt it, but okay)...?

Whatever the answer, it is clear that they neither understand the real meaning of the words "customer service", nor do they have any grasp of the concept of a "World Class Customer Experience".

Even crack dealers understand that, "The first one's free, THEN you have to pay!" (Substitute "Meth" for "Crack" in some markets)

Lead Conversion

Meaning, when someone contacts you with interest in a house, you show it to them, no matter what!

Full transparency: I've never done drugs. Heck, I don't even drink (for that matter, I don't even drink coffee or black tea or even smoke cigarettes or vape!), but that doesn't mean you and I can't learn a valuable lesson or lessons from the dealers of the dark and destructive.

They understand, for example, the need to get "into rapport" with their prospects. They know that their clients must know, like, and trust them before they'll do business with them.

They understand the value of "giving a taste" for free, thus reducing some of the risk to the prospect (what if the product sucks?).

They even understand "risk reversal", which is another key benefit of the "first one's free, then you've got to pay" philosophy.

Frankly, they are so good at selling sultry, seductive, and scandalous stuff; one can only imagine how successful they would be at selling the American Dream of Home Ownership!

In fact, we should all thank our lucky stars the cartels and corner critters don't figure out how lucrative and legally less problematic selling real estate is than their current line of work, or they'd come in and take over our industry with their far-above-average sales skills!

Think about it. If they can convince people to pay top dollar for, and ingest, substances that will MOST ASSUREDLY, and quite often painfully, kill them, maybe we can learn a thing or two from their techniques!

That is, unless, you insist on being right, rather than being rich.

I for one, am taking note, and applying those techniques in my businesses.

When someone reaches out to you, and wants to see a house, SHOW IT TO THEM!!!

Quit making them jump through your selfish hoops first!

Decide and commit THIS MINUTE that you will immediately and forever cease to be a member of the Sales Prevention Team, by giving prospects the first one free from now on!

There is no magic bullet to lead conversion for Real Estate Agents. Yes, we strive to:

- Keep it simple
- Be authentic
- And be consistent

Above all, give prospects what they want, as soon as humanly possible. We get them that pair of Louboutins in their size, a taste of the drug, a first showing of an interesting home IMMEDIATELY, and without questioning whether or not they can afford the product!

Also, always remember there is a real human on the other side of the conversation and they don't have your script! You should always assume they have already talked to 5 other Agents, if not more. There is no such thing as exclusive leads anymore, not even referrals! Therefore, you must be different. How are you going to be different? How will you stand out from the 50 other Agents in your market that they've already talked with?

Hint: it's not by asking them to pre-qual through your lender!

Module 2 -Set the Appointment

As mentioned earlier, all too frequently Agents will tell us, "I don't want to waste my time with unqualified buyers!" Unless you're closing 4+ transactions a month, you don't know what an unqualified buyer is. You have more than enough time to show ANYONE a home, and frankly you need the practice!

You now have two choices: be offended by what I just said, close this book, never open it again, and continue doing what you've been doing,

OR

You can remember: You can be right, or you can be rich. Swallow your pride and understand that, while there is nothing wrong with closing fewer than 48 units a year, you didn't open this book to be "Middle Class", you opened it because you want to be WORLD CLASS! Because you know in your heart that Eagles don't flock with Turkeys, and you want to be an Eagle.

I've got news for you. Eagles close 48+ units a year!

YOU CAN DO IT!

Now read on, and let's get to the business of becoming a WORLD CLASS EAGLE!!

What is my goal when I'm on the call?

- To avoid dropping the ball like most other Agents do, you

have to continually stay in front of the client (be the shoe salesperson standing next to them when they're ready to buy) and work to find their preferred method of communication.

- Use what is called the land, air and sea approach to induce SHOCK and AWE. Basically, hit them in every way possible! Send a letter or postcard via USPS, send an email, text message, video email and video text, make contact via phone, and send them a message via Facebook or other social media account and EVERYTHING else you can think of! Soon, you will discover which they respond to... this is likely their preferred method of communication, and the one you should focus on most (but not exclusively).

- Your goal on the follow-up call is NOT to get a listing or make a sale. Your one and only goal is to **get an appointment**.
- As soon as you set up the appointment, **hang up the freaking phone**! Have you ever talked yourself out of an appointment? I have. It's easy to do! Just set the appointment and say "see you then."
- I may have mentioned this already, but it bears repeating: STOP trying to get them on the phone with your lender! This is not necessary for your initial call. You can refer them to a lender, if they aren't pre-qualified, when you meet them face-to-face. Set the appointment regardless.

Inducing a "Yes" State

There's a great story that's told around the Club Wealth® office about how Austin Hellickson handles stubborn Agents who won't schedule a Strategy Session with one of our coaches.

First, you have to understand these Strategy Sessions are a no-pitch, no-cost coaching call, with an actual coach (not a salesperson), who sells more real estate than the Agent does. In other words, if you were closing 100 units per year, your Strategy Session would be with one of our Coaches who close 200+ units per year in their own real estate business.

Clearly there is a TON of value in that, and absolutely no risk, so who wouldn't want to do a Strategy Session, right?!

Well, surprisingly, there are actually Agents out there who, for whatever reason (maybe they had a bad experience with a coaching company who does things differently, maybe they think they know it all, who knows), but there are still some who choose not to take advantage of a 55 minute call with someone who is more successful at selling real estate than they are.

So, Austin's job is to call Agents and help them to take advantage of one of these free coaching calls.

Keep in mind, Austin began working as an Inside Sales Agent for Club Wealth® at age 14. By the time he was just 16 years old, he had been our top salesperson for over a year!

When making his sales calls, Austin focuses on inducing a "Yes State", by getting them to say "yes" 7-12 times on each call.

This is an NLP technique, and is designed to get the person saying "Yes" so often that it becomes their natural response during the conversation.

To do this, he'll ask questions they can't say "no" to.

For example he might ask a particularly stubborn Agent that refuses to say "Yes" (not too many of those out there *wink**wink*...) the following question: "If you were drowning, and I threw you a life jacket, would you reach out to it? SAY YES!!"

Notice, as soon as he asked the question, and before they could answer, he COMMANDS them to "SAY YES!!"

If a 14 year old can do it, SO CAN YOU! :)

Inducing a "Yes State" can help you get them to set an appointment.

The Mechanics of Going for the Appointment

Now that you've got them on the phone, how do you convert them into an actual appointment? It's very simple: you're going to talk them about what they called about. If they inquired about 123 Main Street, simply set an appointment to see 123 Main Street.

- Don't be the "Sales Prevention Team"
- Don't over qualify them
  - Remember: First one's free, and then you've got to pay!
- Don't send them to your lender
- Don't make them come to you or your office

Remember, if they want to see the house: **SET THE APPOINTMENT.**

AFTER you have scheduled the appointment, then, and only then, have you earned the right to ask the following question that is virtually guaranteed to get the lead to WANT to speak with your lender:

"IF they could save you $10-20,000 on your mortgage, would you be interested in chatting with one of our lenders?"

If they say "No", show the house to them anyway.

If they say, "Yes", and most will, ask "Is this the best number for them to reach you at?" Then, make the connection by introducing them over a 3-way text message (4-way for couples).

Show them the house. Close well. Write it up. Close it. Get paid.

What if the house is pending?

- Set the appointment anyway.
- Meet them in front of the home. Then, and only then, let them know the home is pending, and encourage them to write a back-up offer. If you're not comfortable with this (there is some controversy among some Agents as to whether you should disclose the pending transaction prior to meeting them at the home), then let them know it's pending, and encourage them to meet you to look at it from the outside, and potentially write a back-up offer, as MANY transactions fail to close and become available again. (Note: MAKE SURE you check with your Team Leader and/or Broker on this to ensure you are in compliance with local and state laws, and office and Team rules and guidelines.)
- Suggest viewing one or both of the other 2 homes you have right around the corner that may also be a great fit, or go for a buyer consultation appointment on the spot. This

is a TERRIFIC time to bring up your "Off Market Property List" and your VIP Buyer Program!

Build Trust and Rapport

Before asking information from your prospect, go for rapport. Why?

- People fear being sold to right away. Frankly, they rarely ever want to be sold.
- Be sure that you come from a place of curiosity.
- Reference what they are inquiring about. If they're calling about 123 Main Street, then talk to them about 123 Main Street.
- Your goal is to create a human connection... this requires being human!
- Show them that you really care.
- Be human first, and then set the appointment.
- Above all, SET THE APPOINTMENT!

How do you come from a place of curiosity?

Questions to ask:

- I'm just curious... is this something for investment or a home you're planning to live in?
- I'm just curious...are you looking in any other areas besides this one?
- I'm just curious...what's the ideal timeframe to find your next home?
- I'm just curious...how many bedrooms do you need?
- I'm just curious...what price range are you looking in?
- I'm just curious...do you currently rent your home?

Lead Conversion

Module 3 - Handling Sign and Ad Calls

There are many scripts and many different ways to approach various lead sources.

It is common, and in fact likely, that sign callers are sitting in front of the property when they call, wanting to know the price and to schedule an appointment to see the inside.

The speed of your response time is critical. If you don't answer the phone or return a sign call immediately, the prospect may simply drive away (if you're lucky). Worse yet, the prospect will likely keep calling other Agents until someone answers, and there is a 72% chance that if they connect with that person face-to-face (a showing, for example), they will do business with them, and not you!

Keep in mind; they are just looking for information. They don't care WHO answers their call as long as they get the answers they're looking for and the action they want (in this case, they frequently want to see inside the home, as quickly and easily as possible without being "sold"). This is an easy lead to convert as long as you know HOW to convert their calls.

The easiest way to convert a sign call is to simply say, "Would you just like to know the price, or would you like to see the inside as well?"

Key Points for Online Leads

There are various ways of handling online leads. Zillow and Realtor.com leads already have access to relevant information and are likely looking to set an appointment to see the property sooner than later. Speed to lead is critical with these leads as well, especially since immediately after clicking the link to connect with you, they likely clicked the same on 4 or 5 other listings as well!

That said; RDC and Zillow leads are often going to buy in the next 3-6 months. And remember, as with most buyer lead types, these leads have a home to sell nearly 40% of the time, so ALWAYS ask, "Will you be selling your current home, or renting it out?"

Website, Facebook, and PPC (Pay-Per-Click) driven leads, on the other hand, are just starting their search and likely haven't targeted a specific home yet. These leads are usually very early in their buying cycle, and will require longer term nurturing in most cases.

Some Agents prefer not to work website, Facebook and PPC leads, citing the long term (12-18 months in many cases) closing cycle of these leads as onerous or undesirable. We at Club Wealth® disagree. We believe that you're likely to still be in the real estate sales business in 12-18 months, and you'll probably want some closings then too. :)

You see, you've got to build a FULL funnel with a mix of now, mid, and long-term leads. One of the greatest advantages of these Website, Facebook, and PPC leads is that you have FAR less competition with them than other lead types, and they tend to be some of the best referring clients as a result.

Furthermore, if you're on a team, you'll likely only receive these lead types in the beginning, until you prove that you can convert well.

Think about it: why would your Team Leader give you the best leads when they don't even know if you can convert or will even follow up or not?

Many of these leads will convert in 30-90 days, just like RDC and

Zillow (and other Portal) leads.

So, if your team provides you with leads at all, be grateful, and follow up like crazy!

Scripts that Convert Sign Calls

Agent: Hi, I see you are inquiring about 123 Main Street. When would you like to see the property? PAUSE. Does today at 2pm or tomorrow at 5pm work best for you?

Scripts that convert Realtor.com, Zillow, and Similar Portal Leads

Script Intro:

Agent: Hi...I got your request from Realtor.com on 123 Main Street. When would you like to see it?

Set the Appointment & hang up the phone!!!

Scripts to Convert PPC Leads

Agent: Hi (first name)...This is Misti with the Free Home Search website that you just registered on. How are you?

Wait for reply

Agent: I noticed you were browsing our website for homes. Are you just browsing, or are you thinking about making a move in the next little while?

Wait for answer

Scripts to Convert Older Leads

Agent: Hi Jack, this is Misti. I hope you remember me. We connected a while back when you were looking for homes. I wanted to check in and see how the home search is going?

Wait for the answer

Agent: I totally respect that. I didn't have it in my notes. Is this something for investment or a home you're planning to live in?

Conversion Rules

Here are some great, simple to use tips that will help you convert more leads to appointments.

Remember, ALL they care about is that radio station playing in their head: **WIIFM** - What's In It For Me? What are they getting out of it? How are you going to solve their problem?

The absolutely WILL NOT care what you know, until they know that you care!

- DO NOT talk about yourself. They don't care about you, and that's okay. Don't try to find and articulate common ground. It's counter productive at this point.
- Show them what's in it for them.
- Lead with value, value, value!

Transition Questions

Use transition questions when responding to the lead. When they answer a question, you follow up with another question. Imagine a game of tennis. You lobby a question; answer a question.

- "Do you live in the neighborhood?"
- "How soon were you thinking about moving?"
- "Where do you currently live?"
- "Do you own or rent your current home?"

NEVER ask, "Are you working with another Agent?" They will almost always lie to you, and we never want to create a situation where it is easy, let alone likely that they will lie to us. Lies feel bad, and we want them to feel good when they are talking with us.

INSTEAD, always ask, "WHO is your Agent?" This will elicit an honest response more often than not, and quite frequently, they will struggle with the answer... PERFECT! Even if they are "kind-of" working with another Agent, this indicates to you that, since they barely even remember the name of "their" Agent, it's not a solid relationship.

In such situations (where they mention a name but struggled), follow up with "What documents have you actually signed with that Agent?"

More often than not, the answer is "We haven't actually signed anything with them." This is your clear indication that it is okay to pursue the prospect.

Information Gathering

Dig deeper into the prospect's why. Why do they want to buy a home? Why do they want to downsize? Why do they need a 3 bedroom with an office? Why is a big backyard important? Asking "why" bridges the gap between information gathering, and purpose and vision.

It will also help you do a much better job in finding the right home for them!

Building Relationships on Trust (B.R.O.T.)

You're calling a human being that doesn't have to use you.

- How can you be different? (VIP Buyer Program, Love it or Leave It Guarantee etc.)
- Don't chase the commission! Focus 100% on THEIR best interest, NOT yours!
- People can smell "Commission Breath" from a mile away!

What do consumers want from a World Class Buyer Agent?

- Looking out for **their** best interest
- Showing empathy
- Showing you care the most
- Know, like & trust you
- Human relationship
- Helping get a great deal
- Ensuring no legal or financial challenges
- Avoiding mistakes

Humanize the relationship with your prospect. Using the F.O.R.D. technique when converting a lead is imperative to your success.

We do this by asking them open-ended questions and pausing to actively listen to answers on the following topics in THEIR lives:

F=Family

O=Occupation

R=Recreation

D=Dreams

During this process, they should be doing 90% of the talking, and we should be simply guiding the conversation by asking the open-ended questions like: "Tell me about your family...."

"What do you do for a living?" followed by "Wow! That's interesting... tell me more about that!" and so on...

You don't need to do a TON of this on the phone; there will be plenty of time for building and deepening rapport at the appointment. That said, you need just enough rapport on this call to accomplish 4 things:

- Get them OFFLINE! We need them to STOP SURFING other people's sites.
- Keep them on the phone for 5 minutes so the other Agents don't get through to them.
- Set the appointment!
- Get enough info to set them up on great searches that will yield a TON of listings on a daily basis for them to browse through YOUR listing alerts.

That's really all you need to accomplish on this call.

Module 4 - Learn What NO Really Means

When a buyer says "no," it often means "not right now", or "I'm not sure I'm ready", or even "Convince me you're the right Agent". Remember the Nordstrom example from earlier: when they say, "No, I'm just looking", what they are really saying is "Once I've found what I'm looking for, I'll grab the nearest salesperson and ask for them in my size." Find out what they are looking for and stay pleasantly persistent, so that YOU are the closest salesperson when they find what they want!

By now you've generated and followed up with a lead successfully. Get into the mind of the consumer, and **think about how you shop for services online.** The minute the idea to buy something pops into your head, you jump on Google, you search around, and you submit an inquiry.

You expect instant gratification.

Five minutes later the baby is crying, and you realize you forgot to pick up milk. You're running out the door to the grocery store. The company you inquired with calls you as soon as you're getting the screaming baby into the car. You answer, "I'm not interested. Stop calling me!"

This doesn't mean you aren't truly interested. It only means that "right now" is a bad time.

Heck, even the fact you yelled at them is not necessarily an indication you don't like or even want to work with that salesperson, it simply means they caught you at a bad time.

Frankly, if that salesperson were to call you back a week later, and catch you at a better time, you might even feel a little bad about the way you treated them, which would automatically invoke the Law of Reciprocation! PERFECT!!!

Sadly, most Agents NEVER call back a 2nd time, let alone the 7-10 (often up to 27!) other times necessary to secure the deal, and the prospect ends up buying through someone else.

All other things being equal, the salesperson that follows **up in the magic window** of time will always get the sale!

How to Handle a No

Maybe you've gotten them on the phone, but they just aren't ready to meet, or even talk right now.

If you can't get the appointment:

- Ask if they would like to receive your weekly "Off Market Properties" List.
- Offer to send a list of open houses.
- Ask "Is it okay if I follow up with you down the road? Great! When is a good time to call you back?"
- Rule of thumb is cut that amount of time in half.
- Always set the next step (usually a follow up call) in your CRM!
  - Remember there are only 3 acceptable outcomes for a phone call or appointment:
    - Write a contract
    - Schedule an appointment
    - Decide not to work with this person going forward.
- Always set them up on property alert emails and if possible, text messages
  - Make the initial search really broad (200-400 homes) so that they will actually receive daily email/text updates from you with pretty pictures of pretty homes.
- Continue to provide value on an extremely consistent basis or they will forget you.
- Add them to your pixeled Buyer Audience, so your Facebook and other targeted value-add marketing will be

silently dripping on them day and night!

Find ways to keep in touch - bring value, value, value!

Follow Up is Key

Set them on a solid follow-up plan, and be prepared to nurture them for as long as it takes, even if it is literally years!

Add them to your Client Appreciation Program as a "C" Client.

Remember what Gary Vaynerchuk preaches in his bestselling book - *Jab, Jab, Jab, Right Hook* - You have to bring Value, Value, Value, THEN go for the close!

Most home shoppers are online and most everything is available online these days: school districts, pricing, etc.

Knowing that is the case, then what value do we as Agents provide?

Remember, you're the professional with all the tools needed to access what they want. They've seen the big screen, but you've seen behind the curtain.

You can guide them through this process in a way the Internet cannot, and you can give them a level of service that discounters and online services either can't or won't.

Final Tips for Going for the Close on the Phone

- One goal: SET AN APPOINTMENT
- Go for the close... if they have a concern or objection, resolve the concern

- Restate close
- Resolve concern
- Restate close
- ...Until they buy! :)

For more great scripts, visit www.ClubWealth.com/scripts

CHAPTER 13
THE BUYER CONSULTATION

Module 1 - Why Do a Buyer Consultation?

A buyer consultation is a good way to establish a proper relationship with your client from the start. When doing a buyer consultation, you must be informed and prepared.

Why shouldn't you just skip it? It is a great opportunity for you to cover any buyer objections, answer your buyer's questions and concerns, and address any fears. If you skip this important process, you won't have a chance to head off the dreaded buyer's remorse and any buyer disloyalty that may arise during the sales process. If you properly prepare your buyers during the consultation, you will have a chance to avoid the transactional chaos that is bound to ensue if you DON'T have the consultation.

Purpose of the Buyer Consultation

The strong buyer's consultation should:

- Educate the buyer on the entire home buying process.
- Establish rapport with the buyer.
- Complete a buyer intake form and identify property needs/wants.
- Lay the foundation for a successful working relationship by setting expectations.
- Reduce client questions along the way.

- Have the buyer sign the Buyer Agency Agreement.
- Create a sense of urgency to purchase NOW!

Module 2 - Preparing for the Buyer Consultation

As a World Class Buyer Agent, you should be offering the highest level of service and Customer Experience to your buyers. This includes a strong buyer's consultation coupled with a professional homebuyer's packet. Not only will you have happy clients, you'll reap referral benefits when your clients pass your name along to all of their friends and family. Preparing for the buyer consultation is just one way to offer a higher level of service that is expected of a World Class Buyer Agent.

Buyer Consultation Materials Checklist:

1. Home Buyer Guide
2. Home Buyer Intake Form
3. Buyer Agency Agreement
4. VIP Buyer Program Sheet (Unique Selling Proposition)
5. Blue Ink Pens

You should always dress in a professional manner. That means men should wear a suit and tie. Is it possible to look professional with a nice button up shirt and a jacket, yes? That said, we recommend you stack the odds in your favor, and wear a tie.

Ladies should remember what they ARE selling and what they AREN'T selling.

Get "in state" before the consultation. You should be in the right frame of mind, pumped up and ready to go! You can achieve this by repeating affirmations like:

I am an Awesome Agent!
People love working with me!
I'm getting this Buyer Agency agreement signed today!

For some other great affirmation ideas, visit www.ClubWealth.com/affirmations

Saying your affirmations about 30 minutes before the appointment - whether in the car or at your office - really helps put you "in state" and ready to conquer your goals. Say each affirmation out loud at least 10 times.

If you've never met your buyers before, or if you've only talked over the phone, another good trick before the meeting is to memorize their names. When they are putting you in charge of buying the biggest asset of their lives, it's easy to get flustered. Say their names out loud 10 times before meeting with them. Also, have your first line or greeting loaded up in your mind and ready to go.

If you are someone that is uncomfortable making eye contact with a person when you talk, a great tip is to notice eye color. When you meet someone for the first time, always stop to notice what color eyes they have. It's a great way to remember to establish eye contact.

Logistics of the Buyer Consultation

The buyer consultation should be held at your office whenever possible. You want the environment to be professional and hospitable to your buyer so setting the stage is critical. It also helps that you'll have home field advantage, which will help you feel more in control, which leads to greater self-confidence, which leads to more sales!

However, if meeting at the office is not an option for whatever reason, you can meet at a public place like your favorite coffee shop, deli, or restaurant. Just try and find a spot that is quiet with little to no distractions. Your buyers should feel comfortable speaking with you about their home buying goals and financial information.

Module 3 - The Buyer Consultation, Step-by-Step

When meeting your clients for the first time, these steps may seem a little rudimentary, but they work all the same.

Step 1: Welcome the buyer(s).
Offer water, coffee or any kind of refreshments to the buyer(s). Make them feel comfortable and at home. Walk them through the office, especially if you are on a large Team, so they can see all the different roles involved in getting their transaction closed. Some Agents like to introduce key staff members like the admin, Team Leader, or transaction coordinator before the meeting.

Step 2: Outline the purpose and mission of the meeting.
- The goal is to find and negotiate the successful purchase of the right home for you.
- This consultation helps ensure you choose the right property that fits your lifestyle.
- We want to be the Team and/or Buyer Agent that you want to work with. It's important to choose someone who understands the business, has up-to-date market knowledge, can successfully negotiate on your behalf, and knows how to ensure a smooth close and move.

Step 3: Explain the possible outcomes of the consultation.

There are only 3 possible outcomes today...

a. We will decide if we should work together. If so, we will sign the Buyer Agency Agreement and I'll start looking for homes right away today...

b. You may decide to work with another Agent today... (Ask for referral?)

c. I may decide we are not the right fit for you today...

Any of those is fine, okay?

Step 4: Discover Buyer's Wants and Needs

Your goal is to familiarize yourself with the buyer and find out as much as you can about what they want and need. You'll follow the Buyer Intake Form and ask a lot of questions.

> **Coach's Corner: Listen more than you talk! Asking open-ended questions will elicit the best responses.**

Download a copy of our Buyer Intake Form at http://www.clubwealth.com/buyersconsultation

Review the Steps to Home Ownership Process

Review the home-buying process regardless if this is their 1st home or the 12th home they've bought. This will ensure they understand all that's involved and how you will help them as their Agent.

STEPS TO HOME OWNERSHIP

1 Find a Real Estate Professional
- Meet face to face
- Interview Real Estate Agents
- Go over needs and expectations

2 Are You Ready?
- Get pre-approval from lender

3 Find a Home
- What are your wants and needs?
  (Schools, neighborhoods, amenities)

4 Make & Negotiate the Offer
- Review all contracts - ask questions
- Home inspection
- Escrow deposit - how much?
- Submit a competitive offer

5 Closing Time
- Walk through inspection
- Obtain home insurance
- Set up utilities
- Get ready to move in!

- Explain Agency Relationships

You'll go over this in more detail when you have them sign the agency agreement. Hit the bullet points on how buyers should be made aware of how the agency relationship is impacted in the following situations: how to handle FSBOs, open houses, new home construction, meeting other agents, etc. "If I don't represent you as the buyer, then I'm really working for the seller – no matter who has the property listed."

- Review the Mortgage and Lending Process

Ask if they've already talked with a lender and have received their pre-approval letter. If their lender does not work out, or they do not have one, offer your three recommendations of lenders, all of whom should be Team-approved lenders. Help buyers understand the benefits of working with Team-approved lenders (the leverage the team has due to the volume of business sent to the lender, how much harder the lender is likely to work for the buyer because they don't want to lose all the possible business the Team can sent them, etc.) Educate buyers about the impact being pre-qualified has on purchase negotiations. Help them understand the potential consequences if the lender they choose does not close the transaction on time, up to and including not closing at all, losing earnest money, etc.

Lender Script:

"Mr. and Mrs. Buyer: If they could save you 10-20 thousand dollars over on your mortgage, would you be interested in chatting with one of our lenders?"

- Educate Your Buyer

Educating your buyer is all about discussing current market conditions, and how you will help find them a property. You should also be current on the sales activities and trends for your local area. Know the absorption rates so you can properly explain what type of market the area is experiencing. It's also beneficial to discuss current interest rates, and what a small rise in interest rate could do to their purchasing power and or ability to buy at all. Ask the Team lender for help with this.

- Explain the Love it or Leave it Guarantee

Explain the LIOLI Guarantee and any other incentive programs (Move for Free etc.) and or USP's. This is likely part of your VIP Buyer Program.

- Share Your VIP Buyer Program

Your VIP Buyer Program tells the customer what you will do for them throughout the process. Your program is about the benefits you bring to the buyer and why they will choose you over anyone else.

Step 5: Set Expectations
Set expectations upfront for your buyer.

Establish how you will communicate with them and how often. Does the buyer prefer phone calls? emails? texts? Also set boundaries on when and where they should contact you.

You can also walk the buyer through the Team process. Do you employ a showing assistant? Who will write up the offer? Negotiate with seller? Who will assist with transactional duties? Make sure they are clear on exactly what to expect every step of the way. Ideally, they should receive a flowchart (if you are on a Team) on who handles what, and when, along with their contact information

Step 6: Close for the Agreement
Throughout the consultation, ask for agreement with trial closes to gauge your buyer. When you have established a pattern of "yes" answers, it is easier to get a "yes" when you get to the Buyer Agency Agreement.

Remember to induce this "Yes" state by getting them to say yes 7-12 times during the Buyer Consultation.

Trial Close with Tie-downs*

- Can you see the benefit?
- Would that work for you?
- That's what you want, correct?

- Does that make sense?
- Wouldn't you agree?

Before you close for the agreement, it is also important to explain to your buyer the importance of a signed agency agreement, and how you are compensated for your services.

Where appropriate, share the Club Wealth® "Will work for free" form to help them understand how Agents are paid, and invite a sense of loyalty. It will also help to put their "greed factor" (everyone has one) to work for you, by encouraging them to ensure you get compensated the same no matter what commission the listing office is offering.

You can obtain a copy of the "Will Work For Free" form on our website at www.ClubWealth.com/workforfree

---

Coach's Corner: Have your agency agreement as a separate document or as the first part in your Buyer's Representation Agreement. Once the buyer has signed the agency agreement, there is usually no hesitation from them to sign the representation agreement.

Step 7: What Comes Next

Now you have the agreement and are ready to start working with your buyer. Before you part ways, do the following:

1. Ask if they have any other questions.
2. Establish the best way to stay in contact.
3. Confirm criteria for the house.
4. Send them their first list of homes during the consultation, and make sure they received it before leaving.
5. If the buyer needs to sell a house first, offer to do a CMA.

6. If buyer still needs to speak with a lender, remind them to send over the preapproval letter. Once you have this, let them know you can proceed to the next step.

7. Ask for a referral!

8. Set the next appointment.

Download a copy of the Homebuyer's Packet at http://www.clubwealth.com/buyersconsultation

Add your own information to adapt to your team.

Bonus content: For Buyer Objection Handlers, visit our website for invaluable scripts. http://www.clubwealth.com/scripts

CHAPTER 14

HOW TO CREATE THE ULTIMATE BUYER EXPERIENCE

CLUBWEALTH

Module 1 - Communication With Buyers

Building trust with a buyer requires staying in constant communication with them. Good news, bad news, or no news, over-communicating with them is a very good thing.

Per a recent National Association of Realtors (NAR) study*, 69% of buyers were unhappy with the Agent they used, and the number one reason was lack of communication.

When we talk about how to win over buyers and how to create raving fans and massive rapport, the number one thing that you want to remember is to **communicate, communicate, communicate**.

When working with a particularly motivated buyer, you need even more communication, care, and attention. If someone is ready to write an offer and they are looking at property with you, you'll want to communicate with them all the time.

There's no such thing as too much communication for this type of highly motivated buyer. You'll want to show the buyer that you are an expert, and a true professional, and the best way to do that is with constant follow-up and communication before, during, and after the sale.

If you ever worry that you're going to be bothering someone, and you don't want the buyer to feel like they're being hounded, just call the buyer and say, "I just want to be sure that I'm not dropping the ball on my end."

Part of what makes you a World Class Buyer Agent is consistent follow up with the client. It shows the client that you are there for them and that they hired the right person to represent them.

Module 2 - Communication During Closing Process

Most Agents tend to think that once they get the house into escrow, they're done. When you get a house into escrow and you're starting the closing process, that's typically the time the client feels the most anxious and excited.

Logistically speaking, there is a lot for the Agent to handle during this time, and oftentimes most Agents seem to disappear.

Once you get into escrow, you'll want to continue communication. Whether you are on a Team or are a solo Agent, you must still communicate with the client weekly through the closing process (or whatever frequency your Team Leader has requested).

> **Coach's Corner: Remember, communication doesn't stop just because the showing process has.**

In order to develop a long-term client relationship, your communication should be consistent and helpful. Also, if you're on a Team, you may have a transaction coordinator or office assistant that takes care of the client communication during the escrow stage.

Even if you have a transaction coordinator (TC) or office assistant working with the client during the closing process, it still makes a big difference for you to reach out to your client - even if just to say "Hey, I wanted to make sure I'm not dropping the ball on my end. Is there anything you need? Is [name of TC] taking great care of you?"

At a bare minimum, you want to contact your client once a week during the escrow (closing) process. Most likely you will be talking even more when it comes time for inspections, appraisals, repairs, title issues, and loan problems.

When an issue comes up, don't be that Agent that runs and hides. You need to show your client that you can handle any type of situation that occurs during closing.

Assure your client that if you can't help them, you'll find someone who can! **Keep this valuable rule in mind: If you're going to bring a problem to a client, always be prepared with a solution.**

Your long-term goal is to develop a relationship with this client. You want to be sure they're your clients for life. They only way to do that is through constant and consistent communication.

You want the client to give you their future business, as well as send you referrals. So as soon as you know there is an issue, hit it head on! Never run *from* a problem, run *to* the problems. Get the client on the phone. Send them a text or an email.

Coach's Corner: Bring solutions, not problems!

Bottom line, raving fans generate referrals.

Module 3 - Communication After Closing

An interesting NAR study* found that 80 percent of consumers never went back to their original Agent for one reason: the Agent never called them again!

If you are looking for ways to build your business, keeping in constant contact before, during, and after the sale not only retains your clients, but you may end up picking up other clients whose Agents dropped the ball on them.

If you have a prospective buyer that can't even remember their previous Agent's name that is probably an opportunity to build rapport with them and make them a client for life!

We call this "Adopting an Orphan Buyer".

Coach's Corner: You can acquire the clients of many other Agents because those Agents are not going to be a World Class Agent like you.

Follow up with the sellers after closing, too. Ask them if the new buyers have any questions – may you call them? Stay in touch and put them on a drip campaign.

Not only do raving fans generate referrals, raving fans generate A LOT of referrals!

Module 4 - Sharpen Your Skills

In the world of communication, the first thing you'll need to accomplish is building rapport. The best way to build rapport with buyers and be recognized as a true expert is to ask lots of good questions.

That said, before they begin to know you, like you, trust you, and perhaps even love you - there is only one thing that interests them, and that's themselves! We've mentioned the expression **What's In It For Me**, right?

This is nothing against them - we are all looking out for ourselves. As human beings, we are naturally wired to think about ourselves and put our own needs first. If you continue to ask your clients great questions about themselves, you and they will eventually create a bond. This fosters a truly magical relationship.

What kind of questions should you be asking your clients? You can't help them achieve their goals if you don't know what those goals are. How do you know what your clients want? You ask them the right questions, and then you listen. A lot. It's literally that simple.

Coach's Corner: Every time I walk into an appointment with a client, I use this affirmation. I would say this to myself over and over again. "I'm a creative, solution oriented, problem solving machine."

Key Questions Build Trust

There are a few questions that you can ask clients if you want to build massive rapport and trust. And when you ask these questions, by the way, there's a big difference between a conversation and an interrogation. Ask your questions with a curious tone, not a confrontational one. This will help you get a little deeper and dig out their true motivations.

Key questions that most Agents forget to ask are:

- What are you trying to accomplish by moving?
- How soon do you want to be in your new home?

- Can you describe the home you want to live in?

You can also drill down deeper on these questions by asking: Can you tell me about the living room? What's the backyard look like? When you wake up in this house, what do you do first? What are you excited about when you move into your new home?

These are great examples of open-ended questions that you can ask to get your buyers talking, and to show them you are genuinely curious.

Perhaps the most important question that is almost never being asked: What are you looking for in an Agent? If you are genuine, people will usually tell you exactly what they are looking for. The reason Agents don't ask this question is because they don't want to hear the answer. Now that you've learned this, the next time you sit down with a buyer, take notes and do exactly what they say is important to them.

Elaborate on value elicitation. Values are what determine our motivation and make us happy. A person who works in alignment in his or her values is most likely a motivated person, despite what other things are going on at the time. The secret to value elicitation is to ask intelligent questions and answer them honestly, without interpretation by the conscious mind.

An example of value elicitation: If transaction gets sticky, you can go back to your clients' original motivation, and remind them of that. When you feed information back to someone within his or her value system, it becomes attractive and difficult to resist.

Module 5 - Little Hinges Swing Big Doors

There are certain things that you can do in the process of working with clients that may seem miniscule to you, but are massive to your clients. These things go a long way to generate rapport, which translates into referrals. Remember: raving fans send more and better referrals.

Download a copy of our Buyer Intake Form at http://clubwealth.com/ultimate-client-experience

An example of this would be the Buyer Intake Form that is used when initially talking to a buyer before showing property. On the buyer intake form, there are a few lines that say **favorite snack and favorite drink**. This is also great to use at the buyer consultation.

Once you know what snacks and beverages they favor, arrive with a cooler packed with their favorite snacks and drinks the first time you show them property. It may not seem like much to you - but it's a BIG thing for your buyer! Use a personalized cooler and give it to the client if you have the budget for that, or just buy a less expensive reusable cooler. Either way, your buyers will appreciate this small gesture in a big way.

Just remember that simple is best; don't overcomplicate it.

Another simple but effective thing to do for your client is a Ribbon Cutting Ceremony. Once you find the right house for your client and you're ready to meet them for the big key exchange - make it extravagant. Sometimes the best closing gift is creating a special moment.

For fewer than ten dollars you can purchase a big red bow and drape it across the doorway. Have the buyer and their family stand at front door. You can use a special pair of scissors and have the buyer cut the ribbon to the front door. Snap some photos of this occasion.

Ask for, and if given permission, post the photos to social media, tagging the buyer, and, if they were referred, the person who referred them. This is another great way to generate referrals. Don't forget to film the buyer video testimonials, too.

Take it one step further and take that picture to a print shop. Have them blow up the photo on canvas (this costs around 30 dollars). A beautiful canvas print is a perfect memento of this special event in their life. Now you have an excuse to go back to visit, so you can give them the personalized gift. They will probably hang it up on wall in their new house, and this way they will remember you always.

You are changing people's lives. Where they live is one of the most important aspects of their life, and you are the person that connects them to their home.

One more great idea: Print postcards of the ribbon ceremony and create "Just Moved" cards for your buyers. On one side is the new mailing address, and on the other side you can have printed, "My World Class Agent was <insert your name here>."

Building strong relationships with your potential and current clients by staying in constant communication will help you reach the status of World Class Buyer Agent in no time!

For more great ways to create the Ultimate Customer Experience and Raving Fans, visit http://clubwealth.com/ultimate-client-experience

*Source: https://www.nar.realtor/research-and-statistics/quick-real-estate-statistics

CHAPTER 15
VIP BUYER PROGRAM

CLUBWEALTH

The goal of a World Class Buyer Agent is selling yourself to buyers, so that they will eventually either buy from you or refer you to someone who will. It's a known fact that buyers like to talk to a bunch of Agents. So how do you differentiate yourself from the pack?

You can start by making a promise to yourself that you will not be just a normal real estate Agent, and that you will be a World Class Buyer Agent who gives a ton of value to clients. Developing your own USP is a great start to setting you apart from your competition.

Module 1 - Great USPs Do the Following

What exactly is a USP?

What is a USP? USP stands for Unique Selling Proposition. A USP is an offer that sets you apart from other Agents. The average buyer is talking - and maybe even looking at houses - with several Agents before deciding whom to work with. We should assume a buyer has spoken with at least 5 other Agents by the time we get to speak with them. With this in mind why are they going to pick you as their Agent? Well, because you are going to be different and better. That is where the USP comes in.

Since USPs are best used as a powerful, long-term differentiator, you want to make sure you get it right the first time.

You will need to craft your own USP in order to build your VIP Buyer Program.

3 characteristics of a great USP:

1. It is different than what other people are offering. This seems simple, but by definition a USP must be unique. Sometimes people will pick you simply because you are different. Standing out is the goal here.

2. It shows a true value. Anyone can offer to setup a listing alert, or "provide great service". Things like this are the baseline, not outstanding behaviors. However, offering to pay a fee or offering something special, such as a home warranty, is actual value to the buyer. We will go over examples later in this chapter, but remember, when creating your USP, the S stands for selling, but you could replace that with a V for value proposition - you have to provide a value.

3. Lastly, we want the offer to be memorable. Something that makes the buyer say, "I absolutely want to work with that Agent. I know they are giving me the best value."

Module 2 - Give Clients the 5 Star VIP Treatments

Once you've crafted your USP, it's time to start building your own VIP Buyer Program. To get you started, we're going to share some of the most popular USPs that many of our Club Wealth® Coaches and Clients use as part of their VIP Buyer Program.

Love it or List It - "Don't like your new house in 12 months – we will sell it for free!"

The Love It Or List It Program is really a simple concept. If anybody for any reason buys a house from us, and in the first 12 months of homeownership they decide that they don't want to live in the house anymore, we will sell it for them and not charge a commission on the listing side.

So why do this? It's not something that will cost a lot of money and it will get you - the Buyer Agent - significantly more buyers in the time that you have to sell the house for free.

Love It or List It is one of the simplest USPs out there, and it's probably one of the best type of USPs an Agent can offer because it provides the client with a peace of mind and with no risk.

This is called "Risk Reversal".

Essentially, we want the client to feel that working with us reduces their risk and ultimately feel comfortable choosing us as their Agent.

Real estate clients want to be confident in your ability. The best way to instill confidence in them is to show them how confident you are in your own ability. What better way to demonstrate that confidence than to put your money where your mouth is with a solid risk-reversal strategy like Love It or List It?

Buy from Me, Move for Free - "When you buy your home from me, I'll pay for your local move!"

It's best to have a tight relationship with a moving company that will do a great job and give you a discount when using this USP. Make sure you are covered from a liability standpoint, and market the heck out of this one, as it brings them in!

Unlisted Home Program - "If the home you want isn't for sale, we'll door knock the entire neighborhood until we find someone willing to sell to you!"

As the market heats up and listing inventory is low, some buyers will want to live in a certain subdivision where nothing is for sale. This is an amazing opportunity for you to show value to a prospective buyer.

How it works:

The buyer gives you a couple subdivisions that they want to live in and you find there is nothing listed for sale. Instead of just coming back to them with nothing, you would go knock on doors in that area, talk to potential sellers, and see if there's an opportunity to find a house.

You could also send letters, emails, and texts to all the homeowners in that area, looking for someone who wants to sell. This is a great win-win program for all parties involved. It's also a great opportunity for your Team to get more listings.

Remember one of the major complaints clients have about Agents in today's online world is "My Agent didn't even find my house". This program goes above and beyond, and the buyers will know you are working for them to get them what they want.

One key to success is to never say, "I have a buyer" to the homeowners. They immediately don't believe you, and therefore distrust you from that point forward in the conversation.

Instead, use the following script: "I'm Michael with Hellickson Real Estate. I've been working with SSgt John and Susie Smith to find a home in the neighborhood, and unfortunately, haven't been able to find them the home that fits their needs.

I was wondering: if they were willing to pay your price, pay all closing costs, commissions, repairs, and any fees, and were willing to close whenever you want, and even let you stay after closing as long as you need to move to your new place, would you even entertain an offer from them?"

If the homeowner doesn't say, "yes" at this point, they really don't want to move!

Handyman for a Day - "Get a handyman for the day to take care of all those little repairs"

All too often we go through the inspection process and there's a whole bunch of little nitpicky things that the buyer wants fixed. The buyer will feel like they're important and necessary. The seller feels the exact opposite because the sellers have lived in that house with those problems for the last 15 years and they can't see any value in fixing them.

Handyman for a Day adds value to your buyer so they can solve some of those inspection issues like painting a room, replacing a electrical outlet, sealing a crack in a door, or replacing a fogged window. Most of those little problems can often be solved with Handyman for a Day. Your new buyers are excited to work with you because you offer this great program, and in the end, you end up getting more transactions to the closing table.

Take this to the next level by doing the following:

1. Offer "Handyman for a Half Day"
2. Get your Handyman to do it for free, knowing that NO ONE has a HALF a day's work for a handyman... they almost always have at least 2 or 3 days worth of work, which they will likely hire your handyman to do for them. He'll likely be super happy to do the free half days as a means to acquiring the new customer for subsequent days, and often for life!

Certified Contractor Program - "Make sure all inspection work was done properly by offering a certified contractor to do a final inspection"

More than likely, you are a real estate Agent and not a licensed general contractor (although a few of you may have your contractor's license). There is a good possibility that you may not discover everything that is wrong with a home that your potential buyer is interested in. You may miss something critical that needs to be addressed.

So after you negotiate repairs, and the seller makes those repairs, you can have a certified contractor come out there to take a look at those repairs, and assure both parties that they were done right. The purpose of this program is not to find issues; it is to ensure that issues the seller agrees to repair are completed correctly.

For example, a contractor I know did a repair on a home that cost over $20,000 due to a small piece of flashing being incorrectly installed and water ran down behind the brick on the home and created rot and mold. If the buyer had been offered a similar Certified Contractor VIP program, this whole situation may not have occurred and could have saved the buyer a good chunk of change in the end.

Vendor Support Program - "An exclusive list of high quality contractors and vendors in your area that include discounts as well"

In today's real estate world, it is challenging to get quality people to come out in a quick and timely manner. On top of that, to be professional and efficient and maybe, even offer some potential good discounts. Offer your clients access to your exclusive Vendor Support list so they know they'll be getting quality professionals that will show up on time, and get the job done right the first time - at the best price possible.

Easy-Out Listings Agreement or 100 % Cancellation Guarantee Program - "Cancel anytime for free. No obligations."

This simple program states, "We are so confident in our real estate system, that we will give you a 100% guarantee to cancel your listing agreement at any time prior to receiving an offer to purchase your home, with no penalties or obligations, if you feel we are not living up to our promise." Or any kind of language similar to that. This is mainly for a listing Agent to give a home seller that has been burned before by working with a bad Agent. However, as a Buyer Agent, you can come up with a similar program to give your buyers - or build this language into your buyer agency agreement.

Module 3 - Don't Forget the Basics

When writing your VIP Buyer Program, don't forget to offer the basics. The prospective buyer may not know that all Agents in your market offer electronic signatures or homebuyer alerts, but to them it could be a great benefit that YOU do offer it.

Here are some examples of simple things virtually any Agent can include in their VIP Buyer Program to get started:

- Secure the best financing program for your specific situation with the lowest interest rate and least expensive closing costs.

- Have a pre-qualification/approval certificate generated to give you the best competitive advantage in purchase negotiations, allowing you to compete with and even win out over cash buyers.

- Provide you with regular updates from our Home Hunter Service of all the new properties that match your home buying criteria, so you can drive by and determine which properties you actually want to see from the inside.

- Arrange a private showing of any property you want to see, including new construction, bank-owned, and For Sale by Owner (FSBO) and off-market properties.

- Discuss the best strategy for making an appropriate offer, as well as financing terms, interest rates, cost to close, possession date, inspections, termite/pest/environmental reports, and any questions you might have.

- Help you prepare an offer with terms, provisions, special stipulations, amendments, exhibits and addendums weighted in your best interest.

- Present the offer on your behalf and negotiate in your favor to help you secure the property at the best possible price and terms.

- Recommend extremely competent affiliates that can help with your home purchase, including legal advice, home inspections, appraisals, warranties, homeowner hazard and title insurance.

The things listed above sound simple, but will demonstrate value to your clients. It is also important that we cover these things with the potential buyer or you may end up losing them. For instance, if you didn't cover arranging private showings of FSBO to your buyer. Imagine if your buyer rides by a home that is offered For Sale By Owner.

The buyer calls them and the first thing the FSBO asks is, "Do you have an Agent? If not, we can give you a discount on the price." Are they getting a better price? We don't know for sure. All we do know is that the buyer just walked away because they think they are getting a better deal.

Instead, tell them that you are willing to work with every FSBO, and that you'll negotiate on their behalf. Also, assure them not to worry about the commission and that you will negotiate that from the FSBO. If you demonstrate value, the buyer won't leave you to try to save a few bucks.

Module 4 - Develop a VIP Program

When developing your VIP Program there are a few key strategies and suggestions you can implement.

Use all of the programs or mix it up! You can use all the programs at once or you can mix and match. The key to the VIP Program is showing more value and benefit to the client, but it doesn't have to necessarily cost us more money.

Think about what niche or market area you are working in. If you live in an area that has a lot of vacation or second homes, you may consider the **Handyman for a Day!** Out of state owners don't have time to oversee work on repairs and this is a perfect program to offer them. Think about what niche you are serving and formulate a program to meet the needs of that niche.

Check with your broker. Before you implement and start advertising your new unique selling proposition, you must first check with your broker. As with any powerful strategy, there are many T's to be crossed and I's to be dotted. Failure to do so could create major legal challenges for you and/or your broker.

Make it professional and polished. Be sure to have professional marketing materials to hand to clients, not something that looks like it was just whipped up on a word processor. Everything your client views in connection with you needs to convey that you are the most competent and professional Agent out there.

Have someone proofread it. This is going to sound silly, but make sure somebody proofreads it. Too often you may have one word misspelled, and if you made a clerical error on your marketing materials, someone might make an assumption that you'll be just as careless when it comes time to close.

Also, it helps to read it out loud to someone. This will help you avoid grammatical mistakes.

Here are a few other things to consider when utilizing the VIP Program:

- **Always offer your program to every client.** The last thing you want to do is have someone refer a buyer or seller to you and you don't offer the VIP Program. They know that you offered it to their friend. Why aren't they getting the same service? That makes you look like you didn't care about them, and you're probably not getting any more referrals from that client.

- **Have a VIP loyalty agreement for each client to sign.** Create an agreement with your VIP Buyer Program. An agreement is something that a person signs. The psychology behind having someone sign the agreement is that the person who's willing to sign a piece of paper - even though it doesn't actually commit anything - will be loyal to you as a client.

- **Having someone sign creates a commitment even though it is not a contract to work together.** Here's the best part about getting someone to sign the VIP buyer agreement: Now you can go over a Buyer Agency or Buyer Broker Agreement, depending on your state, and the client is already in the mindset of working with somebody. It will make it easier for them to sign another agreement since they are already committed to working with you.

To give you a quick script that we use all the time at Club Wealth®: "We can work with 5 to 7 people at a given point in time. And we would love to work with you, but at the end of the day, if you're not willing to commit to work with us, we have to go find another person to work with. For us to give you the quality of service you deserve and for us to offer all of the stuff, we need to make sure that you're willing to work with us exclusively, because we can only work with 7 people at a time."

- **It's a great transition from the VIP Buyer program (which has no obligation) to a Buyer Agency or Buyer Broker agreement.** When people sign one that does not obligate them it is easier to get them to sign other documents.

Module 5 - Conversion Scripts

Here are a couple of scripts that work well is for people who call and say that they're working with another Agent. Let's disclose right now that we're not trying to steal clients, but rather decide whether that statement is true or whether they're just saying that.

Essentially, if they have signed a Buyer Agency Agreement with another Agent, they are off limits. If not, they are fair game.

The script is:

Prospective client: I'm working with another Agent.

Agent: Ok, great. Have you actually signed a buyer agency agreement with them, or am I still able to tell you about some of our off-market properties?

Script #2

Prospective client: I'm working with another Agent.

Agent: ok, so... let me ask you quick question... How is their VIP buyer program?

Or you could say, "That's great. I imagine they have a great VIP

Buyer program!"

Then just wait; don't say anything else. Because 95% of the time they will come back with this statement: "What's a VIP Buyer Program?" Or "No, I've never heard of that. Tell me little bit about that?"

All of a sudden the Agent that they had magically disappears. It's a huge opportunity to set yourself apart. Now you've offered something unique to the buyer and they've become your client.

When to Present the VIP Buyer Program –

At Club Wealth®, we try to present the VIP Buyer Program at the buyer presentation. The reality, however, is that doesn't always happen. Another time that it can be presented is during or at the end of the first showing. After you have shown a home, have a copy of your program on the buyer's clipboard.

A script might go something like this -

"So, Mr. Buyer it was really great to meet you today. A really cool program that we have that no one else is offering is our VIP buyer program."

95% of the time they say, "Absolutely, I would love to do that."

It's a great opportunity to stand in front of that person and answer all of their questions.

Another time that we can present the VIP Buyer Program is as a lead conversion technique on the phone. You can certainly use it to convert someone that is not that excited to work with you. If that client won't answer the phone or is not responding to your text messages, you can send a video text followed by a link to your program that says:

1. "Not sure if this is something that you're interested in but I want to send you a link to our VIP Buyer program in case it is something that might benefit you."

2. Send a url (can use bitly link or Google shortener to track)

Coach's Corner: Use your "off-market properties list" to create scarcity and attract interest.

Module 6 - How to Market your VIP Program

Once you develop your VIP Buyer Program (or USP), tell the world! Put it everywhere. You will see a dramatic increase in your response rates and close ratios when you begin using your powerful USP!

The more creative ways that you can get that out there, the more possibilities to convert people.

Put your VIP Buyer Program in your:

- Email Signature Line
- Website
- Signs
- Flyers
- Newsletters
- Social Media

Ultimately, VIP Buyer Programs are one of the most powerful ways to convert a buyer into a client, whether it's a text or in person. Make sure you present it to everyone you meet. Stand behind it, and set yourself up as the World Class Buyer Agent that they want to and will work with today.

CHAPTER 16
SHOWING PROPERTY

CLUBWEALTH

Your goal as a World Class Buyer Agent needs to be to create the ultimate home buying experience. In order to do that, we want to focus on three specific things.

First, we have an eight-step process for showing the house to make sure it's a great experience for your buyers.

Second, we want to focus on "wowing" the buyer every single step of the way.

Finally, we want buyers to understand that we are different than the Average Agent - we are a World Class Buyer Agent!

In this chapter, we will even help you to achieve a higher closing rate than most Agents just by using a simple closing script. But first, it all starts with knowing how to begin the property showing process.

Module 1 - Ultimate Home Buying Experience

Showing property can be the biggest, and most time consuming, task of a Buyer Agent's job.

What is the purpose of showing a house? If you ask ninety-five percent of real estate Agents that question, they would probably give you the answer, "To sell the house!" Of course, we are not opposed to selling a house, right? That's how we get paid. However, that's not the *purpose* of what we are trying to do.

The number one purpose is to build rapport with our buyers. In this situation (the home showing), we have the best opportunity to find out so much more about our buyers and to build a great lifelong relationship with them.

The second thing we set out to accomplish is to capture a client. In other words, when we meet someone for the first time, we can begin to build rapport, have a great time showing property, and then we have the opportunity to make that person a client (and sometimes even a friend) for life.

Another thing we want to focus on is making our potential clients extremely happy! Here's a little secret the average Agent doesn't know....we don't care what house they buy, as long as they use us to buy it. As a matter of fact, a great to script to use is this one:

"Mr. Buyer, I don't care what house you buy as long as you're happy with the house that you choose, and you allow me to help you buy it."

Simple, honest, transparent, sincere, and extremely effective.

The last thing is to, of course, actually sell a house. If we are always focusing on the wants, needs, and desires of our clients and showing up, on time, and 100% ready to help, we can't help but be successful at selling homes. Make your client happy while building a relationship with them and earn your commission.

Module 2 - The 8 Steps to Showing Property

By following this 8-step process to showing property, you will separate yourself from the pack. Every prospective client that you show property to should receive the same World Class service from you every single time. Service that will far exceed what other Agents provides.

Step 1 – **Preparation**

Preparation is not only the first step in the showing process, but it is something that you do long before you shake the client's hand.

Napoleon Hill instructs us to "Begin with the end in mind". This is sage advice from one of the greats.

You should have several generic Buyer Packages already in your office and/or vehicle, ready to go. This way you can add to and personalize the packages once you have an appointment to show property.

Here are some documents to consider adding to your Buyer Packages:

VIP Buyer Program - You want to include a document fully explaining the VIP Buyer Program because it is an opportunity to show value and uniqueness that a lot of buyers don't experience with other Agents. Remember, your VIP Buyer Program is what sets you apart from other Agents.

Buyer Intake Form - This is a form that will determine the exact wants and needs of that client.

Offer Sheet - It is imperative to include this form in your package. If you do have the opportunity to write an offer, this sheet will systemize the offer writing process for you, and it makes you look professional, as a World Class Buyer Agent should.

Purchase and Sale Agreement Sample - Bringing a sample contract with you is a great opportunity to go over a contract with your buyers in person. Nowadays, we often use electronic signature technology software to write and send the offer to our buyers. The very first time the buyer usually sees a contract is on their electronic device.

The buyer is excited to make the offer and may not know or understand what they are signing. So, before they electronically sign something, you want to use this process to review the contract. That way the buyer understands all the components of a sales contract, can ask questions, and begin to get comfortable with what they will eventually be signing.

Once again this makes you a true professional who spends the time to make sure that the clients are informed and comfortable every step of the way.

Once you make the showing appointment with your buyer, whether it's after the initial buyer consultation or after a phone appointment to show a home, you can add to and personalize the packet with research about the neighborhood, local maps, and school information.

Another important thing to have in your arsenal is a 2 clipboard system

Clipboard #1
The first clipboard is for the buyer.

Here is what's needed on this clipboard:

- A pen attached to the top of the clipboard.

- An MLS sheet of every property you are going to look at that day – numbered in the upper left-hand corner from the first to the last house you'll be viewing, 1-x. That way the buyer knows in what order the houses will be shown, and this also makes it easier to keep track of their notes of each property shown. The buyer will appreciate your organized system.

- Any other relevant information to include on your client's clipboard (this is on a case by case basis). For example, if you are showing houses with large acreage you could include any surveys attached to the MLS sheets.

- Property disclosure is another piece of data that you can  give to your client prior to showing. If you have discovered there is something the client should know or be aware of on that particular property, bring the property disclosure with you.

- Lastly, a one-page sheet that details your VIP Buyer program. Make sure this is the last sheet on the clipboard. It's the perfect time to go over what you offer as a Buyer Agent.

Clipboard #2

The second clipboard is for you, the World Class Buyer Agent. This has everything that the buyer clipboard has on it, but for your eyes only. Depending on how your MLS sheets are designed, you may have a more detailed MLS sheet with information like commission, listing Agent's name and contact, property taxes, HOA fees, etc. It also:

- Has a pen attached to the top of the clipboard.
- Has every MLS sheet you're going to look at today in order numbered in the upper left hand corner.
- Has a dream home sheet - same as client clipboard.
- Has an offer sheet - same as client clipboard.
- Has a blank contract.

Other things to keep in the vehicle for an **Ultimate Home Buying Experience:**

Favorite drinks and snacks in a cooler. Always keep bottled water and granola bars on hand. Make sure your buyers are able to get something cool to drink while they're out running around looking at houses with you. The last thing you want is for them to be worn out, and dehydration causes moodiness and fatigue!

Ideally, you have collected their favorite drink and snack preferences at the initial buyer consultation, and are prepared with those in your car.

Have a flashlight. You should try to have flashlights for everybody, including any children coming along. That way everybody gets a flashlight in case the lights are off at a property. Sometimes when you're showing bank owned homes, the utilities aren't working. And besides, kids love flashlights... who doesn't?!

> **Coach's Corner: Carry a tape measure. This may seem like a small item, but buyers really appreciate it and seem to enjoy using it. Again, it's one more thing to set yourself apart from other agents.**

Umbrellas and rubber galoshes. Sometimes you pull up to vacant land, or maybe you're at a property where the walkway up to the house is a mess, or maybe your client just wants to walk around the back yard. Having umbrellas and galoshes will make it really easy for them to take a full and complete look at each and every property regardless of the weather conditions. Depending on your area, you may also want to carry rain ponchos in your car.

A basic First Aid kit is a good idea to keep in your vehicle at all times. It should include Band-Aids, some type of antibiotic cream, aspirin, Tylenol, Advil, Benadryl, motion sickness tablets, and heat and cold packs. You never know when an emergency may arise.

Ultimate Home Buyer Kits for Kids. Yes, you want them for the kids too! This is very important because you want to involve the kids in the process. Put a package together that has their own snacks, such as fruit chews, granola bars, and Cheerios. Also include coloring books and crayons. Maybe even bring a DVD player or tablet so the kids can watch a video while you're showing the house. Anything else you can think of the help get the kids involved in the process will be helpful.

Give the kids a clipboard too. Make them feel special and like a full and complete part of the process. Ask them questions about which houses the like best and why, what is important to them in selecting the home.

Step 2 – **Mental Preparation**

You need to put yourself in a positive mindset before meeting buyers to show property.

Before you meet your buyers to show property, you need to be mentally prepared. This is just as important as being physically prepared for the appointment with your buyers' package.

If you're having a bad day or just not feeling it, your clients will pick up on the low energy you're emitting. Therefore, you need to be able to put yourself in a positive state of mind.

Tony Robbins refers to this as getting "in state".

"The difference between peak performance and poor performance is not intelligence or ability; most often it's the state that your mind and body is in." – Tony Robbins

You can put yourself in a positive state by doing the same thing every time you have a showing or an important appointment. Develop a routine.

There are several ways to do this.

Affirmations –

Coach Brian Curtis likes saying affirmations before meeting a client. An affirmation is just saying a positive statement over and over until your subconscious starts to believe it.

You see, your subconscious mind is far more valuable than your conscious mind and cannot tell the difference between reality and what you tell it to believe.

Repeating affirmations over and over again out loud can literally reprogram your subconscious mind, and begin to change your actual reality.

Some of my personal favorite pre-buyer appointment affirmations are:

- I feel successful today.
- I attract qualified buyers who readily buy from me.
- I believe in myself and so do others.
- I will create a great relationship today
- I will write an offer today.

Playing uplifting music -

Playing music has a way of pumping you up for the appointment and putting you in the right frame of mind. If you like music then pick one of your favorite uplifting songs, and play that same song every time you meet with a client. Make it your thing. Your mood has memory, and if you listen to that song over and over again, it will put you in that "state' without you having to think about it.

Listening to a favorite podcast –

It's the same as listening to uplifting music. Listening to the right podcast (think motivational or real estate related podcasts) will put in you the right frame of mind before meeting a client. It gives you that extra boost you need to close your appointment!

Whatever it takes to get you in a positive mental state – do it. Every single time.

Step 3 – The Greeting
How do you talk to the client?

This is a simple step, but one that I think Agents don't even attempt to do anymore. Most of the time you'll see the Average Agent giving a quick "Hello" or acknowledgement nod to the buyer and unlocking the door for them.

This type of greeting is cold and may give off a vibe that you're too busy or non-caring.

Remember, a Buyer Agent can make anywhere from $100,000 to upwards of $500,000 a year. Ask yourself: Are you a door opener that makes $30,000 a year or are you a World Class Buyer Agent that makes $500,000 a year and takes it to the next level?

Anybody with a real estate license can open a door for someone. Remember this fact as you are reading this book and going through the courses. You can be an Average Agent or a World Class Agent. It's your choice.

So what does a World Class Buyer Agent do when meeting a client for the first time?

When greeting a buyer for the first time, the World Class Buyer Agent will look them right in the eye, notice their eye color, smile brightly, and firmly shake their hand with enthusiasm.

> **Coach's Corner:** The perfect handshake is firm, but not tight. Your hand is parallel with the buyer, not over or under, and finally, 3 pumps is the right number of pumps for the perfect handshake.

Greet all parties the same way. It's professional and courteous.

Step 4 – Get Inside

Once you've greeted the buyer, you should get them in the house as soon as possible. The last thing you want to do is stand around talking in the hot sun, or in three feet of snow, or pouring rain, with your buyer being miserable. You want the buyer in a controlled, comfortable environment where you can have a conversation with them without any distractions.

Step 5 – The Process

Once inside the home it's time to go over the process. Most buyer Agents just start doing what is called the "Vanna White" and begin the showing process by pointing out the kitchen, the living room, and so on.

Wrong! This is prime time to put you in control of the showing process. You'll start it if off the right way by doing the following steps:

Hand out the clipboards and your Buyer Package. Explain the clipboards including the MLS Sheets and go over what information is included in the Buyer's Packet and what the system is for viewing properties.

What is the house rating system?

Explain to the buyer how they are going to rate each house. The prospect can also add any notes to the MLS sheet that will help in the rating system. They will write the rating at the top of the sheet.

Why are we asking them to rate the house? Because elimination is our friend.

Sample script: "I want to explain the 1-10 rating system I'd like for us to use with each house. 1 is the lowest on the scale (I can't believe we even walked in the door) and 10 being the highest (I can't believe we haven't written an offer yet). How does that sound to you?"

Asking the important question of "How does that sound to you?" is a great way to get the buyer to commit to rating each home. It's also what we call a micro-commitment. Micro-commitments lead to major commitments, like signing the contract.

If the house is rated less than a 5 there is a really good chance that buyer is not interested in it. Keeping that MLS sheet is only making the decision to buy a house a little harder for them.

Explain to your buyer that the goal is to help them find the best home for them. You can say, "If you rate one home a 5 and another home an 8, we are going to literally tear up the MLS sheet for the home we rated a 5, okay?"

Some buyers may feel uncomfortable with that. However, you can assure the buyer that you want to make sure that they're getting rid of info that is no longer helpful to the decision process.

Remember, professional sales people take control. They look like they have shown a home before, yet many Agents are afraid to go over the process because they feel like they are being pushy. Taking control and leading is not pushy; it is your job.

Professionals have a plan. Imagine going to your doctor and her sitting back and asking you what you want to do, instead of coming up with a plan of action. That person would not be your doctor very long.

Step 6 – **Walk through**

Don't do the HGTV way of showing a house where the Agent lets the buyer walk through the house alone while the Agent steps outside and waits in the backyard. That's not professional and that's not real life.

It's lazy, and basically ineffective. Remember, goal number one of showing the home is to build rapport. It's hard to build rapport if you and the buyer aren't even in the same room.

On the flip side, while walking them through the house you don't want to be like "Vanna White", pointing out every single feature of the home.

Don't treat your buyers like they are idiots. They've been in a house before. They know what a kitchen looks like. They can probably figure out what a family room or dining room looks like.

You are likely experiencing the home for the first time as well, s do yourself and your buyer a favor, and experience it with them,

So what do you talk about? Use this opportunity to learn more about your clients by building rapport.

The technique we have already mentioned for quickly building rapport is the **F.O.R.D. Technique.** FORD stands for Family, Occupation, Recreation, and Dreams. Let's go a little deeper on each of these and how to evoke great answers on each:

Family. Talk about their needs for housing. Do they want a one story or two story? Do they want to be near certain schools for their kids? Do they want a pool? Do they have pets? Maybe a big backyard is desirable.

Occupation. Where do they work? Would a home office be desirable? Must it have a view, or is any home office ok? What does the commute look like? How much bandwidth and speed will their Internet connection need to have?

Recreation. What do the family members like to do for fun? Swimming, hiking, golf, lake, watersports, etc? Is having a community with amenities important? Where do they currently go for recreation? How far can they be from the kids' dance studio etc.?

Dreams. Have them close their eyes and imagine their perfect home. Does it include a large front porch? Game room or movie theatre for the kids? Craft room for Mom? A big backyard with plenty of room for a garden? A swimming pool? Will this be a forever home? Which of these items are MUST HAVE, non-negotiable items?

By implementing the FORD technique your client will start to relax and give you more valuable insight into their wants and needs.

AVERAGE AGENT VS. WORLD CLASS BUYER AGENT

Here's how the Average Agent handles the walk through of the house:

1. Points out all the features of the house like Vanna White.

2. Points out all the features about the house that THEY think are important.

3. Impresses the client with all of their knowledge of this new thing called a house.

Here's how the World Class Buyer Agent walks a client through a home:

1. Listens with their eyes, ears, and heart.

2. Asks open-ended questions using F.O.R.D. to build rapport.

3. Acknowledges the features the BUYER likes and dislikes without judgement.

During the walk through of the house, start building rapport with the client and ask a lot of questions about them.

Don't stand right next to them or lead them around the home. Keep a respectable distance and let the client explore the home at their own pace. Listen to what your client is saying about the home. Employ the **See, Hear, Feel** method by asking questions like:

"How do you **feel** about the house?" rather than "Do you like this house?"

"Can you **see** yourself spending the holidays in this house?'

Acknowledge their responses by parroting back to them. Whatever you **hear** them say you repeat back.

If Buyer comments, "I love this kitchen."

You'll say, "This is a really great kitchen"

If Buyer comments, "This bathroom is big enough for two people to get ready in the morning."

You say, "Big bathrooms are nice to have for the morning rush."

Oftentimes, people don't feel like they're being heard. So by always repeating their responses you are showing them that you **HEAR** them and that you understand their wants and needs.

ASK BETTER QUESTIONS

"Can you see yourself raising kids here?"

"Do you feel like this would be a good area to raise kids?"

"How do you feel about the house being in a cul-de-sac?"

"Can you see the kids playing in the backyard?"

Step 7 – Rate the house

Go through the rating process on each and every home. It's important that you ask EACH person (if there is more than one buyer), including the kids, so that all parties feel they're being heard.

Average Agents may miss this important strategy, and they fail to realize that people in a relationship don't always communicate effectively with one another, nor do they listen to their kids as well as one might think. They may not know what the other person is thinking about that home and don't even think to ask. Often, they simply assume their partner shares their opinion, or worse yet, they take for granted that their partner has an opposing viewpoint.

Here is a good example:

While Agent Brian Curtis was showing property to a couple, he asked the husband to rate the home, and that husband gave it an "8". Then he asked the wife for her rating and it was a "4". That gave Agent Brian the perfect opportunity - and a perfect opportunity for the couple - to find out why each one rated the home the way they did. That one conversation allowed them to eliminate about half the houses they were looking at, and focus on the things that they both wanted and needed, and get to the point where the Agent could get them to their dream home.

This saved the clients and Coach Brian a ton of time as well as potential frustration!

That opportunity is one that you cannot miss. You need to ask them every single time to rate the house. Give them an opportunity to talk to you and each other if there is more than one person. We are all about professionalism, but we also need to make the process an enjoyable one.

Now for the hard part...

Have them rip up the MLS sheet if the home doesn't rate more than a 5!

That's right. Rip it up if it doesn't meet their needs. Do it right now, together!

Buyers will want to argue and keep the sheets for future reference.

Remind them "this is a process of elimination and refer back to their 'Must Have' list. At the end of today, we need to be down to one or two houses, so that you can easily choose which of them you'd like to make an offer on. So, to make this easier, let's go ahead and rip up any sheet that rates lower than the last house that we have viewed so far."

Step 8 – The Last House - Write Up the Offer!

Hopefully, the buyers are down to one or two houses by the time you have viewed the last house.

Now is the time to ASK the question:

"Would you like to write an offer on any of the houses we saw **TODAY?**"

-OR-

"Which house that we saw **TODAY** would you like to write up?"

Today being the key word in both questions so you can build buyer urgency. Assuming you have pre-programmed their subconscious mind with urgency by avoiding words like "think" and "ponder", and instead have been consistently saying the word "today" a minimum of 7-12 times throughout the appointment, they should naturally elect to write an offer on one, or perhaps even two, of the homes they have viewed today.

Remember, you have one goal before you end the tour: get them to write an offer on a house TODAY.

The buyers aren't hanging out with you on a Sunday because they need new friends. They are looking to find a house, write an offer, and move into their dream home. Give them permission to write an offer. HOW do we do that? We ask them.

The number one question that will give you more closings is "Which of the homes we viewed today would you like to write an offer on?"

Remember: there are only three acceptable outcomes from a showing appointment:

WRITE the **OFFER**

-OR-

SET Next **APPOINTMENT**

-OR-

FIRE THEM, after deciding that you **DO NOT** want to work with this person going forward.

Writing an offer is the ultimate goal. Don't forget to use the offer worksheet to ensure you get all the correct information.

If they're not ready to make an offer, then **make a plan**. If this is the first time showing and you have not done a buyer presentation, then concentrate on doing the following:

Go over buyer presentation.

Explain your VIP Buyer Program.

Help them fill out the buyer intake form. The Agent usually fills out the form by asking the buyer questions.

Script: "Let me ask you a few questions so I can make sure we are focusing on getting you exactly what you are looking for, and so we don't waste any of your time looking at homes that won't fit your needs for one reason or another."

Go over a sample contract - remember, be unique. The majority of Agents are just opening doors and don't have a plan. The fact that you have a plan makes you a professional. The buyer will want to work with you - not the Average Agent, aka "door opener".

Coach's Corner: As 3rd party technology companies seek to remove Agents from the home buying/selling process and to "Uber-ize" the industry, it is the Agents who differentiate themselves in the ways discussed here who will not only survive, but thrive. Most of the "door openers" who call themselves "Agents" will end up either working for the tech giants, or simply looking for work in other industries and memorizing new scripts like "Would you like fries with that?" That is, until automated checkout stands completely replace those jobs, too!

While setting up your next appointment, be sure to go over the buyer wants and desires - keep them focused on where we are going. This is particularly important if they did not find the perfect house today. They may be feeling dejected, frustrated, overwhelmed, or they may just plain lose interest in the process.

It is incredibly important to make sure they know they are not alone. This is not your first rodeo, and you know how to get this done for them and will not rest until they have exactly the home they want and love!

You will be a "Pit-bull on the pant leg of opportunity" on their behalf, and will do the heavy lifting for them, so all they have to do is look at a few more homes and sign the agreement. Talk about the things they liked today and ensure them you will find them what they are looking for. You know this because you have been doing this a long time and have helped many others just like them accomplish their dreams as well.

Let them know that what they are feeling is absolutely normal at this point in the process, and that once they are in their new home, watching their kids play in the backyard with their friends and dog, they will be glad they stuck it out and made it happen.

They'll be even happier when they begin to realize the benefits of the tax-deductions and appreciation this investment gives them, and will be glad they are no longer throwing money away on rent.

Do not leave the buyer without making the next appointment or writing an offer, or deciding that you never want to deal with them again.

You have spent a large amount of time and money getting to the point where you can meet people in person. This is your chance to create a client for life, and when you go in with that mindset, you can't lose. If they don't want to write an offer, you set an appointment to look at more houses or to meet at the office to look online for properties.

If they say, "We want to think about...."

If the buyer won't commit to an appointment then make an appointment to make an appointment.

Script: "I'm going to go back to my computer and find some homes that may work for you. I'll email them to you and then give you a call tomorrow would 3pm or 5pm work better for me to follow up?" Using an "Alternative Choice" close allows you, the Agent, to remain in control. Because it is not a close-ended question, it doesn't leave them the option of leaving us hanging.

Let them sleep on it and ask if you can follow up later. "Shall we meet tomorrow at noon or 3 pm to discuss your options?"

If they are ready to make an offer, now is the time to pull out your offer worksheet and review it with them. If it's the first time to show property, go over a sample contract so it's not the buyer's first time they see the contract. We go over a sample contract because we don't want the buyer seeing this for the first time when they are signing it. They should already have an idea of what they are signing long beforehand.

Here are some simple guidelines to follow when your buyer may seem hesitant to follow through with writing an offer.

Guidelines to Assisting in the Decision Making Process:

1. Engage a lender's help if necessary. Ask the buyer to contact their lender to calculate how much they would have to pay on a 30-year note if the rates go up. You'll want to emphasize the importance of locking in today's rate.
2. Remind the buyer that if they want to "sleep on it" that they may not be "sleeping **in** it" if they wait too long. There is no way of absolutely knowing when another buyer toured the property before them and is working on writing up an offer right that second. The ones who "slept on it" last night may end up buying it first.

3. Sometimes being direct is best. Ask the question, "How would you feel if this property was taken of the market tonight and was no longer for sale?". The buyer's response should give you a pretty solid indication of how they really feel about making an offer on the property.

The third option, deciding to fire the client, should be an extreme scenario that doesn't happen often. That said, there are definitely people out there that you don't want to work with, as they are cancerous to your life and well being. It is okay to decide NOT to work with these people.

Normally, however, every single tour should end with writing an offer or setting up an appointment. Don't walk away without knowing how you will connect with the buyers again. Make an impression. Be the Agent who has a plan and appears professional. Be the Agent everyone wants to work with. A World Class Buyer Agent.

Remember, the hardest part of our business is simply getting the appointment. Many Agents think that once the hard part is done, it's smooth sailing until closing. Not true.

A World Class Agent knows that each appointment to show a home is an opportunity to stand out and let the buyer know they picked the right Agent. It's an opportunity to solidify a client for life, who is capable of referring literally hundreds of thousands of dollars in commissions over your/their lifetime.

The potential lifetime value of every client is MASSIVE. Treat them as such.

CHAPTER 17:

MASTERING KEY SALES
AND NEGOTIATING SKILLS

CLUBWEALTH

Mastering your sales and negotiating skills are MISSION CRITICAL tasks for the World Class Buyer Agent. There are only two ways to get more sales. First, talk to and meet with more people. Second, close a higher percentage of the people you talk to and meet with.

It's that simple.

Module 1 - Building Rapport

The number one thing you can do to build rapport is to ask questions. However, before you go to meet or even call someone for the first time, you should do some research. The beauty of the world that we live in today is that we can do that easily now with social media. We've got so much information at our fingertip today that wasn't available 10 years ago.

For example, you can go on Facebook and find information on anybody you might want to be friends with. You may be able to look at the things that interest them. Just having the opportunity to find out a little bit about somebody can pay huge dividends later.

When you meet for someone for the first time, they really don't want to talk about the weather - that makes you seem uninteresting. You really want to find an opportunity to talk to somebody about the things that *they* are interested in.

282

Get people to talk about themselves. Ask questions that are unique and unexpected. People love to talk about themselves. It's their number one favorite subject. For example, instead of asking someone what they do for a living, ask why they love or hate their job?

If you have read the book *How to Win Friends and Influence People* by Dale Carnegie, there's a great story in the book about Dale going to an event and asking a question to basically everybody in the room. He wasn't really talking at all, just asking a very simple question and letting other person talk. The best part about the story is the next day Carnegie talks about how throughout the entire day people keep talking to him and telling him what a great conversationalist he was. The reality is he didn't talk - he listened.

A popular saying that we have mentioned before in this book, and you will probably hear over and over again because it's so important to remember, is that you've got two ears and one mouth. That is so you can listen twice as much as you talk.

Another thing to remember about a good rapport - stay appropriate. Sometimes you'll find yourself around people who may be a little bit inappropriate, but that doesn't mean you have to cross that line, too. Stay appropriate, stay professional.

Clearly, you don't want to make them feel uncomfortable, or like you look down on them in some way. That said, just because they curse, drink excessively, do drugs, make off-color jokes or speak ill of others, etc., doesn't mean you need to do the same to establish a good rapport with them.

It is important that you "stand for something" at some point in your life. This doesn't mean you don't love the people who live life differently than you do. It simply means that once you have decided what your goals, values, morals, mission and vision are, you need to stick to them in all ways and at all times, and allow others their God-given right to Free Agency and the right to exercise it without judgment.

Here's another example of a great rapport question. "So you're from New York City? What do you miss most about living there?" By getting them to talk about themselves, you're giving them the opportunity to share something that they may be excited or passionate about.

What if they were born and raised where they are looking, or have even just lived there for a long time? Here's a great question for that person: "So you were born and raised here? I'm always looking for good recommendations for restaurants for my clients to hang out on Friday night. What's your favorite nearby restaurant?"

People love to help people, so if they feel like they're helping you, then you're building rapport with that person, and they don't even realize it.

Lastly, none of the other things that you will read in this book will work as well as they should if you do not have a good rapport. Without it, you're basically running into a wall. Before you work on any of these other things, work on building rapport with people.

Of all the skills we teach, it is the most important and will help you in your career and your life more than all the scripts, dialogues and other skills combined.

"When people know, like, and trust you, they will more likely do business with you."

Remember, the person asking the questions is really the person that is in control.

Module 2 - Matching and Mirroring

Another thing we can do to build rapport is called matching and mirroring. What is matching and mirroring?

Essentially, it is doing exactly what the other person does. If the person is raising their hand, we raise our hand. If someone is smiling at us, we smile back. Again, very simple.

Why do this? It makes people feel comfortable. Matching and mirroring the physical body movements, if you're presently in front of someone, is by far the simplest way to establish rapport without them even knowing.

As you hone this skill, you can even get them to match and mirror you subconsciously! This is my FAVORITE technique for building rapport!

Examples:

Inducing a "Yes" State - As I ask them questions like, "Won't that be great?" or "Does that make sense?" I look them square in the eye and nod my head up and down as if to get them to nod their head in agreement and say "yes". And guess what they almost always do? They nod their head up and down and say, "yes", almost as if they were in a trance and had no choice!

The Close - When I say, "Are there any other questions before we get started on the paperwork?" I look them square in the eye, and I shake my head back and forth as if to encourage them to do the same and respond with a "no". And guess what they do 99% of the time? They shake their head back and forth and say "no".

You can also match and mirror their speech. This is extremely important if you're on the phone, where you can't match their body language. You can, however, match their speech patterns while they're on the phone.

Match and mirror their rate of speech, tone of voice, voice inflections, volume, even their accent if they have one.

Things to consider with rate of speech: People who talk slowly are often considered "slow" or less intelligent by those who talk faster. People who talk noticeably fast are often considered to be a "fast-talking salesperson", and are perceived as less trustworthy.

The key to success is mirroring the rate of the person talking. It builds rapport and helps the other person feel more comfortable. This is the goal. If you as the sales person are a little uncomfortable, you are probably doing it right.

The flip side of that is, if you talk extremely slow, someone may make assumptions that you are a person who is slow, or someone who may not be as intelligent. It doesn't really matter which side that you fall on, as long as you're staying in concert with the person you're trying to build rapport with.

It is also important to match and mirror the tone of their words. If you want to match their tone and their volume, and you're a person who talks loud, you need to be careful that you're not scaring somebody out of the room. At the same time, if you talk too softly, they might not be able to hear you. Matching and mirroring their tone and volume will make them feel comfortable with you.

I am a very loud, and some might say obnoxious person by nature. I normally stand when making my calls. When I am doing a Strategy Session, however, for an Agent who is more quiet and reserved, I will deliberately change my delivery to match and mirror them.

I remember one particular Agent I did such a call with. When he picked up the phone and said "hello", it was in a very low, almost monotone voice. He was so quiet; I struggled to even hear him.

I was, at the time, standing at my desk, and immediately moved to a sitting position with my feet up on the desk as soon as I heard this man's voice.

Instantly, even effortlessly, my voice changed as a direct result of my new body positioning. Although, I immediately recognized it, I doubt it even registered for the Agent on a conscious level.

Interestingly, even though it slowed me down and automatically brought low the tone and volume of my voice, it still wasn't quite enough. I found myself having to still put further effort into matching and mirroring this nice gentleman.

I asked tons of questions, many of which were open-ended, so as to get him talking (not an easy task, as he wasn't a big talker like me). I listened to his responses, and responded, repeating what I had heard and affirming that his answers made sense to me and were acceptable to me.

Soon, we began to deepen our rapport with one another, and before I knew it, he was a raving fan of our conversation, and more importantly, of Club Wealth.

He later became a coaching client.

Module 3 - Language Techniques to Master

Learning to master language and understanding how that can help you is essential to your success as a salesperson, particularly if you want to go BIG with your sales. Communication is the cornerstone of all sales.

Since the majority of communication is not the words we say, but the process of delivering them in a way that conveys the most information, studying and mastering these techniques will go a long way toward helping you become truly World Class.

Here are several language techniques that you can use to better communicate with people, and ultimately achieve your sales goals.

A.R.P.

Not to be confused with A.L.F. which, as we all know, stands for "Alien Life Form", A.R.P. stands for Acknowledge, Respond, Pivot, and is much more useful to you and your career, and is less likely to be found on late night cable TV show reruns.

It is also not a discount program for seniors, there is no membership card, nor does it indicate entry into your Golden Years.

A.R.P. comes from a book called *The Conversion Code*, which was written by Chris Smith (VERY intelligent guy, by the way...) and is a relatively simple concept.

A = Acknowledge.

Acknowledge means repeating things that are said to you. This is one of the most powerful things we can do as a listener. It is an integral part of "Active Listening Skills" we teach our coaching clients, as it proves that you are actually listening to the person who is talking.

Oftentimes, people do not feel that they are being heard. This is an extremely common complaint from consumers about real estate Agents, as noted by the National Association of Realtors. The number one thing you can do to assure them that you're listening is to repeat back what they're saying.

For example:

Prospect: I was just wondering the price of the home at 345 Lincoln Street?

Agent: Great, so you are just wondering what the price of 345 Lincoln Street is, let me look that up...

It sounds simple, right? Acknowledging what people say can be very helpful. This process may be very awkward the first couple of times you do it, but believe me, YOU find it much more awkward than they do.

After practice it will actually become second nature to you, and your clients will appreciate what a good listener you are.

R = Respond.

Respond is as simple as it sounds: answer their question.

Agent: ...the price of 345 Lincoln Street is $330,000.

This is where things can get hairy. Some Agents don't want to tell someone the price of their house, because then they might not qualify for the house. However, failure to answer someone's question can be frustrating to them.

Prospect: Would you be willing to reduce your commission?

That's another question some Agents will dodge. You need to know that it's okay to answer the questions. As a matter fact, it's required.

Agent: No. Are there any other questions before we get started on the paperwork?

Here is another example.

Prospect: What is the price of the home on 345 Lincoln Street?

Agent: So I understand that you're looking for the price of the home? (Acknowledge) The home is $353,000. (Respond)

Acknowledge the question, and then respond. I know that seems truly simple but please, for the love of all that's good in this world and for the sake of your career and everyone's sanity, please answer people's questions. Keep in mind, it shows that you care.

Next up is the most important part: we learn about Pivot.

P= Pivot.

Pivot is about turning the conversation into what you want to talk about, not what they want to talk about. With the Pivot, there's no pause. Pivot should also **not** be a closed yes/no question.

Agent Pivot: Out of curiosity, what price range are you looking to buy in?

Let's try the Pivot with our previous example.

Prospect: What is the price of the home on 345 Lincoln Street?

Agent: So I understand that you're looking for the price of the home on 345 Lincoln Street... (Acknowledge) The home is $353,000 (Respond). Out of curiosity, what price range are you looking to buy in?
(Pivot)

The last question was the Pivot. Now, instead of asking them a yes or no question, we are directing them to find out where they are at. There's not an opportunity for them to just hang up the phone or for them to move on.

Acknowledge - Let them know that you listened to exactly what they said.

Respond - Answer their question.

Pivot - To something that you want to talk about.

As a young candidate for the City Council many years ago, I was asked to participate in a debate. The other candidates were either more qualified or more deserving of the position, and likely both.

I had no business even being in the race, let alone the debate. Everyone thought I didn't stand a chance, but using A.R.P. (even though I had never heard of it since this was decades before Chris' book came out), helped me tremendously.

You see, my 3 platform values were: Public Safety, Transportation and Accountability in Government.

So, in the debate, when asked, "Michael, wouldn't you agree that allocating 2% of every city tax dollar to the arts would beautify our parks?" I calmly responded.

"Yes, Barbara, I do believe that donating 2% of all city tax dollars to the arts would beautify our parks. As I am sure you would agree, it is important that our citizens be safe, particularly as they experience our parks after dark, which is why I'm sure you'll agree that it is important to first fund our already understaffed police department so they can patrol our parks after dusk. It is also important to ensure our parks are adequately lit and funded. Where would you suggest we make cuts to fund this extra 2% that is not currently in the budget, or are you suggesting that we should increase taxes to pay for it?"

Clearly, I won both the debate, and subsequently, the election, much to the astonishment of the "establishment".

Obviously, we don't want to debate our clients, nor put them on the defensive or become argumentative. That said; you get the point that you must Acknowledge, Respond, and Pivot the discussion to where YOU want it to go.

Module 4 - Embedded Commands

An embedded command is an opportunity to literally deliver information directly into somebody's subconscious mind. As a note of caution - we are not using this to get people to do things that they don't want to do. If you start using embedded commands, please use them responsibly. These are very powerful techniques that can easily be used for the wrong purpose.

This is not about getting someone to do an inappropriate thing, or something they don't want to do. This trying to get them to go where they already told you that they wanted to go. And one of the great things about that is it actually feels like their idea. We like to call this the Jedi mind trick.

Let's talk about exactly what an embedded command is.

First and foremost, it's a command. You are literally telling someone to do something.

- Sell your house

- Feel good

- Feel comfortable with me

- Buy a house with me
- Work with me

- Sign the offer today

Those are actually some of the commands that we are telling people to do.

Secondly, an embedded command is embedded. This means it comes in the middle of two thoughts. If the embedded command is *"work with me,"* then you might say something like, "Most people who... *work with me...* love our VIP buyer program."

The third important thing is it needs to end on the downswing. A downswing is what happens to the pitch or tone of someone's voice at the end of a sentence. If the tone drops, or gets deeper, it's a downswing. It if goes up, or gets higher in pitch or tone, it's an upswing.

When you listen to someone speak, if their voice ends on an upswing that implies a question. If they end on the downswing, it implies a command.

"Go to your room!" Clearly ends on a downswing. Go ahead; try it. Say it out loud right now.

"Would you like fries with that?" Clearly ends on an upswing. Try it, but don't get too comfortable with it, unless, of course, you don't plan on following the advice in this book. Then, you'll want to memorize it! ;)

This is the part that most people have problems with. For whatever reason, when people are practicing embedded commands they have a tendency to accidentally create a question by ending on an upswing. It is important to pay attention to your speech pattern.

Here is a simple trick that you can use when practicing embedded commands. This might seem a bit silly, but you practice this by holding your hand up, saying the embedded command, and pushing your hand down. It's a mental trigger for you to end on a downswing, and it works!

The next thing you must make sure you do is to pause before and after your command.

"Most people who...[PAUSE]...*work with me*...[PAUSE]... love our VIP Buyer Program."

Here are some more advanced examples that you can try:

"Thanks for meeting with me! I'm guessing you don't necessarily want to just...*INTERVIEW ONLY ONE Agent*...out of curiosity what do you expect from your Agent?

Let's break that sentence down. I told them that they didn't want to "interview only one Agent" but, of course, that is exactly what I want. I'm telling them they don't have to, but their brain lingered on "interview only one Agent," even though it was wrapped in a negative.

Finally, change your volume, tone or pitch, and rate of speech during the embedded command, even if ever so slightly.

Here is another favorite embedded command:

"So we have already seen nine houses...*BY NOW*...you should have a really good idea what you like and don't like."

By (buy) have two meanings. You use the term "by", and that is what they will hear on a conscious level, but the client's subconscious mind will hear and retain the word "buy."

What you've done is actually told them to "buy a house now" but they don't even know it because all they consciously heard was "by now."

That's the difference in hearing BY NOW and BUY NOW.

It's an interesting strategy to use.

Practice embedded commands and get good at them.

To get started, use a couple that is very simple to use like:

Work with me

Feel comfortable

Have five embedded commands that are memorized and in your toolbox that resonate with you as something you will use regularly.

Practice makes perfect.

To recap, here are the steps for embedded commands:

1. It is a command
2. It is embedded between 2 thoughts
3. Ends on a downswing
4. Pause before and after the command
5. Change your rate of speech, tone, and volume on the embedded command

Module 5 - Tie Downs

What are tie downs? Tie downs are questions of agreement.

What you're doing with the tiedown is getting somebody used to saying yes. This helps you induce the "yes" state we have referred to.

We will cover two different types of tie downs:

Simple tie downs

Emotional tie downs

Emotional tiedowns are tiedowns that are associated with an outcome the client desires and that is personal to them. "Didn't you say you wanted a den or office?"

Simple tiedowns can be literally anything else that gets them into agreement with you: "Did you just say you like tacos?"

SIMPLE TIE DOWNS

QUESTIONS THAT USE WORDS LIKE:
Isn't • Wouldn't • Wasn't • Aren't • Won't

TIEDOWN EXAMPLES:

- Won't that be great?
- Don't you agree?
- Haven't you?
- Isn't that what you want?
- Can you imagine that?
- Isn't that great?

- Right?
- Shouldn't we?
- Wasn't that?
- Weren't you?
- Didn't you?
- Does that work for you?

Please understand that while I'm asking these questions, I'm asking questions that I probably know the answer to.

I don't want to set myself up for this and then get the wrong answer so I'm using these in situations where I feel like I know the answer the question.

Agent: "Wouldn't that be great?"
Client: "Yeah, that would be great."

Agent: "Don't you agree?"
Client: "Yeah, I agree with that."

That's what you're looking for, so remember, when using a tie down it actually serves two purposes. First of all, it gets people in agreement, and if they're not in agreement, the big advantage is that it will flush out any objections they might have.

So, tie downs should be used all throughout any presentation that you have, and also when you're showing property or doing buyer presentation.

Another thing is you can do is actually include a tie down with simple embedded commands.

Here's an example:

"We use an electronic signature so you can more easily...**sign our contract**... and get an immediate copy sent directly to you!"

The embedded command was "sign our contract".

Then you can follow up with:

"Won't that be great?!"

" Isn't that convenient?"

"Wouldn't that benefit you?"

" Does that work for you?"

The tie down embedded script would be:

"We use an electronic signature so you can more easily...**sign our contract**... and get an immediate copy sent directly to you! Won't that be great?!"

This is an advanced technique that works really well.

Once again, you should practice these tie downs until you feel comfortable with them, and they don't feel like that you're just doing them for the first time.

Don't wait until you're with a client. Add this to your daily scripts and role-play practice.

Emotional Tie downs

With this idea, you want them to remember where they're at. You want the client to remember why they're doing it, or hitting a pain point. Talk about what's important to them.

It really makes it personal and it also lets people know you're listening to them.

Here is an example of an emotional tie down:

"You did say you wanted to move in the next 3 months so you could spend more time with your grandchildren, didn't you?"

You can hear the emotion in that. It's about what they want.

Another example:

"Great! I can send our photographer over at 10:00 am tomorrow to take pictures so we can get the house on the market and you can get moved before winter. Won't that be great?"

You are using things that they are already tied to in order to ask questions so you can get them emotionally involved.

Remember, people rarely do things from a position of logic. People do the things they do, 99% of the time, from a position of emotion. Bringing that emotion into your questions helps them carry lasting, subconscious weight.

Here is an emotional tie down with an embedded command:

"Great! Why don't we ...SIGN THE CONTRACT NOW... so you can get moved before winter comes... that is what you want, right?"

Remember, practice, practice, practice. Start with a simple embedded command and then work your way up to including emotional tiedowns with embedded commands.

Module 6 - Words of Wisdom

One of the things that Agents don't pay attention to is the words they use daily.

There are 3 great words you should use over and over again.

- **TODAY** – You should say the word "today" no less than 3 times every time you are with a client, and ideally 7-12 times.

Some examples:
"Hello, Mr. Buyer. How are you today?"
"Would you like to see any properties today?"
"What questions do you have for me today?"
"I was just thinking of you today…"
"A new listing came up today…"
"I was watching the Today show today..." (lol, just kidding, sort of...!)

It shows that you are interested in doing things NOW. Remember, that you are in the TODAY business.

- **AND** – This is another word to say over and over again. "And" is a coming together word. And is word to show people that you are on their team.

- **BECAUSE** – This word gives people a reason to do things.

As you go about your daily activities, you want to use these words consistently. Add them to your vocabulary: Today, And, Because.

Module 7 - Three Words to Eliminate

The one word you want to really eliminate is THINK. Weak Agents show property all day long to a buyer and constantly say the word "think":

"What do you 'think' about this house?"
"What do you 'think' about this neighborhood?"
"What do you 'think' about the backyard?"
"I 'think' we should write it up..."

It's no wonder when they ask the buyer at the end of the day, "Do you want to write an offer today?" their response is "I don't know. I want to THINK about it."

Get people to act. Instead of asking:

"What do you THINK about the house?"

Say instead:

"How does this house FEEL for you and your family?"

They will respond:

"It FEELS great, it FEELS like home!"

"Could you SEE yourself living in that house?"
"Yes, I could SEE myself living here."

Replace the word THINK with the words FEEL and SEE.
The word THINK comes out just as naturally.

NO is another world to eliminate.

The word NO shuts people down.

Replace NO with statements like this:

"That may not be in our best interest, why don't we look into another way to do it."

"I'm not 100% sure, why don't I look into that?"

It's better than just saying NO and then giving a reason. NO slams the door closed and we don't want to ever do that to our clients.

BUT is another word that weak Agents say constantly.

BUT – NEGATES everything we JUST SAID

When you say, "I love you, but...."

What you are really saying is that "I don't love you."

Replace BUT with the word "AND". It works just the same as BUT.

"I love you, AND..."

"I want to buy this house, AND..."

AND opens the door to additional possibilities and never blocks progress.

My favorite "AND" script: "Let's make an offer on both this house AND that house, and pick the one that comes back with the best price and terms for you. Won't THAT be great?"

Module 8 - Isolate the Objection

We've covered some great techniques so far. Now, we want to talk about objections. Oftentimes, as sales people, we make assumptions about our clients based on our bias. The main issue this causes is closing the wrong objection. Let's look at some ways to flush out objections.

WHAT SPECIFICALLY?

What specifically allows you to isolate an objection and figure out what the client is really concerned about?

The 5 PHRASES to use just before "What specifically" are:

1. I'm CURIOUS...

2. I was WONDERING...

3. Just of out CURIOSITY...

4. I'm CONFUSED...

5. So I UNDERSTAND...

Note - Be carefully when using "I'm confused" because that could backfire on you and frustrate the client. Use this word very sparingly.

When the market has been hot, you'll see that bidding wars are very common. We will use this example for an isolation objection.

If your client doesn't want to be in bidding war on a property, you can isolate that objection by using this statement:

Client: I'm not interested in being in a bidding war.
Agent" "I definitely get that... I'M CURIOUS... WHAT SPECIFICALLY makes you feel like a bidding war or multiple offer situation is bad for you?"

They may respond that it makes them nervous or feel uncomfortable, or that the price will end up being higher than what they want to pay.

Next, say, "I totally understand how you might feel that way... Why don't we just... **write our best offer today...** and, if that doesn't work out, then we will go find something else, okay?"

By saying that, you've eliminated their uncertainty that they are in a bidding war with someone and that the seller will either accept, reject, or counter offer.

Another example:

Client/Prospect: ""I have not picked an Agent."
Agent: "I understand... most people we talk with have talked with several other Agents... I WAS WONDERING... WHAT SPECIFICALLY you feel you are looking for in an Agent?"

Once again, you've given the client an opportunity to explain what their needs and wants are. This is great because they may have something very simple that you could cover for them immediately.

Prospect: "We are not sure we need an Agent."
Agent: "That's great I completely get that... just out of curiosity, if you were going to work with an Agent... what specifically would you be looking for?"

What specifically does an amazing job as an objection isolator, so you really know what to talk to the clients about. It gives you an opportunity to resolve their specific concern, and give them exactly what they are looking for.

Module 9 - Objection Handlers Scripts

Practice these Objection Handlers every day as part of your script practice and role-play. You'll be a World Class Buyer Agent in no time!

Objection: "We are just looking right now . . ."

Handler #1: "That's good to hear. How many homes have you looked at so far?"

Handler #2: "Great...I understand... what are you looking for?

Handler #3: "Perfect! I understand you are just looking - out of curiosity, if we found you the perfect home today, how quickly could you move?"

Objection: "Our credit isn't good enough yet . . ."

Handler #1: "Ok. I understand there are many people who don't think they qualify - do you happen to know your credit score, because our lender has quite a few programs for people with less than perfect credit?"

Handler #2: "Actually, I hear that a lot. I've also had several clients find that their credit is better than they originally thought after speaking to a lender. I would love to get you with our lender partner and see if you qualify. If not, we can put together a plan to get your credit score up and get you ready to buy - how does that sound?"

Handler #3: "Other than credit, if we could get you a loan where credit wasn't an issue, what specifically concerns you about buying a home?"

Objection: "We aren't ready to work with an Agent yet . . ."

Handler #1: "I understand you are not ready yet. Do you have a specific timeframe for buying in mind?"

Handler #2: "I get that you are not ready yet. Out of curiosity, in your mind when specifically would be the perfect time to close on your new home?"

Handler #3: "Got it! Okay... I'm curious, what specifically is it about working with an Agent that concerns you right now?"

Objection: "We are going to wait. We aren't ready now . . ."
Handler #1: "Okay, so I understand... what specifically are you waiting for?"

Handler #2: "Okay, I see. I'm curious... When specifically do you want to move into your new home?"

Module 10 - Closing Questions to Memorize

These are great closing questions for you to practice or add to your role-play.

"Are there any other questions before we get started on the paperwork?"

"At what price would this be a great deal for you?"

"If spending thirty minutes with me could save you hours of time and thousands of dollars in your home search, would that be of benefit to you?"

"I've enjoyed talking with you today. To be honest, I'm not sure if I can be of help to you or not, but I would love to meet to find out. Would that work for you?"

CHAPTER 18
WRITING THE BULLET PROOF OFFER

CLUBWEALTH

Writing and negotiating a strong offer is where you truly earn your commission. Constructing a bulletproof offer that will meet your buyer's criteria *and* appeal to the seller so they accept your offer is a skill that requires preparation, strategizing, and excellent negotiation tactics.

This chapter will show you why and how writing a bulletproof offer will help you achieve this. It is part of the sales process that is often forgotten. By now you know that to be a World Class Buyer Agent, you need to lead generate, follow up with leads, convert leads to appointments, show property, and do all the tasks required to close the property.

However, some Agents don't consider how to write the best offer to get your client their dream home. Let's talk about some things that are important when writing a bulletproof offer.

Module 1 - Constructing a Bulletproof Offer

First, you need to ensure that the offer meets all of the buyer's needs. Oftentimes, Agents get caught up focusing on what they want, which is obviously to get to closing, and they miss that they need to make sure they are meeting the buyer's needs. The buyer needs to feel comfortable and well represented by you.

Next, make sure the offer appeals to the seller, because ultimately you are looking to create a win-win situation. A situation where the buyer is happy and the seller is happy, because that is the best way for you to get to closing.

These skills require preparation. They require you to be strategic. They require you to have excellent negotiating skills. You will need to study and master these skills so you can write an offer that is most likely to get accepted.

Module 2 - Ask All the Right Questions (of the Listing Agent)

The very first thing that you're going to do before constructing the offer is talk to the listing Agent. This step is overlooked almost every time by most Buyer Agents. Be that World Class Agent who is going above and beyond and talking to the listing Agent BEFORE submitting, or even writing the offer.

When you call the listing Agent, ask them about the needs of the seller. This is something that you don't typically think about because you're representing the buyer. It just may be that satisfying one or more of the seller's needs are just the thing that will make your offer better than the rest. Remember, it's not always about money.

As real estate Agents we make the assumption that the only thing that matters to a seller is getting the most money. However, there are two parts to this. The first part is how much money the seller will end up with. The second part is the terms and conditions of the offer.

For instance, a term or condition could be related to "occupancy". Does that seller want to stay in their home an additional week, or month, or six months? Having an occupancy agreement in the offer may be more important to the seller than netting more money at closing.

Another important term for the seller could be escrow or earnest money. Sometimes a larger than normal escrow deposit is more attractive to a seller because they think it means the buyer's offer is strong and/or that the buyer is more serious about buying the home.

Closing time frame is another important term to many sellers. The seller may want to close quickly or they may want to delay the close three or more months out.

Many sellers are concerned with who the buyer is that wants to purchase their home. You may find that the seller wants someone to love their home as much as they do. Especially if the seller has lived in the home for most of their lives, raised their children there, and had a lot of good memories in the home.

That type of emotionally attached seller is going to want to be assured that the next owner will take of the home just like they did. While we will discuss ways to meet the emotional needs of the seller, it is important that we carefully avoid potential Fair Housing Law violations. Be sure to discuss plans and strategies with your broker to ensure compliance.

These are examples of why it's so important to get to know who the seller is. The only way you're going to accomplish that is by asking the Listing Agent all the right questions.

It is also important to begin building rapport with the Listing Agent. Remember that a sale is two people communicating to achieve a common goal. And, if you look at your conversations with the listing Agent in that manner, you will create a win-win situation. That will put you way ahead of the Average Agent.

This should NOT be an adversarial relationship, but rather a symbiotic one, wherewith each party and their respective clients benefit.

When you present the offer to Listing Agent, they have the opportunity to be biased with that offer in a good way, a bad way, or maybe not at all. When it comes down to it, you're dealing with a human being, and the Listing Agent is going to have an opinion about you, the buyer, and whom they're working with.

Help them know they want to work with you. Help them know, like, and trust you, the buyer, and even your lender. The best way to do that is by building rapport with the Listing Agent so they will want to work with you and your buyers.

Ask in-depth questions and really listen to their responses. A favorite saying of Club Wealth® coaches) is, "As a salesperson we have two ears and one mouth. And the reason that we have two ears and one mouth is so that we can listen twice as much as we talk." The majority of us fail at doing that on a daily basis, so you have to really keep it in mind when you're working with the Listing Agent.

Coach's Corner: When talking to the Listing Agent, I do more listening than I do talking. It's amazing what most Listing Agents will tell you if you just stay quiet and give them a chance to elaborate. Keep asking questions. The more you know, the better for your client. Come from curiosity.

In-depth questions to ask the Listing Agent:

Start the conversation like this: "Hi [listing Agent name]! Michael Hellickson with The Hellickson Team here... I'm getting ready to write an offer on your listing at 345 Lincoln Ave and wanted to make sure I write it up in a way that works well for you and your seller. Do you have a few minutes to help me get it right for you?...You do? Awesome, thanks!

Is there anything specific, like forms, terms and such, that you feel needs to be in the offer? Particularly with institutional sellers, like banks, hedge funds, corporations etc. they will likely have their own addenda, and even instructions on how to write the offer. For retail sellers, the Listing Agent often has strong feelings about things like escrow, title, closing dates and more. That doesn't mean the seller feels the same way. That said, strive to give on the small things to make the big ones happen. Sometimes, losing the battle to win the war really does work.

Have you received any offers yet? You want to know if the seller has had any low ball offers and that may have irritated the seller. Or have they had any offers at all? Clearly, you will be sharing this information with your buyer.

How many showings have you had? I know that might not seem important, but if the house is getting shown three or four times a day, obviously the house is not going to be on the market very much longer. More great information to go back to your buyer with and let them know that you need to write a really strong offer - and do it quickly.

Why is the seller moving? This can provide all kinds of motivation for that seller. Most times the buyer is going to ask you that question anyway. The answer may not be all that important to you or make a difference in the offer, but most likely, your buyer is going to want to know the answer to it.

How would you like the offer delivered? They may sound like a silly question, but the common goal is to build rapport with the Listing Agent and get the house sold. The Listing Agent may want it hand delivered for whatever reason, emailed, uploaded to a specific portal, or even faxed (yeah, I know… lol). It's common courtesy to ask, and shows them that they are working with a World Class Buyer Agent.

Would you notify me if any other offers come in? A lot of Buyer Agents have encountered a frustrating situation where they write an offer, and 24 hours later still have no response from the Listing Agent. Why didn't the Listing Agent let them know there was another offer? Because the Buyer Agent didn't ask him to. You should never make the assumption that Listing Agents are doing their job and trying to get the best for their clients. You don't know that. And, they're imperfect human beings just like us, so please ask this question each and every time.

What is the one thing that could make or break the deal? Or what is the one thing that is the most important to your seller, so that we can make sure that we're going to include that, if possible, in our offer?

Module 3 - Why Write the Bulletproof Offer?

Why is this whole process so important? Your homebuyers deserve the best. As a World Class Buyer Agent, it is up to you to provide the best service for them. The Average Agent just fills in the blanks on the contract, and submits the offer. As a World Class Buyer Agent, you're bringing value and showing clients how to get what they want in the quickest and easiest way possible.

The initial offer is an introduction to negotiation. Remember, the offer is a way to introduce yourself and your client to the seller. Unfortunately, you do not have the opportunity to sit across from the seller and have a conversation with them like we did back in the good old days. So basically, your presentation of the offer to the Listing Agent is going to be a representation of you and the buyer.

Lastly, writing a bad offer can cost your client the home, especially in multiple offers situations. Worse yet, creating an enemy of the Listing Agent can cost subsequent buyers you may work with the opportunity to purchase this Agent's future listings.

Relationships matter in this business. Take care of the Agents in your marketplace, and treat them like clients.

Module 4 - World Class Buyer Agent

What does a World Class Buyer Agent do when they write an offer? First of all, they use an offer form checklist.

The offer form checklist contains all the details of what's in an offer.

It makes you look professional. With all the things you need to remember when writing an offer for a buyer, it's easy to forget something like asking the buyer if they want a home warranty. Or what the closing date is. The offer form checklist has every question that you need to ask so that when you get back in front of your computer to write the offer, you have all the information at your fingertips.

You don't want to be the Average Agent, who calls the buyer several times to ask questions about the offer that you should've already known - if you'd used a checklist to begin with.

Type the offer; NEVER handwrite it. As a Selling Agent you want to make it as simple as possible for the Listing Agent to present the offer. If they can't understand your handwriting, the Listing Agent is going to get frustrated and then they have to call you back. Furthermore, a typed offer looks clean and as close to perfect as possible. Remember, this is your introduction to that seller and their Agent. Make your offer stand out by presenting a crisp and clean offer to the seller.

Module 5 - Points to Cover with Buyers

What points should you cover with the buyer when writing the offer?

What's the purchase price? Did you go over your CMA with the buyer to ensure they are offering the best price possible for them to get an offer accepted?

Are the buyers pre-approved for the loan? If not, get the buyer on the phone with one of the Team's preferred lenders.

How much earnest money do they want to deposit? This amount may make or break the offer. We recommend 5% or more when possible.

Is there an option period?

What conveys with the property?

Remember, each state is going to have their own rules on what conveys with a property, so please check with the state you are licensed in. For example, in Texas, permanently installed and built-in items such as appliances, valances, screens, shutters, and awnings, to just name a few of the things, would convey with the sale. When you talk to the buyer about what conveys with the property, it helps to clarify every single item they want so there is no confusion at closing time.

Are there any contingencies? For example, there could be a financing contingency, home inspection contingency, or appraisal contingency.

Do they need to sell their current home?

There are a number of contingencies that could go into a contract. Make sure you cover them all.

Closing costs is another item to go over with the buyer. If you don't know how to calculate closing costs, ask your preferred lender how to do this. Also, asking a seller to pay all closing costs is a great way to get that offer turned down. Knowing a specific number that a buyer needs for closing allows the seller to determine their net profit. If the seller knows their net profit, it's easier for them to make a decision.

How long are you going to give the seller to reply to the offer? This number of days will differ depending on the area you are located in and what the buyer and seller needs are. Is the seller out of state or out of the country? You may want to give them plenty of time. If there are a lot of offers expected, a shorter response time may be best for your buyer. Typically, 48 hours is a good timeframe for a response.

When does the offer actually expire? When you are going back and forth in negotiations, always be aware of when the offer expires so you don't lose the deal because you didn't respond in the time allotted.

Module 6 - 17 Strategies to Writing Bullet Proof Offer:

Your homebuyers deserve the best strategy possible, especially when in a multiple offer situation. There are certain tactics that you can employ in order to get your offer accepted, and more importantly, closed without any issues. Although there is never a "magic pill", the strategies we're about to share with you will have you feeling like you just found one!

1. **Minimize contingencies.** Eliminate as many contingencies as possible. They are usually not a huge deal, but can be confusing to sellers. Clean offers are strong offers. The more contingencies that you can eliminate, the stronger the offer becomes.

2. **Always submit a preapproval letter or proof of funds.** The seller doesn't want to take their house off the market for over 30 days if they don't know that the buyer has the capacity to buy it. A pre-approval letter or proof of funds letter is helpful to instill confidence in the buyer that they will actually be able to successfully close the transaction.

3. **Put up high earnest money.** Sometimes putting up a $500 earnest money is almost no better than no earnest money at all. So if the buyer is going to put up earnest money, put up a significant amount. 3-5% is a good rule of thumb. At the same time, make sure your buyers are protected.

4. **Cancel inspection contingency.** You can write up an offer that says no inspection contingency or repairs if you have a very

confident buyer. Keep in mind that it could be very challenging, so make sure that your buyer understands what that means. Ultimately, if you put together an offer with no inspection contingency that could definitely win in a multiple offer situation. Note: You need to be very careful when using this technique. Another similar thing you can do is offer to request no repairs, but to still do an inspection so your buyer can still opt out if the home has major issues. Additionally, if the buyer is super confident and really wants the house, you could perform the inspection during the showing, or before the offer is submitted, to enable the waiver of the inspection contingency.

5. **Use an escalation clause.** An escalation clause is typically used in a multiple offer situation. It's intended to eliminate the competition from a competitive bidding process. An escalation clause states that a buyer will pay X amount of dollars ranging from $100 to potentially thousands of dollars above and beyond the highest offer received by the seller. It also generally includes a ceiling cap. It is important that it includes the requirement for the seller to provide evidence of said additional offer(s).

There are many Agents who've never heard of an escalation clause, so be mindful of that fact. If you are going to use one, make sure you explain how it works to the Listing Agent. They need to understand why you are doing it and how it works. This is not something that is universally used or taught. Explaining to the Listing Agent why you're doing an escalation clause is in your client's best interests and their client's best interest. Remember, we're always selling.

6. **Proof of funds with offer.** This is very simplistic. If the buyer were paying cash, you would submit a proof of funds letter from

their banking institution so the seller knows that the buyer can adequately pay for the home.

7. **Delayed closing and closing penalty.** This is when you set the closing date to close on January 15th, for example, and the buyer will have to pay fifty dollars a day for any day after that when the closing is delayed. That's a great way to show the seller how motivated you are to get to closing.

8. **Short closing time frame.** Everyone loves to see a short closing, especially the listing Agent. Accommodating the seller's desires is the easiest way to make a strong offer. Note: some Sellers might want to occupy the home post-closing. Making that easy for them can also increase your offers value.

9. **Ask listing agent how they want offer written up.** People are more motivated to seek a winning outcome when they like the person they are dealing with.

10. **Letter from buyer to seller.** Having your buyer write a letter to the seller is a very popular practice. Keep it to 3-5 lines, make sure they use a broad-tipped blue ink pen, and have them embellish on why the home is a perfect fit and why they love it, and why they are the perfect buyer for it.

I've seen MANY scenarios where sellers took an offer that netted them less because they fell in love with the family buying the home

In one notable example, the buyers offered to allow the seller to remove and take with them the piece of door trim upon which they had been tracking their children's growth by marking their heights over the last 2 decades! Talk about sealing the deal! They were substantially lower than the best offer, which the Listing Agent wrote, and got the home anyway!

11. **Record a video of the buyers in front of the home talking about all the things they love about the home.** If you want to take it to the next level you could record video of your buyers in front of the home talking about how much they love the home. Can you imagine the seller seeing that? This is bringing your emotional leverage to a whole new level. This is also something that most Agents and their buyers will never do. It will separate you from the Average Agent, and your buyers' offer from all the rest.

12. **Offer to pay seller closing costs or make allowances.** For the seller, it's often all about what they will net. Crunch the numbers and explain the different scenarios to your buyer. Explain how closing costs and other allowances can affect the offer.

13. **Present the offer immediately.** As soon as an offer is ready, let the Listing Agent know how you will be sending it over, and then do it immediately. Don't wait. Time really is of the essence.

14. **Contingency plan on low appraisal.** Write up a contingency that is based on the possibility of low appraisal. If you are in a market that low appraisals frequently happen, go ahead and plan for that contingency instead of waiting for it to happen and then re-negotiating the contract. Maybe the buyer will pay the difference, or ask to split the difference with the seller, or have a reduction price agreed ahead of time.

15. **Submit credit score.** If you want to really show somebody that

you've gone over the top and your buyer's got a great credit score, (only do this if your buyer has a credit score over 700), then put that credit score information in the offer. Remember to redact any information like Social Security numbers because you don't want to be putting buyers in a situation where they can have their identity stolen.

16. **Pre-approval from lender that Listing Agent uses.** If you know that the Listing Agent has a lender that they love to work with, ask your buyer to get preapproval letter from them. A preapproval letter from a lender that the listing Agent loves is far better then a preapproval letter from an online bank that no one has heard of. This doesn't mean your buyer must use the listing Agents lender, just that they have gone through the pre-approval process with them to reassure the Agent and their seller.

17. **Reduce commission due from seller.** Reduce commission due from seller, and have buyer pay it on payments through a buyer agency agreement post closing. Check with your broker or Team Leader first for approval.

Next time you write up an offer on a home for one of your buyers, try one or two new strategies and see what a difference it makes!

Module 7- Presenting the World Class Offer

When presenting the offer to the seller, you'll want to include an executive summary with all the details of the offer. The more organized you appear the better chance the other Agent will work with you. Remember, every little thing matters.

The executive summary should include: price, contingencies,

inspection time frame, financing details, down payment information, pre-qualification or pre-approval letter, and credit scores.

Other things to remember when presenting an offer is that time is of the essence. Your buyer has an expectation that that offer will be submitted as quickly as possible. Make sure that you explain that process to them thoroughly, to ensure the offer gets received by the Listing Agent as quickly as possible.

Obviously, our goal is for your buyer to get the house. When you discuss this with your potential client, you will want go over with them what to expect after the offer has been presented.

Let the buyers know that your goal is to have one of two possible outcomes. One, to get a counter offer back from the seller, or two, for the seller to accept the offer. Those are your goals. If you followed the above steps in writing a bulletproof offer, chances are good you will have one of those two results - and not a flat-out rejection.

Module 8 - Submit and Negotiate Offers

Once you get the offer submitted, then the real negotiation begins. Again, the communication is paramount in this process. Always follow up with the Listing Agent, either by phone call or text or both, to let them know that you sent them an offer. Don't just assume because you hand delivered it or emailed it that the Listing Agent got the offer.

Always give the other Agent adequate time to present the offer to the seller. Don't give a listing Agent two hours to present an offer. In some states, Agents are not even technically required to submit it for twenty-four hours, so give that Agent an opportunity to get in front of their seller.

Give that person adequate time to do their job. Always ask if there are any questions that they need clarified, or if there's anything on that offer that doesn't make sense. It probably made perfect sense to you when you wrote the offer, but it doesn't mean it will make perfect sense to the Listing Agent. Communication, communication, communication.

Throughout this process, there are three outcomes that can potentially happen. The first one is obviously the offer is accepted. If that doesn't happen, hopefully you'll get a counter offer. And the third potential outcome is a rejection.

Our goal is always to avoid rejection. Presenting the first offer is about opening up a conversation. It's about beginning to communicate with that seller. We want to write an offer that is not going to be offensive to the seller.

Obviously, it's really simple if it gets accepted. But what happens if you get a counter offer? Your job is to explain the counter. Show the buyer exactly what it would mean for them if they were to accept that counter offer.

Accepting the counter offer will remove the risk. If they sign the counter offer, you're good and can move toward closing. Sometimes a seller may counter offer with just a few thousand dollars higher than the buyer actually wrote the offer for.

The buyer may not understand the impact for them, so this is where you can use your skills to show them the benefit of accepting the offer. For example, maybe the seller counter-offered $4000 higher.

You can show that buyer that is only going to cost them approximately $20 a month by accepting the counter offer. Then you follow up with the question: Are you willing to lose this house over $20 dollars a month?

It gives them the opportunity to see the real hard cost of what they are going to live with day in and day out and are they really willing to lose that house over $20 a month? If we don't present that reality to them, if we don't let them know the exact consequences of accepting or not accepting, then we are not doing our job very well.

Most importantly, remind them above all that you are their Agent. Why is that? During this process we can appear as if we're trying to get them to accept something that may not be in their best interest or may not be what they want.

Always finish with this statement. "I will do whatever you guys want. This is your house, you're the person who's going to have to make the payment every month and my number one goal is for you to feel comfortable in this process. And, of course, that you get home that you want."

Next step - after the offer is accepted, go over the process.

Module 9 - After Offer is Accepted

After you get the offer accepted, it is time to go through the inspection. This will happen usually within the next week or two of the acceptance. To ensure the buyer understands that process and feels comfortable with it, have the buyer come to the last 15 minutes of the inspection. That way the inspector can go over any problems or concerns with the buyer in person.

Remember, a home inspector talking about something in person often softens it and makes it seem like something that is not quite as critical as it appears on a piece of paper.

Here is a great example of that. A home inspection report may state that there is a cracked or broken cover plate for electrical outlet. Now, technically that is a fire hazard, but on the flip side of that, it is really only a $.49 repair.

You can see that actually taking a look at something and understanding what it really means versus having a third party explain what that really means can often calm a buyer down. Instead of that buyer receiving a daunting 75 page report that makes them freak out, ask the inspector to talk to them, and have them take the opportunity to explain any questions or concerns.

Once the inspection is completed, you will want to estimate and submit the buyers' request for repairs. Be clear with the buyers that you are looking for critical items, safety items, and deal breakers. You never want to nitpick the seller over little things.

If you nitpicked them over little things, the seller will become unwilling to do the big things. Go over that with your buyers and explain the goal is to get to closing. You may need to remind them why they love that house, and chose to write the offer in the first place. Are they willing to lose that house over an item that cost three hundred dollars to repair? Remind them that a week ago this was their dream house.

Lastly, make sure that the buyer knows once again that you are on their side. That you will submit whatever repairs they feel are important. Make sure that they know that you are doing the best you can to get them the deal that they want, without losing the house of their dreams.

In conclusion, keep this in mind when you're going to write an offer. Each step of the real estate process is extremely important. From lead generation, to showing the property, to getting the client to commit to work with you.

You've gone through all of the steps and you spent a bunch of time and most likely, a bunch of money to get here. Take the time to do the last step. That last step is to write an offer that is strong and powerful. Do it in a way that is professional, so that you will get your buyers the house of their dreams.

World Class Buyer Agents work HARD to put, and keep, transactions together. They swallow their pride, and set aside the need to be right for the greater need to be rich, or at least successful on behalf of their clients.

"You can be right, or you can be rich." - Michael Hellickson

CHAPTER 19
WRITING OFFERS ON
SHORT SALES & REO

CLUBWEALTH

While working in real estate you'll find that a majority of sellers are just regular people looking to sell their house. However, some sellers can be banks, insurance companies, corporations, developers/builders, trustees, and government entities. No matter what kind of seller they are, they all have one thing in common. They need to sell the property, and that requires a buyer - and maybe a Buyer Agent!

Buying a foreclosure or short sale home might hold the promise of a great deal, but it's important for the Buyer Agent to be aware of who the players are in the transaction, and what the sales process entails.

This chapter is divided into several modules that define Short Sales, REO properties, HUD, and Institutional sellers. It explains how the Buyer Agent should approach each type of sale and how the sales process works with each one. This makes for a handy reference guide when it comes time for your buyer to make an offer on a unique property. You may even find yourself specializing in selling to investors who like to purchase bank-owned properties, short sales, or probate homes.

Module 1 - Defining REO, Short Sales, and Institutional Sellers

If your goal is to get more of your offers accepted when you are writing offers on an REO or a short sale, or even to an institutional seller, you first have to know the vocabulary. You have to know both whom you are talking to, and what you're talking about.

Let's first start with the definition of REO.

REO stands for **real estate owned**. It's also known as a foreclosure. Banks use this term to describe houses they have repossessed through foreclosure.

What is a **short sale**? Short Sale is when the seller owes more than the home is worth. If you are a buyer or a Buyer Agent, it's important to understand that this type of sale occurs only with the lender's permission.

The difference between an REO and a Short Sale is that in a Short Sale, the owner still "owns" the house. They just need the lender's approval to sell the home at a price that will not satisfy the entire lien amount. This could, and often does, involve multiple lenders if there is more than one loan on the property. It may also involve other lien holders such as HOAs, legal judgments, and more.

In an REO, the former homeowner no longer owns the home. They have lost the house and now the bank owns it. In this instance, the bank is now the seller.

An "institutional seller" refers to large categories such as banks, asset management companies, insurance companies, REIT's, iBuyers and hedge funds. Some lead generation providers today function more like asset management companies or institutional sellers than lead gen companies. This is particularly true for those whose compensation is largely referral fee based.

Depending on your local board and how your local MLS defines these types of sellers, you can usually identify an REO, Short Sale, or

Institutional Seller by looking in the MLS notes or category section.

Also, you can check your local county records to see who has title to the home.

Their Way, Not Yours

Basically, what this means is that you have to do what the bank or lender asks of you. They don't mess around, and have absolutely no patience for Agents who can't follow their directions.

Whether you are working with an REO or Short Sale, it's their timeline that you are on. It's a "hurry up and wait" situation. You have to put in an offer quickly for your buyer to beat out other potential buyers. If the bank or bank's rep asks for something - a form or letter - they usually want it quickly.

Then, you have to wait - sometimes days or weeks, potentially even months or in extreme Short Sale cases, it can take years - for a response back from the bank or conclusion to the sale. That's the "hurry up and wait" mentality of working with REO and Short Sales. You have very little control over the timeline.

In terms of their forms, REO and Short Sale sellers will have their own contracts and addendums. Always ask the Listing Agent BEFORE you write up an offer - what kind of contract or form do I need to use to write up the offer?

Also, find out what kind of terms and conditions are needed for that offer. There are rarely any negotiations when it comes to the bank's required terms and conditions for an REO or Short Sale property. That said, with Short Sales, with pleasant persistence, you could often get some movement out of the underlying lien holders.

Managing your client's expectations is very important. Since the bank requires certain forms, addendums, contracts, and terms and conditions for offers, it is crucial that you let your buyer know what they can expect when it comes time to write an offer.

If you have a high maintenance client or a big investor that is used to getting their way when it comes to buying property or making lower offers on properties, let them know up front that the usual negotiations and strategies will not work for these types of transactions.

Submitting the offer takes skill and confidence. When you submit the offer, make sure you are submitting the cleanest offer possible. This means making an offer with the least amount of contingencies. If it's a well-priced REO property and needs a little work, it's probably safe to assume that you'll be competing against cash buyers.

So you'll want to have your inspection period as short as possible or, if feasible, no inspection contingency period at all. If your client has already looked at the property and is willing to turn in a cash offer with no inspection period, this can be a great way to make an offer even stronger.

This is often the case when the buyers are contractors themselves or have other experience with home repairs, but before you go forward with this plan, make sure your buyer fully understands what 'no inspection contingency period' means.

Module 2 - What is HUD?

HUD stands for Housing Urban Development or, the Department of Housing and Urban Development.

This is a home that has come into HUD's possession as a result of an FHA loan default.

You can search for HUD homes in the MLS or you can go to www.clubwealth.com/HUD to search for ALL HUD homes in your area.

Your broker must have registered with HUD in order for you to put in an offer on the HUD website. Your broker must also have an NAID number - there is no cost to do this - in order to write an offer on a HUD home. If your broker doesn't have a NAID number, please encourage them to go to the HUD website and register for free.

There are two terms that you need to know before showing and writing offers on HUD home:

Exclusive Listing Period - That's the first 15 days where you can only buy the house if you are an owner occupant. It helps if you are an owner occupant because you aren't competing against other investors. The goal of HUD is to encourage the owner occupants to buy the home.

Extended Listing Period - This comes after the Exclusive Listing Period. As a note, you can see which type of listing period is on the HUD website. During the Extended Listing Period, any buyer can put in an offer on the property, including investors, and other non-owner

334

occupants.

Module 3 - Writing an REO Offer

A house goes through foreclosure when a homeowner either stops making or falls behind on loan payments. In some states, the foreclosure process can take a few months, and in other states, it can take years. Once a house goes through this process, the bank owns it and can sell it without the prior homeowner's permission. An REO Agent is a Listing Agent who sells REO properties for banks and asset managers. The asset manager is the main contact between the Listing Agent and the seller.

As a Buyer Agent, knowing what goes on with both sides of the transaction will help you understand what it takes to successfully sell an REO property.

Submitting REO Offers

If a house is priced correctly, the Listing Agent usually gets offers right away, and sometimes multiple offers. Communication is important to maintain between you and the REO Listing Agent. You want to build a relationship with the Listing Agent – and anyone on their team like the office manager or transaction coordinator. Because selling REO properties can take time and patience, the Listing Agent will want to work with a Buyer Agent that is well versed on how the process works, and is easiest to work with.

Before you write an offer on any property, especially an REO property, you want to make sure that you're asking the right questions. The goal is to get your buyers' offer accepted, so you need to do everything that you can to build a rapport with the Listing

Agent. You can even go as far as giving a gift to the Listing Agent. It doesn't have to be anything super expensive. Send them flowers or chocolates. Be super friendly on the phone. Whatever it is, it should have a high-perceived value, but be low cost.

People do business with people they know, like, and trust. So getting them to know you and like you, and with any luck, trust you, is very important to your success here.

On the flip side, you don't want to drive the Listing Agent crazy by calling them every day and bothering them with questions about the offer. There is a fine line between being annoying and staying on top of your game, building a relationship with that other Agent and/or their Team. Make sure you're alert to signs that you might be crossing that line and adjust accordingly.

A couple of questions to ask to before you submit an REO offer:

Other than price, are there any other terms that are important to your client?

Ask the Agent, "Do you have any other offers"?

- Follow up question to that if the answer is yes: "I don't want to step on any toes or ask any hard questions, but are you representing any of those buyers?" If they say yes, you can probably guess that they're not going to give out any additional helpful information. If they say no, at least you know that your offer may have a shot of getting an answer or an acceptance. Then you can follow-up with "Awesome, what price do you think I need I come in at?" Or "What do we need to do to put this together". Now, they aren't required to tell you, however, you'd be surprised at what the Listing Agent may tell you. If you slowly build rapport with that Listing Agent, they may tell you exactly what you need to do to get your offer at the top of the pile.

Sometimes it's just being at the right place at the right time, which just takes time and consistency.

As a Buyer Agent, you should always submit the highest and best offer the first time. Clean contract. No contingencies is ideal, however, sometimes that isn't possible. The fewer contingencies, the better the chance the bank will pick your offer.

Cash is king. If you are submitting an offer with a contingency on financing, some banks will require you to submit a preapproval letter. NOT a prequalification letter, but a preapproval. There is a big difference. A prequalification letter is just the bank saying, "We've pulled credit and it looks like the buyer can qualify for a loan." The pre-approval letters states, "You are approved for a loan based on conditions."

REO Timelines for Listing Agents

The last and most important thing to know when you list REO properties is the bank's timelines. Each bank has different requirements for when tasks are due, and completing those tasks on time is very important. Usually, it's 24 hours for initial inspection, 48 hours for BPOs, 24 hours for MLS sheets, and 72 hours for HOA info. But, there are many, many more tasks. If you do not complete tasks on time, the bank will find someone who does. Many Agents want to get into REO, and banks do not have to look far to find a replacement.

Module 4 - Writing a Short Sale Offer

While the short sale process is long and arduous, it is really no different than selling any other home. No need to worry or lose sleep over getting your buyers through the transaction. Knowing the short sale process along with some tips on how to handle a short sale will get you and your buyers over the finish line.

Knowing how a short sale works on both sides of the deal is imperative to a successful transaction, and will save you and your buyers an enormous amount of frustration. It's also helpful to have a Listing Agent that has experience in listing short sales. One of the first questions you should ask the Listing Agent when considering an offer for your buyer is "What experience do you have in short sales?" or "How many short sales have you sold in your career?"

If you really want to get good responses, try "You seem to know a lot about short sales. Have you done a ton of them?" They'll likely jump right into telling you all about their extensive and storied history with short sales. If they don't give you an actual number, simply follow up with, "That's awesome! So, tell me, ballpark, how many short sales do you think you've closed overall?" Taking the extra step here will keep them OFF the defensive, and IN your corner. Stroke that ego! :)

An experienced Agent will have already contacted the bank, received an approval for the short sale and have the checklist and forms in place to coordinate this type of transaction. If the Agent isn't experienced in short sales, this is the perfect opportunity for you to take control and guide the transaction with your knowledge on how to facilitate a short sale.

Most banks or lenders will agree to a short sale because it takes less time and may save them money over completing a foreclosure. The Listing Agent will list the house like a traditional listing, but also must help the seller communicate with the bank. The bank will need the seller to provide certain paperwork and it may take weeks or even months for the bank/lender to decide if they will accept an offer. Short sales come with many tax and legal implications, and Agents must be familiar with it all. Short sales take a lot of work and patience on both sides of the transaction. Working with banks is not always easy, and these situations can be very frustrating for the buyers and sellers.

Keep in mind this is an emotional time for the seller. It is your job to keep all parties calm, cool, and collected. Remember that you and the Listing Agent are on the same side and both of you want the offer to get approved and the transaction to close successfully.

Submitting Short Sale Offers

Here are some sample questions that most Buyer Agents will ask the Listing Agent. Knowing the answer to these questions will help your buyer get their offer accepted.

- Are they going to submit a single offer to the bank, or will they submit multiple offers?

    - Single offer to bank is best. The loss mitigation department (what the bank's short sale division is usually called) will most likely prefer that only one offer is submitted at a time.

- How many loans and HOA or other liens are on title? The more loans the more complicated and slower the process will be, and the less likely that it will close.

- Has the bank done a BPO (Broker Price Opinion)?

  - BPO's are very similar to doing a CMA (Comparable Market Analysis). A BPO is completed by a licensed real estate Agent or Broker. Check your state law on who is able to complete a BPO. Some states only allow a licensed real estate broker, and some states have a rule on how many years you must be licensed in order to perform a BPO.

  - A BPO is a report used to provide a market value on a property, and typically consists of three recent sales, three active homes, and three pending homes that are comparable properties to the property being valued. The BPO also includes commentary and certain statistics. BPOs usually require an inspection (property visit by the Agent, NOT a professional home inspection by a licensed home inspector), with some requiring only exterior pictures and others requiring interior photos.

- Do we have an approved sales price? If the lender has an approved BPO on file there may be an "Approved Sales Price". That is a set price or price range already determined by the loss mitigation department that they would accept. There is no need for you to submit a $100,000 offer on a short sale when the approved sales price is $125,000. You will just waste your time and more importantly, your buyers' time.

Short Sale Timeline

To better understand how the short sale process works, here is the flow of a short sale:

- Seller submits a complete short sale package to the bank/lender.
- Sometimes there is an offer attached. Sometimes it is just the homeowner getting the process started while they wait on an offer.
- When the bank receives the package that will trigger a BPO request.
- If there is an offer attached, the lender will compare the offer price to the BPO value.
- At this point, one of three things could happen:

1) It will get approved.
2) The bank will counter and ask for a higher number. Or alternatively,
3) They will turn the offer down completely (due to various reasons depending on what the offer entailed).

The range to get the short sale closed is anywhere from one month to one year. Buying a short sale requires patience. Just remember to manage a buyer's expectations and make sure that a buyer understands what is involved, including the timeline.

The number one question to ask a buyer is how long they will wait for a short sale approval.

There is little reason to start the short sale process if the buyer is not committed to the transaction or unmotivated to wait. Buyers who will not wait or can't wait, for whatever reason, should buy a home that is not a short sale. Very few can get approved within 30 days, even if the house is "Short Sale Approved" by the bank.

The Longest Short Sale in History

Ok, truth be told, I don't know what the ACTUAL world record for longest short sale is, but I can tell you about my longest short sale ever... Listed in early 2007, it was still listed for sale in late 2010! While we never sold it, we DID sell somewhere in the neighborhood of 19+ other homes to buyers who called on that listing (60% of which called on the BACK of the flyer in the flyer box on the sign!). Furthermore, the homeowner got to live there, without making a payment, for over three years!!

We went through seven buyers on that property.

That said, we averaged over two sign calls per week per sign in the ground, so as you can see, even on a listing that will never sell:

"A sign in the yard beats a sign in the car EVERY TIME."
-Michael Hellickson

At one point in time, we had over 750 listings in active and pending status!

During that time, we were receiving 6352 sign calls per month. Assuming we gave each of our Buyer Agents 40 sign call leads per month, and each closed just 5% (2) of those leads (should be able to easily close 10%, but we'll be conservative and use 5% as our guide), we could have been closing over 317 transactions a month as a team. The problem was we weren't able to hire the 159 Buyer Agents, closing 2 units per month each; it would have taken to service all those leads!

Module 5 – What is Probate?

A home is sold in probate court when someone dies without

bequeathing their property to one of their heirs. To simplify, if someone dies without a will and they own property and don't designate an heir, that property is sold through probate court.

Sometimes probate sales have to go through court approval where there is an overbid process, which is like an auction.

This can be a complicated legal process, and having a licensed probate attorney to help guide you through the process is recommended.

If you find a property for your buyer that indicates it is a probate sale, ask the Listing Agent a few key questions.

How many decision makers are on the property? If there are a lot of family members or siblings, the process may take longer. If there are three or less siblings or family members, the better your chances are the process will go quickly.

Each state is different on how probate sales are handled, so it's best that you check what those laws are in your city and state and seek the advice of a probate attorney.

Club Wealth® has a forthcoming book on REOs and Short Sales (there are a total of 19 Club Wealth® Books in the works). Keep updated on all the books at www.ClubWealthBook.com.

CHAPTER 20
WORKING WITH LUXURY BUYERS

Module 1 - Attention and Intention

If you want to work the luxury real estate market, you've got to start by telling yourself, "I'm going to do this, and nothing is going to stop me!"

All great growth comes from doing things outside of your comfort zone. Otherwise, you'll be nothing more than ordinary. You have to decide that this is what you're going to do and then you dive in headfirst without hesitation.

You must have your attention, intention, and actions toward getting into the luxury market. You cannot dabble. You have to be all in!

To start, set a goal. Whether it's "I **intend to** sell 10 homes over a million dollars in one year, or work with 5 luxury home buyers in a six month period, put your **attention** on the luxury market. Make a vision board, talk about it, and take an **action** every day that will move you toward that goal. Be intentional! What action can you take TODAY?

LUXURY DEFINED

Triple the market average.

High end is double the market average.

Understand what makes the difference in your market and why.

Module 2 - Breakthrough Limited Mindset about Luxury

Breaking into the luxury market is 98% mindset.

Most agents are afraid of going after high net worth buyers. What they don't realize is you most likely have less competition. Agents don't try because they're afraid of talking to high-end clientele. As a matter of fact, a lot of agents think that way. The Average Agent's mindset is: "They are fancy, and I'm not." Or "I'm not wealthy, so I'm not going after someone who has more money than me."

Yes, money CAN be intimidating. But it doesn't HAVE to be.

Wealthy people are just like us. Most are the most humble, down-to-earth people you'd ever meet. They don't care if you are rich. They care if you are THE expert. They care if you are competent. They care if they can TRUST you.

They are also often the easiest, most appreciative people to work with.

With a little direction and advice, you can break into the luxury niche market, too. Don't be intimidated. Just go for it.

Module 3 - Educate Yourself

How do you educate yourself on the luxury market?

Get comfortable walking into million-dollar homes. Whatever price range is considered "luxury" in your market, you have to get comfortable walking into those types of houses.

The best way to educate yourself is to go preview luxury properties. Find vacant properties or do an office caravan. Bring a notebook and take notes. Take a lot of pictures and do research on each listing. Walk inside as many houses as you can. This way you can get familiar with the technology of luxury homes. You know what kind of countertops, appliances, flooring, and construction materials are typically used in luxury homes.

Get obsessed with learning. A great way to do this is to meet with other luxury agents. Ask to co-list properties with them or host open houses on their listings or luxury FSBO's. Knowledge in the luxury market is confidence, and confidence closes.

Module 4 - Walk the Walk and Talk the Talk

You have to know what you are talking about when it comes to selling to high net worth clients. Luxury buyers expect you to be competent. They expect you to know the things about their house that an Average Agent wouldn't know, like different architectural styles, cool technologies etc.

One way you can shortcut your learning curve on luxury homes is to start reading LUX Magazine or Architectural Digest. Test-drive the cars they drive like a Tesla or a Ferrari so you know what you're talking about.

Coach's Corner: You don't have to BE luxury, just carry yourself like a Luxury Agent.

When two people meet, as long as there is any form of rapport maintained, the person with the most certainty will eventually influence the other person. - Anthony Robbins

Attire: Dress appropriately for where you are. For instance, Seattle is a very casual place. When showing 3 million dollar homes in Seattle, the typical buyer will show up at a listing in a Prius, shorts, and flip-flops! That said, you can never go wrong being "Overdressed".

If you are in a market area where people expect you to dress like them, then go upgrade your attire. If you can't afford Gucci or Prada or any other luxury brand, go to consignment and buy a few pieces at a time. Start to upgrade yourself little by little until you get to where you want to be. That will give you more confidence and you will feel more comfortable meeting luxury buyers.

Guys, when in doubt, wear a suit. Ladies, let's again remember what we are, and are not, selling.

How do you find high net worth individuals?

Luxury clients don't usually find Agents on Yelp or Facebook or

Craigslist. They find Agents through referrals from other high net worth individuals. They have friends that KNOW Agents to recommend. You have to go find their community. Go talk to "their people." Meet their attorneys, managers, Family Office Managers, financial planners, designers, or architects. Find the people who rub shoulders with the types of people that you would like to sell houses to.

Read *Networking with Millionaires* by Thomas Stanley, and implement his teachings.

Be the master of your game. Know all the pieces of the luxury market. Find people who are already masterful in their game. Get to know THOSE people who are already working with high net worth individuals. Go by their office and drop off marketing materials so they can start to refer you.

Coach's Corner: Put yourself in the way of luxury.

Rubbing Shoulders

Hang out where high net worth individuals like to hang out. Play tennis, join a golf club, go to culinary events, and attend a polo match. Instead of pitching them or coming from a marketing standpoint, concentrate on building a relationship with them. Get to know them first. It has to be an authentic relationship, though. If you don't know how to play tennis, then find something else you may have in common. Sailing? Horseback riding? Art auctions?

Take care of those relationships. Set up a Facebook page just for your luxury clients. They don't have to know it's a special group set up for just them. This way you can respond to them, interact with them, and just focus on building relationships.

Take it a step further, and set up a Facebook Group for Luxury in your area. Invite luxury clients, and those who serve high net worth individuals to participate in the group.

Module 5 - How to Communicate

Once you meet someone, find out as much as you can about them. You should always know whom you are talking to. Google your clients. Know what makes them passionate and what their life is about. Track this data in your CRM.

Of course, you don't want them to know that you checked them out beforehand. However, if you see that you have mutual friends on Facebook that is a benefit. Know as much about your client BEFORE you meet them.

It's a bonus if you know what their DISC profile is. Know WHOSE house you are walking into. Are they a "D" profile? If they are, you'll know ahead of time HOW they like to communicate. Be sure that you are mirroring them. If they are "D", you will know ahead of time that they don't want to hear any "fluff". They want straight to the point answers - the bottom line.

You can find a lot about someone just by Googling them. (Careers, hobbies, associations, etc.). If you're talking to a high "C" you know you need to talk about market statistics, absorption rates, and what percentages of listings sold in a certain amount of time.

Make sure when you walk into that home that you're prepared with all the information needed to know how to talk to your client. That goes along with knowing all the luxury terminology.

How you talk is also just as important.

Most high net worth individuals are very busy. They've got their careers, social calendars, and businesses. Be direct and to the point. Ask them how they would like for you to communicate to them. Daily? Weekly? Monthly? Or only when something important happens? Do you want me to call you? Only text? Don't do a lot of socializing. Again, get to your point.

That said, do it with a smile.

If you don't reach them, leave them a voicemail. Have no expectations of response. This means don't get your feelings hurt when your luxury clients don't return your call. Most luxury clients are highly driven. They are really busy. If you leave them a message with all the details that they need, don't expect a return call. They don't want to be drowned in minutia.

If you are talking to a highly driven individual, they are going to listen to your voicemail and then forget about it unless there is something they need to do. That can't offend you. Mastering your communication is the key to being successful in the luxury market.

Master active listening skills, knowing what they want, and speaking to them the way they want to be spoken to.

Module 6 -Advocate, Consult, Advise

Advise your client. This should not be a "transactional relationship". Instead, be their "consultant" like their CPA and attorney. You have to be educated, competent, and trustworthy to do that.

Once you get into the "consultant" category, you can find a reason to talk to them about the market. You have to keep providing information even after the transaction is done.

They have to know you as the expert. Luxury clients will only refer you out to their friends, family, and associates when they know they can trust you. So talk about their real estate portfolio. It is the long game that you are playing.

Begin by being their advocate; ensuring their best interests are cared for. Then, consult them on what you recommend they should or should not do. Finally, advise them on what to expect based on the course of action they have chosen

Module 7 - Be Seen!

Be seen as the luxury agent around your marketplace. Hang out at the local country clubs. Co-sponsor charity events. Be out and about in the community. If you want to be a luxury Agent you have to be seen by high end net worth individuals. You have to be in the same environment they are.

Other ways you can do this:

Sit luxury open houses in your community. Then invite all the neighbors to "exclusive twilight open houses". Make the neighbors feel special when they do come to your open houses. Give them the opportunity to meet you - and take care of them! Remember to be authentic - do the things that you are passion about.

Invite other businesses who cater to high net worth individuals to participate in your Luxury Open Houses, like: Luxury Car Dealers (have them bring several AWESOME cars), art dealers, caterers, jewelers, etc.

Turn Your Database Into a High Membership Club

Clients should feel lucky that they are doing business with you. You can accomplish this by knowing everything about your clients. Acknowledge special occasions in their life. Know their anniversary, birthdays, and special events. Send them cards or gifts that don't look like you are "marketing" to them. Make it personal.

One great idea is to do *"My Favorite Things"*. Things like food, slippers, candles...what are all the great things that you love? You can share these things with all of your clients. You can do this quarterly for all your luxury clients. You can send them a box and inside of it put a card that says, "Here are a few of my favorite things this season."

For example, you can do a Fall themed box with a Pumpkin candle, branded matches, homemade jelly, etc.

This will acknowledge the relationship with them and it keeps it special.

Turn your database into a private membership. This is a great reason to stay in touch with your clients.

Other ideas you can do: When you get a referral, you can send your client a special gift. Flowers, chocolates, or any kind of customized gift. Something that shows the client that you care.

You can even use a gift app that allows them to tell the app THEIR favorite things, at which point your gifts to them will be tailored to their desires.

You are rewarding your client for thinking of you.

You should do this whether or not you got the referral to buy or sell or do business with you. Include a card that lets them know they've been entered into a drawing when they attend your client event. You can give away a trip, a spa day, golf lessons, personal chef for the night, or whatever you like. Do the drawing at your event!

Invite them to events that THEY love.

Get box seats to a sporting event. It's not an opportunity to talk shop with them. It's an opportunity to build that relationship with them.

Get known so when people ask, "How do I get invited to one of your parties?" you can simply answer, "When you become a client."

Luxury SWAG

Everyone loves a SWAG bag! Order merchandise that has your brand. When you show up a client's house, never go in empty handed. Bring them a thoughtful gift or flowers.

Or you can give them engraved key chains, branded slipper, or a glass jar of branded matches with a nice scented candle. Even your SWAG is marketing. Brand your name so it pops up everywhere they look.

Luxury clients appreciate luxury branding, including your SWAG.

Module 8 - Hosting Events

Throw a Client Appreciation Party and invite all your clients. (Read our Chapter 22 Client Appreciation Program). Holding a client appreciation event for luxury clients may cost more money than doing your usual event. That said; the return on your investment would be well worth it.

Client Appreciation Party Ideas for Luxury Agents

Food Trucks are HOT right now. This is a fantastic way to upgrade an outdoor event or open house by adding a food truck service. Depending on location, some offer exquisite selections such as Asian fusion cuisine, Cajun delights, and lobster rolls. Coaches Kellie and Linda Revoir, Andy Kontz, Tim Ray and other Midwest Coaches may need to find a substitute for the Lobster rolls… just saying (those of us Coastal Coaches tend to avoid seafood in the states too far inland). ;)

Sporting Clinics, such as tennis and golf, are a favorite past-time of retirees and high net worth individuals. Call your country club and arrange for one of their best instructors to hold a private clinic for you and your clients. Spend one or two hours learning a new hobby or perfecting your skills with your clients.

VIP Exclusive Tours with a local museum, art gallery, or zoo can usually be arranged through the public relations or customer service department. Imagine taking 25 of your best clients through an exclusive backstage tour of their favorite museum. This is one event that would be talked about for a long time.

Your clients aren't going to be able to say yes to every event, BUT you have an excuse to call and invite them to your event. You get to "touch" them 3-4 times a year in a meaningful and selfless way.

Charity events are especially nice events to organize and add to your client events list. High net worth individuals usually have the means and the money to attend these types of events, and will often bring other, new high net worth people you can meet and add to your SOI.

Find a local charity that you are passionate about. Create occasions where they want to be present. Give back to the community and rub shoulders with the people that you really want to be working with.

Just remember, breaking into luxury is all about mindset. Create a goal for yourself and be intentional about fulfilling your dream. It's possible. All you have to do is conceive it, and believe it, and it will happen!

CHAPTER 21
SAFETY FIRST

Module 1 - Risks and Dangers of the Career

Most people starting out in real estate would believe our occupation is safe compared to being a firefighter or police officer. While it's true that we don't put our life on the line every day like they do, real estate Agents are still exposed to risks and dangers.

The 2014 murder of Arkansas real estate Agent Beverly Carter rocked the real estate community. It is believed that Mrs. Carter was targeted for her perceived helplessness and wealth.

Most recently a new homes salesman was shot & killed in a model home in Maryland.

While it is very uncommon to become a victim such as Mrs. Carter, it is important not to let your guard down - working in the real estate business can be perilous. Not many careers require you to consistently meet strangers in isolated locations, sometimes during evening hours, in situations that even law enforcement officers deem risky.

The National Association of Realtors commissioned the 2015 Member Safety Report, which found that "while 96 percent of Realtors have never been the victims of crime, 40 percent have found themselves in situations where they have feared for their safety or the safety of their personal information."

What's the best way to protect yourself from being the victim of a potential crime? Always trust your instincts, for starters. Don't worry about offending a client if you don't want to meet them alone. If something doesn't feel right, remove yourself from the situation. Your safety is paramount.

Coach's Corner: Don't sacrifice safety for a commission. Trust your gut and have a smart approach to safety.

Module 2 - Safety Rules for All Agents

Here are some other safety tips that should be followed:

1. Before leaving to show property or hold an open house, let your team members or office staff know where you are at all times.

2. Be prepared to deal with any type of threatening situations by having an out. Use a fake backup if you don't have a real one. For instance: if you are in an uncomfortable situation, say, "My coworker is dropping off some documents," or "I have to meet another client outside," and leave as quickly as possible. If they believe someone else is showing up soon, they are less likely to act on any harmful plans.

3. Don't agree to a private showing without getting information on the buyer first. This means meeting in a public place like your office, obtaining a copy of their driver's license, and having them fill out a Buyer Information Form. At the very least, snap a picture of their driver's license (and/or their vehicle license plate) with your phone and send to a Team member.

4. When in doubt, bring a team member, a lender, or a friend to all showings. For open houses, always ask a lender or title rep to sponsor the event and attend with you.

5. Never lead a person during open houses and showings. Let the client proceed in front of you while keeping a safe distance, or let them explore the property on their own, and offer to meet them in the kitchen or living room when they're done. Never leave a client in your blind spot.

6. Before holding an open house or meeting a new client at a property, take a quick trip around the neighborhood to lookout for any safety concerns. Take note of anything suspicious, like an occupied car parked in the street for an extended period of time.

7. Always have two exits identified prior to an open house or private showing. Keep exit doors unlocked. Make sure that if you plan to use the back door as an escape, you can also escape the backyard. High walls and padlocked fences are things you should take note of.

8. Take a self-defense class.

9. Don't wear expensive jewelry.

10. Leave your purse and any valuables in the trunk of your car.

11. Dress professionally, never provocatively.

   Remember what you ARE and ARE NOT selling. – Michael Hellickson

12. Buy a personal security app for your cell phone and always keep your cell phone in your hands. Check to make sure you have service and have emergency numbers on speed dial. If in immediate danger call the police before you call spouse or coworker.

13. Be ready to defend yourself. Travel with pepper spray and know where it is at all times. Pepper spray is useless at the bottom of your purse or in your suitcase.

14. If you feel like you're being followed while driving, stay calm. Drive to the nearest police station or a busy public place. Don't drive home unless you are sure it's safe.

15. Don't assume that everyone has left the premises after an Open House or Client Event. Check all rooms and the backyard before closing up. Also, check the locks on all windows and doors before you leave.

16. Never park in the driveway where you can get blocked in by another vehicle. At the very least, make sure you can drive out safely. Park in well-lit areas.

17. Ask sellers not to leave out any valuables and medications during showings. Keep those locked up safely at all times.

18. When posting on social media, don't let others know your daily schedule. Especially if you're going to be alone – you don't want others to know where you are and how long you will be there.

19. Purchase a panic button type device that will alert authorities immediately when you are in danger.

Coach's Corner: When prepping a house for showings, be sure to lock the door immediately. Don't leave it open or unlocked for someone to follow in behind you. Go through the house turning on lights and doing your prep work, and open/unlock the door at the last possible minute.

For more safety tips, and links to safety device providers (there are some pretty cool ones now) visit http://www.ClubWealth.com/safety

CHAPTER 22
CLIENT APPRECIATION PROGRAM

CLUBWEALTH

A client appreciation event is an internal marketing strategy to gather more referrals and repeat business. It's the ultimate way to connect with the most important assets in your business - the people in your DATABASE, a.k.a. your Sphere of Influence (S.O.I.)!

A client event focuses on nurturing the business and relationships you already have, which accomplishes two things: Keeps you "top of mind" with current clients and your SOI, AND gets you referrals from both!

Module 1 - Why do a Client Event?

Client events are an integral part of your overall Internal Marketing Strategy (IMS). They help you get to the low hanging fruit on your business tree quickly and easily.

In 2013, approximately 61% of the average Agents' business came from their SOI. By 2018, that number had dropped to around 44%, a significant decline of over 17%!

On the surface, and without full understanding of WHY this dramatic shift occurred, this might cause you to consider abandoning the thought of growing this part of your business.

It is imperative that we fully understand both the cause of the drop, as well as the go-forward solutions that can actually help you

INCREASE your SOI-based business.

The Cause

The root cause of the 2013-2018 Referral Recession, or "RR" as we'll call it, is the prolific rise of the Internet as the primary starting point for consumers in search of a home.

92% of all buyers now begin their home search online. Of those, 72% work with the first Agent they come in contact with. Exacerbating matters further, 40% of homebuyers have a home to sell.

So, as you can see, a LARGE portion of home purchases and sales originate on the Internet. Now, while this should concern uneducated Agents, World Class Agents need not fear, because they have and will continue to embrace technology, and learn to hone their online lead conversion skills. This will enable them to capture more and more of this business.

Furthermore, they will learn the skills necessary to stay in front of their SOI online, through retargeting and other key online marketing strategies.

As if the pressures of the online world weren't enough to drive SOI based business downward, downward shifting markets (recessions) virtually kill this part of most Agents business. Why? Because no one calls their friend and says, "Hey John! We're behind on our house payments, and the bank is threatening to foreclose on the house. I was wondering if you had an Agent you could refer us to?"

Instead, they hide their troubles from the world, especially their friends, and continue on with their Facebook Lives (the ones that seem perfect and trouble free) until the bank repos the house.

Savvy Agents, however, know this, and specifically run targeted ads online to their SOI, including, but not limited to, distressed property and situational ads. They will also take full and complete advantage of maintaining deep relationships with their SOI by hosting regular Client Events, and calling EVERYONE in their SOI before each and every event.

This sounds like a lot of work, and it is, but it is EXTREMELY rewarding. In non-recession markets, you get repeat and referral business. In recession markets, you get to continue to work with your SOI at a time when they would otherwise easily forget about you or bury their head in the sand in avoidance of the real issue, because they don't know where or who to turn to.

So, regardless of where the market is or is headed, make sure you work this important part of your business, and Client Events are one of the best ways to do that.

The Secret

Let me share a secret with you about client appreciation events. The event itself doesn't matter. Don't get me wrong, they are a fantastic way to build and deepen rapport, renew connections and so forth, but it wouldn't matter if no one showed up. It's great when they do, but you can still be wildly successful even if they don't.

You see, each event is an excuse, no, THE PERFECT REASON to touch your sphere 5-6 times a year, in a way that is selfless and that comes from genuine, authentic contribution! As long as you stick to the system, you will never annoy them. You will never have to ask for their business. In fact, we recommend you NOT use cheesy "anecdotal" scripts that ask if the person has a referral for you, or at least severely limit the use of these extremely self serving scripts.

Instead, focus on building the relationships and occasionally and subtly reminding your SOI that referrals are appreciated. One of the best ways is not to ask for them, but to thank publically those that give them.

Client events are a great opportunity to do this, by, for example, announcing your Client of the Year, and the prize with which you are rewarding them. (Check with your broker to ensure RESPA compliance).

The Myths and Truth About Client Events

There are many misconceptions about client events. Let's explore and debunk some of the more prevalent ones.

Myth #1 Client events are just for past clients.

This is limited mindset thinking. Your family, friends, past co-workers, neighbors – they all know someone who will be moving within 1 year. Any and all great referral sources should be at your event. They can introduce you to someone in their SOI who may need your services.

Inviting everyone in your database to a client appreciation event allows them to see you in a professional light. You want to show that you are the "go to" Agent for all their real estate needs. You also want them to see a ton of others at the event who place their trust in you. The more the better. This is one reason why many Agents turn their client events into Community Events, inviting not only their SOI and their entire database, but their Geo Farm area and often the community at large as well!

Myth #2 Client Appreciation is just throwing a party for your clients.

Not true. Client Appreciation is not just about parties or events. It's showing that you are serious about recognizing and developing the lifetime value of your clients.

This means showing up at your client's doorstep after the sale with a basket of goodies. Or delivering pizza on moving day with a custom pizza box complete with your branding. Or sending a happy birthday or happy anniversary card to them. Knowing all there is to know about their family so that when their son graduates from college, you've sent a congratulations card. And, of course, inviting them to your events.

People feel special when –

1. They get something just for them
2. They know you went above and beyond
3. They know you haven't forgotten them
4. They get invited to events just for them and other people they know are important to you (they like to be part of the "in crowd" or "insiders club")

Client events should be fun for everyone. Your clients don't want to sit through an hour-long seminar about buying and selling homes. The event should be about them, and appreciating their business.

Make your events exciting and enticing to your invitees so they get

FOMO (Fear Of Missing Out) if they don't attend. No worries if you aren't sure how to do this– we will cover what you need to know to have a World Class Client/Community Event.

Myth #3 If I Invite My SOI to a Team or Brokerage Client Event, Other Agents Will Steal My Clients

First, this is "Scarcity Mindset" at it's best... STOP IT! Particularly if you are a solo Agent, or a member of a Team, combining efforts can be a huge advantage for you! Think about it... when people show up for your event, they have no idea if all the people there (including the ones other Agents brought) are your clients or not. They simply assume that everyone there is a client of yours, which gives you massive credibility!

As to other Agents stealing your clients: if your relationship with your SOI is that weak, you probably don't deserve to keep them anyway. Furthermore, do you really believe the other Agents in your office or on your Team are that unethical? Is your relationship with them that bad that they would knowingly steal one of your clients? If so, maybe we need to examine your efforts, or lack thereof, to build relationships within the industry.

Mechanics of Client Events

Client events should be held about once per quarter, and they don't have to cost a fortune. We have tons of affordable ideas for events that are tons of fun, ranging from kid friendly events to adult centered events!

Remember, your clients will always be thinking "What's in it for me?" so make the event all about them.

5 KEYS TO A
SUCCESSFUL CLIENT EVENT

1. Hold Every Quarter

2. Involve Vendors

3. Involve a Charity

4. Theme Based and Simple (*Don't Over Think*)

5. Give Them a Special Memento from the Event

Here are some other ideas for client appreciation/community events that are budget friendly:

Backyard BBQ – Have friendly hoedown BBQ party at your house or clubhouse (if you live in a large community/neighborhood that has one). This may limit your invites depending on the size of space. This should be cost friendly. You can even ask your lender or title company to bring the food and drinks. Don't forget about the little ones. Pony rides, hayrides, and piñatas, and other kid friendly activities should be considered.

Fundraising Events – Pick a fundraiser that benefits your community or that is near and dear to your heart. This should be relatively inexpensive because your sponsors would be donating towards the cause and invitees could pay money at the door. Club Wealth® Coach Christine Andreasen likes to throw a Bubbles and Puptails event that raises money for pet owners that have huge medical expenses and can't afford to take care of their pets any longer. Club Wealth® Client Faculty Member Mike Bjorkman hosts upward of 12 charity events per year, and is especially successful at trading the use of his trailers and moving truck for a free table and advertising at the events. If you are passionate about a cause it will show and your clients will appreciate you all the more for it!

Holiday Events– Pictures with Santa (EXTREMELY popular - great in farm areas too), Easter Egg Hunts (VERY popular, and a great community event), Halloween Trunk or Treat, and Spring Fling are just a few themes you can work with. These are budget friendly parties that you can use to market your business and bring families together for a day of fun. Think of it as solving a problem for parents. Parents don't want to stand in line to get their kid's picture taken with Santa. You can throw a Supper with Santa event at your office or a community center and offer a photo booth with Santa. Or hold a Trunk or Treat for Halloween in your office parking lot. Make it a safe place for kids to go Trick or Treat. You can also do a carnival style Halloween with bobbing for apples, cotton candy booth, and more.

Movie Theatre Rental – One coaching client rented out a movie theatre for the showing of Star Wars. She had her team dress up in costumes as Darth Vader and Chewbacca and had her clients pose for pictures. It was big hit that cost her only $500. Her sponsors chipped in to cover the rental costs, plus popcorn and drinks for the attendees. This event was talked about for ages. Parents were excited because the movie had been sold out and they were able to "score" tickets to this event and bring their kids. It was a true VIP experience.

Coach Dan Baltzer recently had 750 people sign up for his team's movie night, before they had to declare it "SOLD OUT" with over 250 more people wanting to attend. Talk about creating scarcity and

Client Appreciation Program

FOMO (Fear of Missing Out) for subsequent events!!

How much should you spend on a World Class Client/Community Event?

The answer is as much as it takes, within your budget. This also depends on your Tier Level, or, if you're on a Team, the Tier Level of your Team. Number of people in your SOI is also a major factor.

Some rough numbers, but as always, check with your coach before spending more than $250 in your business:

Tier 1: Under $500 out of pocket

Tier 2: Under $1,000

Tier 3: Under $2,500

Tier 4: Under $5,000

Tier 5: Under $7,500

Tier 6: Under $10,000

Tier 7: $10,000+

That said, with some creative thinking and leveraging strategies, a client event doesn't have to be anywhere near that expensive. It's not uncommon to hear about Agents that spend tens of thousands of dollars for huge blow out events. This doesn't mean that you have to spend the same, nor does it mean that was a good move on their part.

Also, think about any strategic partners you can leverage. Lenders, closing attorney, title company, pest control, home inspection services, lawn company, handyman services, etc. You can have them sponsor your party and in exchange, they can invite their database for free. You can also get local businesses: bakeries, restaurants, donut shops, coffee shops etc. to donate their goods to your events and even help promote.

This strategy is two-fold. You get money to help throw the event and increase your overall attendance. It's a win-win because you have the possibility of making a huge impact on your business with potential new customers.

Module 2 - Marketing the Event

Marketing a World Class Client/Community Appreciation Event takes time and energy, so you will want to take a very hands-on and aggressive approach and start marketing it VERY early. You want as many clients to attend as possible, and you want everyone to know that it is free! You want your clients and others to know that you take care of them before, during, and after the sale, and make them feel secure in their choice as you as their real estate Agent.

A helpful timeline of preparation before the event:

6-8 Weeks Before Event:

- Select a date and location & book the venue
- Identify which team member will run the event
- Friend every client on Facebook
- Post on Facebook every 3 days
- Run targeted Facebook ads to the emails in your database
- Vlog/blog about the upcoming event, make sure this link is shared and boosted
- Email the link to the video and blog post to your entire

database
- Notify vendor/partners and solicit their support

Getting your event organized and your social media postings set up is the first step in getting everything together and ready to send to your clients.

4 Weeks Before Event:

- Call your clients, let them know the who, what, when, where, and why of your event
- Email your clients
- Snail Mail your clients (Postcard/Brochure)
- Post the event on your personal Facebook page, and personally invite your clients. Use as much video as possible, but throw in some image ads as well. Be sure to run ads targeted to your pixeled and custom audiences!
- Text A+, A and B clients to invite them to the event (video text is best!)

3 Weeks Before Event:

- Social Media Posting (every three days, keep it up!)
- Email out a reminder to your database

2 Weeks Before Event:

- Email out another reminder to your database
- Call your A+, A, and B clients, remind the of the event
- Snail Mail a reminder

1 Week Before Event:

- Start confirming attendance, via phone and email.
- Text your A+, A and B clients for confirmation of attendance (again, video text is best!)

3 Days Before Event:

- Confirm the attendance once more via phone
- Confirm attendance via text as well!

Coach's Corner: The most important thing you can do to increase attendance is to make a phone call and give them a personal invite. Remember, the most important reason we hold Client Events is to have a great reason to CALL our clients.

During the Event

When you are at the event you need to take photos **with** EVERYONE. Take a photo with each and every client if you can, and photos of just the clients having a great time. Also, you should take lots of video of the event for use for future event marketing. It also shows what the event was really like, and how much fun your clients were having, thus inducing FOMO on non-attendees! At the event you can also handout postcards or flyers for your next event, to ensure that your clients can plan to attend it.

After the Event

There are a few things you need to do after the event, because after all, the fortune really is in the follow up!

Those who helped set up the event, and helped at the event, deserve a personal handwritten note. Either hand-deliver or mail the note.

Sharing the photos in your newsletter and on your Facebook is very important! When sharing the event photos on Facebook, you need to spread them out over a week's time, or more, to ensure that you get consistent traction on your posts. Tagging the clients in the photos will also help with this, and get the conversation going about how much fun your event was! (Don't forget about Instagram, SnapChat, and other social media sites).

Video posts are KEY here.

Email your entire database pictures and links to the pictures, so they can go look at what they missed out on, AND for the clients that attended, they can look back on how much fun they had!

Last but not least, calling all of the attendees and thanking them for coming to your event. This is also a great opportunity to mention your next event and personally invite them ahead of time.

Coach's Corner: If you treat them like a client long enough, they will become clients.

If you haven't already, visit http://www.clubwealth.com/clientevents, as it includes ideas for client appreciation events and a step-by-step guide detailing what you should be doing before, during and after each event!

Hosting a client appreciation event is a way to build and strengthen your relationships with your network. I would recommend this over buying leads from third party marketing companies any day of the week, wouldn't you?

That said remember, we need TONS of lead sources on autopilot to ensure consistently great lead flow and, in the end, commission checks!

CHAPTER 23
BUILDING WEALTH

CLUBWEALTH

Every real estate Agent achieves wealth in different ways, depending on where they are in the business. Commissions, splits, recruiting bonuses, and referral fees are just some examples of income streams for Agents. And when it comes to managing your income, any seasoned real estate Agent will tell you that it's very difficult to maintain a budget when your income is wildly fluctuating, especially during shifting markets and lean times. You may see twenty-five thousand dollars in commissions one month to literally zero the next.

However, if you learn the rules for building wealth, you can put yourself on the road to financial freedom. Regardless of your current level in the real estate business, there are simple steps every Agent can take to build wealth.

In this chapter you'll learn about the importance of building wealth and how to do it by saving your hard earned money, investing wisely, and putting your money to work for you.

Coach's Corner: It's not what you make, but what you keep, that creates wealth.

Part 1 – The 5 Rules for Building Wealth

5 RULES FOR BUILDING WEALTH

1. Pay Your Quarterlies First

2. 30/70 Plan

3. Reduce and Eliminate Debt

4. Always Lead With Revenue

5. Put Your Money to Work For You

"If your outgo exceeds your income, then your upkeep will be your downfall." – Bill Earle

Rule #1 Pay Your Quarterlies First

A lot of Agents think that by paying their quarterlies, they are giving their money to the government when they could be using it to grow their personal wealth. Until you get your budget organized and you've developed effective strategies and habits for your finances, it's better to just pay your quarterlies.

The pennies you MIGHT earn in interest are NOT worth the risk of not paying your quarterlies regularly and on time.

Follow this guideline for paying your quarterly taxes:

- For income received Jan 1st through March 31st, estimated tax is due April 15th.

- For income received April 1st through May 31st, estimated tax is due June 15th.
- For income received June 1st through August 31st, estimated tax is due Sept. 15th.
- For income received Sept. 1st through Dec. 31st, estimated tax is due January 15th.

Taxes include all local, state, and federal income taxes.

Rule #2 Follow the 30/70 Plan

All budgets will begin on your adjusted gross income (AGI), not your gross income. This is your income once your taxes have been removed and set aside to pay quarterly.

30% of your income is what is called Sacred Funds. Sacred Funds puts you in alignment with your core values and should be **paid before anything else** from your net income.

70% of your income is what you live on. Living on less than what you make, and investing the difference in cash-flowing assets, makes you wealthy.

It takes commitment and self-discipline to create true wealth. This is why it's called a "PLAN".

The 30% of the 30/70 Plan Breakdown:

The 1st 10% of the 30%
The first 10% of the 30% should go to charity. The charity you choose should be something you support, believe in, and that ensures the vast majority of your contributions go to those in need, and NOT to administration. It should align with your standards and beliefs.

Some possible examples are tithing and offerings to your church or religious center, or a contribution to a charity or nonprofit. Sacrificing these funds will build discipline and help you learn to live on a budget.

The 2nd 10% of the 30%

This should go to reduce and eliminate debt. The best way to do this is to use the "Debt Snowball System". You'll want to stick to it until all debt is eliminated. Here's how the system works:

Start with smallest debt and add the 10% from Sacred Funds to the minimum payment.

When smallest debt is paid off, take the amount you were paying to it (10% plus your minimum payment) and add to the next smallest debt.

Then you rinse and repeat until all debt is paid off.

Once you have paid off all your debt, take the amount you were paying and invest it, and don't ever go back into debt.

Coach's Corner: If you can't pay cash for it, you can't afford it. This goes for EVERYTHING excluding your home and investment properties. Cars should be paid for in cash.

Warning! This does take commitment, discipline, hard work, and planning for your future, but the rewards you'll reap will be worth it.

The 3rd 10% of the 30%

This should go to building a reserve. You should be putting it into a secure account and then forgetting about it. This money is **not** for bills, business, or to spend on fun things. You should continue to accumulate until you have 6-12 months of expenses (highest in past 3 years) in reserve.

An example of a reserve account is a certificate of deposit (CD) account or a money market account. You want the reserve funds to be accessible, but not easily accessible to you. For example, don't put it in a regular checking or savings account or hide it under the mattress where you can put your hands on it at any time.

When you have six to twelve months in secure reserves, put that 10% to work for you. Invest in what you know, like real estate or your business.

As your income increases stick to your current household budget and adjust your percentages to become a 40/60 budget with 10% to charity, 20% to investments and 10% for emergency, or investment, if emergency is already funded. The goal is to get to where you get to 70/30, which again is 70% to sacred funds and 30% to live on.

Eventually, when your passive investment income exceeds your monthly expenses, you are "Out of the Rat Race", and can choose whether or not you want to continue to work.

The idea is to ask yourself, "What am I willing to give up to get what I want?" Eliminate bad practices and habits by creating good wholesome practices and habits that will sustain you throughout your life.

Sacrifice your early earning years to pay for a longer-term stress-free wealth filled lifestyle with passive income. You then can choose to work when and how you want to rather than be a slave to work and your bad habits!

Just remember: to succeed at the 30/70 Plan you have to be consistent, stick to the plan, and start on a small scale if you have to.

"Do not save what is left after spending, but spend what is left after saving." – Warren Buffett

Parkenson's Law

"A part of what I earn is mine to keep". Paying yourself first is the savings, not the income. If you start with paying your expenses first, your expenses will rise with your income and you will always find it difficult to save. This is called Parkenson's Law.

Now you understand why putting 10% straight into savings first is so important. Next, set your budget. What amount should you pay yourself each month in order to live? If you don't already have a budget, figure out what amount you need each month to live. What is your "survival" needs and then distribute from there.

For budget planning, ALWAYS plan to apply this formula and live on less than the lesser of the last 3-year rolling average or last years income.

Example:
Year 1: 100,000 in adjusted gross income
Year 2: 200,000 in adjusted gross income
Year 3: 300,000 in adjusted gross income

So, I would plan to apply the 30/70 rule on $200,000 in adjusted gross income (AGI), because it is less than this year's AGI. Essentially, just because I'm having a good year THIS year, does NOT mean I'm ok to spend based on this increased amount… BE CONSERVATIVE.

IF, however, the numbers looked like this, I would use THIS year as the basis for application of the rule:

Year 1: 200,000 in adjusted gross income

Year 2: 300,000 in adjusted gross income

Year 3: 100,000 in adjusted gross income

Essentially, since this year my income is down, not up, I need to be extremely conservative and immediately cut back on expenses.

> **Coach's Corner: Financial planning is key before you get into real estate. If you're already an Agent, it's never too late to get your finances in order.**

Rule #3 Reduce and Eliminate Debt

Most of us have been there. Broke. Scared. Don't know how to get out of the financial hole. Reading financial self help books like *"The Richest Man in Babylon"* by George Clason and *"Rich Dad, Poor Dad"* by Robert Kiyosaki have helped millions of people find what really works, which is unbelievably fierce and focused intensity on climbing out of that financial pit.

As discussed in the 30/70 Plan, you need a plan in order to reduce and eliminate debt as quickly as possible. By doing the Debt Snowball Method, you will be able to see how close you are getting to financial freedom.

However, just remember this is just one method in many that can help you get out of debt. Research other programs and do the one that you know you have a shot at succeeding with.

Rule #4 Always Lead with Revenue

Leading with revenue simply means don't pay more than you can afford.

For example, car leases or buying a new car with credit is not a good idea.

I drove a 1998 Toyota 4Runner for most of my real estate career. If I were going to buy a new car I wanted, I would first ensure that I could pay cash for it. When I bought my first (and likely last) luxury vehicle in 2017, I paid more cash for it than I did my first several rentals combined. It felt wonderful.

Some coaching programs will teach the opposite and encourage Agents to spend more than they can afford as a motivation tool.

Coach's Corner: You should find motivation within, not pressures from without.

Rule #5 Put Your Money to Work for You

Be a smart investor. Remember what you are good at. Consider real estate investments and only invest in what you know and understand well.

The goal is to maintain your lifestyle with the interest, dividends, or cash flow from your investments, as your other investments continue to grow.

And finally, remember to keep your monthly expenses as low as possible – no matter how well your business is doing - because in real estate things can, and do, change really fast.

CHAPTER 24
COACHING AND TRAINING

CLUBWEALTH

The evidence that coaching and consulting has a MASSIVE impact on agent success is incontrovertible. According to a recent NAR survey, agents who have a coach outperform those who don't by 8X!!

That said; it's important to understand the different types of coaching offered in the industry.

Module 1 - What is Coaching?

Whether you are already a Club Wealth® coaching and consulting client, plan to become one, or choose to go a different route, it's important that you understand a few things about coaching, consulting, mentorship, networking, and training, and the differences between them.

Traditional coaching really involves more encouragement and accountability. Traditional coaching is asking the agent: how many calls, contacts, contracts, and appointments did you get? It's more of a repetitive accountability program where you focus on scripts and repetition more than anything else. It also teaches discipline, and progress is measured and recorded. Now, these are important things and they are helpful, particularly for people who are in Tier 1 and below.

However, when you start getting into one-on-one coaching, you are really serious about your career, and you want to take it to the next

390

level, you have to realize that accountability and motivation need to come from within. That's when you're ready for true **consulting** designed for agents, brokers and teams at Tier 1 and higher.

Module 2 - What is Consulting?

Consulting is one-on-one coaching at a much higher level. It is where we analyze your business, study your strengths and weaknesses, and examine your opportunities and your threats. We understand and fix the holes in your business. We advise you on next steps. We provide you with step-by-step instructions for exactly what you need to do to get to that next level.

We assume that the client is self-disciplined; we assume that the client is self-motivated, and we assume the client will implement what is taught. We also understand that this kind of coaching and consulting is best for agents and team members where progression is reported and measured as well.

Module 3 - What is Training?

Well, if coaching is "go make more calls", and consulting is "let me show you exactly what you need to do" then what is training?

Training is not one-on-one but "one to many". For example, when you watch the Club Wealth University® courses online and an instructor is teaching several people at one time, that is training. It is not specific to an individual or a team but it is usually topic specific.

Module 4 - What is Networking?

Networking is one-on-one, but in a group setting. For example, when you go to an event, you are networking with all these different people in person. It's informal contact with other agents. Ideally, it's with agents producing at or above your level.

It is said that you become the socio economic average of the five people you spend the most time with. Networking is a very important component of increasing that average.

Module 5 - What is Masterminding and how is that different than networking?

Masterminding really involves three or more people formally sitting down to discuss specific topics with other agents producing at or above your level. Someone who truly understands where you are and what you're experiencing - someone who has been at a level above you and knows how to get there, usually moderates it.

It is generally, in best-case scenarios, limited to 25 people per discussion. If it's live or if you are doing a webinar format for masterminds, which we often do at Club Wealth®, then we limit the number of speakers to 25 or fewer. You may have 200 people on the webinar who are enjoying the mastermind as it's happening, but you only have, at most, 25 people actually doing the talking. Of course, the other participants can also be asking questions through chat or Q&A boxes, which further helps to develop and invite topics.

Module 6 - What is Mentorship?

What's **mentorship** and how is it different than all of these?

Mentorship is also one-on-one.

It's usually a marathon, not a sprint. Mentorship is not something that happens only once and then it's over with. The mentor also ideally sells way more than the mentee.

Wherever you are in your business, your mentor should be way further in their business. Ideally, the mentorship involves payment. If there is no payment involved with the mentorship, you're probably getting what you paid for, as there are both no incentives for the mentor, and no skin in the game for the mentee.

Mentorship is often confused with coaching and consulting.

It often involves advice.

It rarely follows a prescribed plan, and yet it is very important that you are involved in a mentorship in your career that **does** follow a prescribed plan.

Module 7 - Which Type Do You Need?

All of them. Every single one of these.

Why?

First of all, to shortcut the learning curve.

Second, to expand your thinking and create synergy.

How many coaching companies do you think offer all of these? The answer may surprise you. Only one, and its Club Wealth®. And it's really important that we offer each of them, and not just one or two. It is very strategic. It allows you to experience all the different methods of learning and growth in an environment that offers just enough structure to ensure you are getting what you need, but which doesn't inhibit freedom and creativity that come along with true mastermind, networking, and all the other things we mentioned. In a nutshell, it strikes a delicate balance with all of the key personal and professional growth and development methods.

It's important to know that everyone goes through a progression, and each of us is at different stages in that progression. At Club Wealth®, we've broken each of these stages into different tiers, as we've discovered there are vast differences between each.

Module 8 - What is the Club Wealth® Tier System?

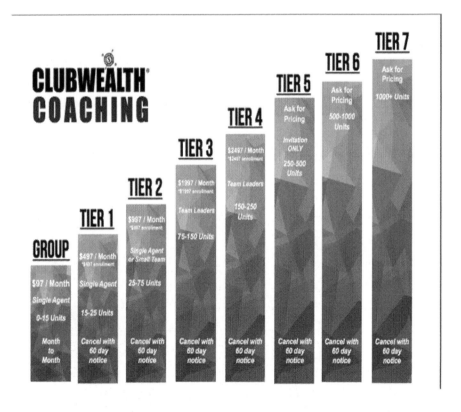

When designing the Club Wealth® Tier System, we recognized that units are more important than the commission.

Why is this?

Because in some markets you may make a higher commission on the same number of transactions than someone in a market that has lower average sales prices.

You will also recognize that Work-Life Balance is a major theme in ALL Club Wealth® Coaching Programs.

Remember: No success in the world can compensate for failure in the home.

Group Coaching

Criteria are 0-15 units closed in a single year. Generally speaking, agents in Group Coaching, whether it is with Club Wealth® or any other company, are not yet financially or professionally ready for one on one coaching or consulting. They are likely still scrambling to figure out the basics, and simply need to get some transactions closed, so they can have a fighting chance at survival in this business.

Quite often, we recommend that these agents consider joining a team, where they will get both instruction and leads, as well as the accountability they need to develop the right habits early in their careers.

Tier 1

This tier is designed for individual real estate agents who are looking for greater profitability with less hassle. It helps you get the basic systems and habits in place, and helps you build a solid foundation upon which you can construct your own Real Estate Team or solo-agent-career.

Criteria is 0-25 units per year

Tier 2

Tier 2 helps you with everything you may not yet have in place from Tier 1, and goes deeper. The focus here is beginning to build a team.

Criteria is 25-75 units

Tier 3

This tier is designed to take you from six to seven figures while working fewer hours/days than ever before. It's personalized coaching for your entire business. We work with you, your agents, and your admin team members to begin scaling your business in a meaningful way.

Criteria is 75-150 units

Tier 4

Tier 4 is also where we usually begin growing your local and national brand and celebrity presence, which creates new business opportunities AND helps your existing marketing efforts, produce more profit!

Criteria is 150-250 units

Tier 5

By the time you reach Tier 5, you've figured out that Eagles don't flock with turkeys! Working with one of our top coaches who have closed 500-1000 units, we'll focus together on how to fully automate as much of your business as possible, while continuing to scale. We're likely helping you grow in several markets by now as well.

By now, we are also working hard to help you grow your celebrity status in the industry, as we have with so many others.

Criteria is 250-500 units

Tier 6

You're a national celebrity now and well on your way to real estate world domination! You're attracting business, and giving back in a way that is sure to leave a legacy. We're now focusing on profitability, and your expansion teams are doing well.

Criteria is 500-1000 units

Tier 7

At this point, your primary focuses are building wealth and leaving a lasting legacy! We will be with you every step of the way.

Criteria is 1000+ units closed

In addition to our Tier System Coaching, Club Wealth® has several very important special interests groups we are focused on. One of them is Brokers-Owners, for whom we have specialized training and coaching.

Instead of focusing on number of units like we do in Agent Coaching, with Brokers/Owners, we focus on number of agents within their team/company.

For example, Tier 1 would be for broker/owners with 0-25 agents, Tier 2 has 25 - 75 agents and so forth.

We also have special programs for Buyer Agents, Listing Agents, and Administrative Assistants. And last, but not least, we even have a Youth Leadership program. All of these things are very important, not only to take care of the clients we have today, but to raise and train the future leaders of tomorrow.

Module 9 - Buyer Agent Training

As you can see, for the World Class Buyer Agent, Club Wealth® has coaching, training, mentorship, and consulting, just for you! Other things you can do to propel yourself into World Class status:

Attend Team Huddles, Meetings, and Call Nights

It's imperative that you attend your daily huddles with your Team. This is a chance to ask any questions, build rapport with your teammates, and show accountability to your Team Leader.

Team Meetings are just as important. Most Teams have a meeting weekly or monthly. This may be an opportunity to go over new listings, new buyer clients, wants/needs of your clients, to learn a new skill, script and role play practice with your Team, or learn something new about your local market. Awards and accolades also may be given during Team meetings.

Call Nights are a great way to obtain new clients. This can be done in a Team setting or with your brokerage if they do a Call Night. (May also be called Dialing for Dollars or some other play on words). Generally, you are given a list of prospects to call – FSBO, Expireds, Geo Farming list, etc. You should bring your Sphere of Influence list to call, regardless of if you're given leads or not.

Daily Script Practice and Role Play

A good Buyer Agent should be able to convert leads into face-to-face meetings for buyer consultations. One of the most important trainings you will need to attack is going over what you should say to potential buyer leads.

Focus on "how to sell without selling" by providing value to someone first, then asking for an appointment later. You need to focus on educating your buyer.

Attend Club Wealth® Events

Club Wealth® hosts free and low cost events all over the country. We offer many different events, for all kinds of Real Estate Agents! We offer a Listing Agent AND a Buyer Agent Bootcamp. We also offer events for assistants and Team Leaders! Our FREE half-day events are very popular, as are our full-day events. We encourage you to find one in your area! For a list of upcoming events, visit www.clubwealth.com/events.

If you would like to schedule an event in your area, please contact our office.

Attend Local or National Conferences

NAR, Keller Williams "Family Reunion", Re/Max Events etc.

Check with your brokerage to see if they have any local or national events

Attend Local and Office Training

Coaching and Training

Your local association is a wealth of information for training events. A lot of associations will hold monthly and yearly training. They bring in talented speakers and professionals where you can learn everything from how to work with VA buyers to why home inspections can be beneficial to your buyers.

Attend Mastermind Groups or Calls

Local Mastermind Groups

Facebook Mastermind Groups

Join the Club Wealth® Real Estate Agent Mastermind Group at no cost. With over 25,000 agents and growing, it is filled with highly intelligent agents and coaches who are eager to help you succeed. Join now at www.Facebook.com/groups/clubwealth

Complete the Club Wealth University® Buyer Agent Certification Course

Go online at www.ClubWealthU.com to see all the courses we offer!

Have Regular Calls with Your Team's Club Wealth® Coach

If you aren't already a Club Wealth® client, you can sign up for a FREE strategy session with one of our elite coaches at www.ClubWealth.com/StrategySession

As you can see, there are a lot of resources available, but here is the key. You have to take advantage of those resources.

Remember: knowledge without implementation is like rowing a boat with only one oar in the water.

Take what you've learned and implement it. Remember, all of the things we've talked about are important. Make sure you implement them and add them to your calendar so that they happen on a regular and consistent basis.

The important thing to remember is that continuing your training and coaching is a LIFETIME of learning. Never stop learning. You will be on your way to being a World Class Agent in no time at all!

"If you'll work for 5 years like no one else will, you can do for the rest of your life what no one else can!" – Michael Hellickson

CHAPTER 25
SCRIPTS & ROLE PLAY

CLUBWEALTH

Module 1 - Using Scripts to Improve Skill and Performance

Would you like to wave your magic wand and have your clients do exactly what you'd like? It sounds impossible, however, we have been developing and working on scripts and dialogue systems for many years. We're going to share with you tips and tricks that will help you develop that exact same skill. Reading this will put you well on your journey to being an amazingly persuasive salesperson.

One important thing to know before we begin: Scripts are like jazz. There is no exact science. However, you have to learn the basic rules before you start.

Look at the script as being designed as a system. A system that will give you the same results every time. That's the reason you use a script: the consistent results. I'm sure you've heard other agents in your office that say, "I don't need scripts! I just wing it."

If you wing it, and consistently get great results, technically you have a script. You've just internalized it without realizing it. It no longer feels like a script. It's just like you're having a conversation.

The goal is that the script will just disappear and you internalize it enough that it just feels like a conversation. This way you can authentically listen to your client. This is when scripts become dialogues.

The only way to do this is to practice your scripts.

Let's go over some ways that you can practice and learn your scripts. If you are someone who already loves scripts, that's awesome. If you are someone who loathes scripts, that's okay, too. Just take a few minutes and set aside your disbelief, and delve into what it looks like to practice a script. What will it take for you to become a script master?

Module 2 – Practice Makes Perfect

Practicing scripts builds muscle memory. It's no different than any sport you've learned to play or any activity that you've ever learned. Let's think about walking. Most everyone reading this has learned to walk. You probably just don't remember that first couple of steps when you were learning to walk because it was so long ago.

Learning to walk is a series of repetitive practices building muscle memory so you know exactly what to do without even thinking about it. That's the goal of a script. To turn it into muscle memory. You'll use the scripts so frequently that eventually you'll go back to just having a "conversation" with your client.

Scripts allow you to become more efficient in converting more leads to clients in less time. That's why we love scripts. Duplicable results. Your whole goal is to make more money in less time, and scripts are one way to do that.

Using scripts will allow you to hit the key points and not get distracted during a conversation. Think about turning on a GPS for navigation. Even though you know where you are going, when you have clients in the car, you still turn on the GPS for navigation.

This way, you can go back to talking with the client with no distractions and let the GPS show you the way. Before you know it, you've arrived at your destination without even thinking about all the turns you had to make. Scripts work the same exact way.

Even seasoned realtors who have made thousands and thousands of prospecting calls still use scripts and keep them close by when prospecting. It's like a security blanket that you had when you were a baby. It keeps you comfortable and assures you that you're on track.

Keep this in mind. If your initial call to a buyer is longer than 10 minutes, it's probably because you don't have a script in front of you. Or if you have a script, you're going too far off of it. Either way, your conversation with that client is taking too much time. Your first initial call should be 2 minutes to 10 minutes.

Even though you've read a script a thousand times, take your finger and go down through it, physically moving your finger down the page as you do so. This lets you focus on the questions. Remember, the client doesn't know you have a script. The client may turn the conversation around and lead you down a rabbit hole. However, if you stick to the script, it will keep you on track. You should always be able to bring that client back to the place in the script that you need to go.

Don't ignore what they're saying, nor ignore their questions. Just guide them back to the script by re-focusing on your script questions. This is why you internalize the script: so you always know where to come back to you if get off track.

- Scripts allow you to be more efficient, converting more leads to clients in less time

- Using scripts will allow you to hit "key points" and not get distracted throughout the conversation.

- Think of scripts like turning on a GPS for navigation, even though you know where you are going.

- Scripts increase your sales.

- Scripts reduce your individual call times (call times should be between 2 minutes to 10 minutes total).

Module 3 - Rules for Using Scripts

Be open-minded towards learning scripts. The fact that you are reading this section in the book let's us know that you are open-minded. You would not be reading this book if you didn't have a strong desire to increase your sales skills. Every page you read is increasing your bond with clients and increasing your ability to make sales. This book is already doing that for you.

Know your overall goal for the call, which is typically to book a face-to-face appointment, even if it's your initial call.

Remember: There are only 3 acceptable outcomes for a call or appointment:

1. Schedule a face-to-face appointment
2. Schedule a follow up call
3. Decide you never want to work with this lead

Using the **feedback technique** will demonstrate to the client that you are listening and that you care. This is a simple technique where you basically repeat back to the client what they just said. For example:

- o **You**: In what area are you looking to buy?

- o **Client**: San Diego or Carlsbad.

- o **You**: Okay, so you want to buy a home in San Diego or Carlsbad? Great. How many bedrooms do you need?

- o **Client**: 4 bedrooms and 3 baths.

- o **You**: Great. So you need to have 4 bedrooms and 3 baths. Got it.

- o It's a very short recap that repeats and affirms exactly what you heard and what the client has said (see Chapter 17 *Mastering Key Skills and Negotiating* for more information).

This is also called **active listening**.

Have you ever been to a restaurant where the waiter asks what you want to order, and the whole table gives the waiter the order but he doesn't write it down? It gives you anxiety because you are used to waiters writing down your order. Even if they get the whole order correct, you are still anxious about them remembering everything that you just ordered. As you order, they repeat the order back to you as a short recap. The waiter is practicing the active listening technique.

When you practice active listening, you can also use words like "that's wonderful" or "terrific" to help bridge the client's response with your next question. Using these keys words make you feel less like a sales robot. It also makes your interaction with the client more like a conversation, and not an interrogation.

- On the flip side, when you recap the conversation, make sure you only use 1-2 words maximum. You don't want to sound like you're repeating everything word for word. If you repeat

3 minutes of conversation back to them, that's overkill. Frankly, it makes the conversation way longer than it needs to be.

Use your pause points!

You need to know when to pause, and know when to keep on rolling. In certain instances, when you want a response, you need to pause. It's that simple.

Human beings are afraid of awkward silences. So, as a salesperson, when you ask a closing question and you're waiting for the client to respond, zip it up and shut your mouth. Wait for that client to respond.

Now, when you are at the intro of your script, don't throw any pauses in there. That's when you might get thrown off your script. Go through your intro and why you are calling. Then ask the question - and pause for an answer. For example:

"Hi, I'm Jesse from Live Love San Diego. I'm calling because you inquired about our listing at 123 Main Street on our website. Would you like to see the home or set up an appointment to meet at my office?" PAUSE.

When you do PAUSE - make sure you Listen for a response.

- Make sure your script is 80% open-ended questions in general. There are times for **Yes/No** (close-ended) questions, and times when you want to use more open-ended questions to get the client talking with you.

- If the client won't open up, use more open-ended questions. If the client is giving you a lot of **Yes and No** answers, and you're having trouble establishing rapport, try using more open-ended questions.

For example - "What's important about moving to San Diego? What will moving there do for you?"

- Don't forget to always close during the script (for appointments, referrals, showings).

When making an initial call to the buyer, you almost always want to close for an appointment. This is a face-to-face appointment unless they live in another state. And when you close, make sure you use the **PAUSE** technique.

Module 4 - Anatomy of a Script

There are 3 parts to every script: The intro, timing and motivation, and the close.

The goal of the entire script is to get to the close or book a face-to-face appointment. Or to get hired (if face-to-face appointment).

1. The Intro - the goal of the intro is to get out of the intro. Most people don't care who you are, or what company you work for. It's probably a state requirement for you to say those things when you first call a prospect. That said, the goal is to get to why you are really calling them, and the things that really matter to the client, which is not you -they don't care about you. They care about themselves, their needs, and their home search. That's all the client cares about. Now, once they get to know you, they may care about you, a little. :) The goal is to have the prospect let their guard down so you can fly

410

under the salesperson radar.

The goal of the ENTIRE script is to get to the close and book a face-to-face appointment, or if you're already in person, to get hired!

- The goal of the intro is to get out of the intro.
- To have the prospect keep their guard down by flying under their radar.
- Talk to them as if you were talking to a friend.

For Bonus Points: Role Play with the "Hello" game!

Do this game with your role-play partner. It will help deepen your matching and mirroring skills.

- Partner picks up the phone and says "hello" and you do your best to match their tone. It helps you to get quickly in rapport with them by matching their tone. Think of how you talk when you call a friend or family member. You're not stiff or formal, right?

For Double Bonus Points: Role Play with "Anti-Rapport" game!

- Practice getting out of rapport.
- Whatever they do you do the opposite. Rate of speech, tone, etc. If they start slow - you talk fast. If they talk upbeat and fast - you talk very slow.

Module 5 - World Class Opening Statements

Opening statements make all the difference. The first few seconds are critical. The people are deciding...Are you a friend or a foe? Are you a sales robot? Why are you calling? Are you some kind of scammer?

State your purpose. Don't get caught up with the intro. Remember, the goal of the intro is to get out of the intro.

Example of Opening Statement:

"Hey it's Jesse from Live Love San Diego. I'm calling you because I got your request from Homes.com about the home on 123 Main Street."

- Who I am, where I work, why I'm calling. That's it. Keep It Super Simple (K.I.S.S.)
- Side note - you don't have to know the person's name you are calling. Studies in large call centers have shown that it doesn't matter if you address people by first name or not... It DOES NOT matter. They get the same results. Using the first name gets you in the state of being friendly, however, you can skip the first name, especially if it's a difficult one to say!

- Who are you?
- Where do you work? (Team or broker name)
- Why are you calling? State your purpose.

- Remember, it doesn't matter if they remember who you are or why you are calling...doesn't get caught up in this.

- The goal of the intro is to **get out of the intro**...

- And then ask your first question.

Questions = Control

The first few seconds of your phone call are the most critical. The quality of the questions you ask determines the quality of your life. In this instance, the quality of the questions you ask determines the quality of the engagement of the client. In other words - the outcome of the call.

Before you can ask your first question, let's give some "intro" examples:

"Why I'm calling...we met at a client event..."

How do you hook 'em?

- "I'm Jesse Zagorsky at Live Love San Diego Homes. We met at a client event last week and I wanted to let you know about recent changes in the marketplace...."

- Hi __(first name)___, I got your request on 123 Main Street, did you have any specific questions or just want to set up a time to see it?"

- You want to make sure your intro matches the lead type.

- Lead types that are earlier in their search process (like a PPC, Google or FB lead) need an intro that removes pressure.

- Example: "Hi, I saw you registered on our Free Home Search Site. Are you just browsing around? Or are you thinking of making a move in the next little while?"

- You are taking off the pressure so they can just say, "We are just browsing...".

- Again, the goal of the intro is to get out of the intro and into your 1st question.

Module 6 - The KISS of Death

NEVER, EVER begin a phone call with...

"Is this ___prospect first name___?"

90% of the people you are calling are answering a cell phone. Of course it's the person you are calling for! Who else would be answering their phone?

Asking for "Is this Mr. Johnson?" for example, just signals you are a telemarketer and may trigger the client's fight or flight mechanism.

"How are you today?" is another "don't do"!

In general, there is no benefit to asking this question.

That is the kiss of death for any agent.

Depending on the client you are talking to, and the culture of your geographic area, it may actually be "acceptable" to ask a client how they are, but typically it doesn't add much benefit to the conversation, and most of the time it gets in the agent's way of connecting and building rapport.

Remember, the intro has no pause. State your name, company, and the purpose of the call. That's it.

Module 7 - Collecting Valuable Info from Prospects

World Class Agents are collectors of valuable information.

Think of this like being like a helpful "spy". You want to learn....

- Everything you can about the prospect, including, but not limited to: expectations, wants, needs, and authority. Do they

414

have the authority to make a decision?

- Acquire as much understanding of your buyer's situation as you can before your appointment.

  - Use your Buyer Intake Form to get all the information

Module 8 - Controlling and Guiding a Prospect

The only way to take and keep control in a situation is to ask questions.

When asking the questions, you have the power. Questions equal control.

- Think of it like a tennis match.

- Give a piece of info, ask a question.

- Never pause before asking a question if you want to keep control.

The best example of this is a sign call. When you answer the call, there is a prospect sitting in front of one of your listing.

Prospect: "Hey, what is the price of 123 Main Street?"

Don't give them a piece of info without asking a question. Instead say...

Agent: "It's 588k - is this the price you are interested in?'

You never want to pause. The question is what keeps you in control.

Don't frustrate them and not give the answer. Just answer and ask

415

another question. Keep the match going. Then pause after the questions.

Think about the tennis match.

- Always pause after offering a compelling value statement and closing.

- Once you've put a closing question out there...you have to keep your mouth shut until the other party responds.

- That's the time when it's okay to have that awkward silence.

"Does 2 o'clock or 4 o'clock work better for you?" **PAUSE**.

Module 9 - Practice Tips

Here are some great tips for practicing your scripts! Daily script practice is a must.

- We recommend 20 minutes daily. You should see dramatic improvement in using scripts by practicing 20 minutes daily x 4 weeks. Try it! Consistency builds muscle memory. One day a week won't work. Do it daily to become a Jedi salesperson!

- Role-play with a partner.

- Stand when you practice your scripts.

- Use a mirror – and SMILE.

Role-play by yourself - if you must. But role-play with a partner is best.

Module 10 - Anatomy of Role Play

Begin by internalizing your script by reading it out loud and/or to yourself hundreds of times. Print out multiple copies and place everywhere. On your mirror, in your office, on your chair, in your kid's lunch box - (just kidding, but you get the idea).

- Read it forwards and backwards. Go up and down the script.
- Read it quickly and slowly.
- Read it quietly and loudly.
- Read it consistently, multiple times a day.
- Read it until it is ingrained in your head and you don't need to think about using it and what you're going to say next.
- At that point you can go back to actually having a conversation with your client.
- Bonus Points: Record yourself saying the script out loud. Use your cell phone. It may be painful at first. There's no judging. Just do it.
- EXTRA Bonus Points: Send the recording to your Coach or Team Leader for feedback!

"When performance is measured, performance improves. When performance is measured and reported, the rate of improvement accelerates" - Thomas S Monson

Remember, every time you record yourself, you are moving more quickly along your journey to becoming a World Class Buyer Agent.

- Role Play Basics To Remember:

  o Find a partner.

o Groups of 2 people are usually the best.
o Listening to others role-play does help, but there is no substitute for saying the words out loud.
o Try to role-play with people better than you as often as possible.
o You can role-play in person or on the phone. However, if simulating an over-the-phone scenario, but you and your partner are actually in person, make sure not to look at your partner.
o Seeing someone will give you visual clues with their body language, etc. that you wouldn't be able to see if just on the phone.
o Role-play is typically harder than talking to "real" people because pretending is hard. That's okay though.
o That's normal, you're right on track.
o It will get easier…
o Some day you will actually think it's fun.

• First, figure out the skill level of you and your partner.
• When you begin Role Playing, your goal is just to get through the scripts without objections, and with your partner being "easy".
• As you gain experience, your partner will increase the "difficulty", throwing out more and more objections you'll need to resolve.
• ALWAYS give your partner the appointment in role-play.
• If you are role-playing DIRECTLY before prospecting, the goal is to get your mind warmed up, not tear each other apart and make your partner feel stupid.
• However, as you advance, you will need partners who test you and give you a run for your money.

You can find role-play partners on Club Wealth® and other Facebook groups.

- Remember, your clients don't have a script.
- Create some client "avatar" cards with examples of the most common buyer types you meet:

  o Edgar - the Emotional Buyer
  o Amy - the Accountant (detail-oriented)
  o Frank- the First Time Home Buyer

Here is an example of how the role-play should work:

One person says "Ring Ring", the other agent answers.

The person who says "Ring Ring" is making the outbound call. Prospect says "Hello".

Don't overthink role-play.

It's a "safe" place to try things you'd never say in the "real" world and see how they go.

Ask your role-play partner - "Was that really as pushy as you thought it would be, or did it go better than you hoped?" You usually will find you sound normal.

The key to role-play is consistency!

Practicing scripts and role-play can be a game changer in your business. Embrace the script. Incorporate role-play in your daily schedule. It's all part of your journey to becoming a World Class Buyer Agent.

CHAPTER 26
WRAP IT UP

CLUBWEALTH

Using the tools and strategies that you've learned in this will put you on the path to becoming a World Class Buyer Agent. We are constantly adding and updating all of our books and courses, so check www.clubwealthbook.com often for new edition release dates to make sure you have the most recent versions of each book. You can always look forward to new content and other materials, such as ancillary checklists, forms, videos and more!

So, you've finished reading the book, what now?

- Practice your scripts and role-play.

- Download all of our free content at www.ClubWealthBABookDownloads.com

- Go to www.ClubWealthU.com to check out all of the courses that we offer.

- If you haven't done one this year yet, reach out to us at www.ClubWealth.com/StrategySession, and as our way of saying "thanks for buying this book", we'll give you a 55-minute coaching call with one of our coaches who sells more real estate than you do. They'll look deep into your business, figure out what you are doing well, where you need improvement, where the holes are in your business and how to fill them, and they'll build you a roadmap for your next 12 months to help you take your business to the next level! All this at no cost to you...

At Club Wealth®, we will do everything in our power to help you take your business to your best level, a level where you can really have a great life, take care of your family, make a ton of money, and build a wealthy empire.

Write this down or highlight this right now. If there is only one thing that you get from Club Wealth®, let it be this:

"No success in the world can compensate for failure in the home."

Everything that you've learned and practiced will put you on the path to becoming a World Class Buyer Agent.

However, the choice is yours. We can give you all the knowledge in the world. If you don't implement it – it won't help you. You know how the saying goes – you can lead a horse to water but you can't make it drink.

Knowledge without implementation is like rowing with only one oar in the water... you just go in circles and get nowhere.

Go teach someone what you've learned and recommend this book to him or her.

It would be awesome if you would give it a 5 Star review if you liked it.

Make this your best year yet!

GLOSSARY

Glossary of Terms

A.R.P. - Acknowledge, Respond, Pivot

BPO – Broker Price Opinion

B.R.O.T. - Building Relationships On Trust

CMA - Comparative Market Analysis

CRM - Contact Relationship Management

CWGRLS - Club Wealth® Guaranteed Responsive Lead System

DISC - Dominance (D), Influence (I), Steadiness (S), and Compliant (C).

DPA – Dollar Productive Activities

FORD - Family, Occupation, Recreation, Dreams

GIGO - Garbage In and Garbage Out

HUD - Housing Urban Development

IMS - Internal Marketing Strategy

ISA - Inside Sales Agent

IVR – Interactive Voice Response

MAP – Massive Action Plan

NFUD -Next Follow Up Date

NLP - Neuro-Linguistic Programming

PDS - Perfect Daily Schedule

PPC - Pay Per Click

RDC- Realtor Dot Com

REO – Real Estate Owned

RR - Referral Recession

SOI – Sphere of Influence

TC - Transaction Coordinator

USP - Unique Selling Proposition

WIIFM - What's In It For Me?

Affirmation - Saying a positive statement over and over until your subconscious starts to believe it.

Glossary

Batching - Essentially doing the same thing over and over and over again.

Consulting – It is a one-on-one coaching at a much higher level, where we analyze your business, study your strengths and weaknesses, and examine your opportunities and your threats.

DISC Profile - A behavior assessment tool based on the theory of psychologist William Marston. It focuses on four different personality traits, which are: Dominance (D), Influence (I), Steadiness (S), and Compliant (C).

Embedded command - An opportunity to literally deliver information directly into somebody's subconscious mind

Escalation clause - A clause in a contract that allows for an increase or a decrease in wages or prices under certain conditions

Institutional Seller - Refers to large categories such as banks, asset management companies, insurance companies, REIT's, iBuyers and hedge funds

Mastermind - Involves three or more people formally sitting down to discuss specific topics with other agents producing at or above your level.

Mentorship - a period of time during which a person receives guidance from a mentor.

Networking - It is one-on-one, but in a group setting.

Nudge text – A text you send to a client that motivates them to respond to you

Off Market Properties – Properties that are for sale, but not on the market yet.

Probate - A home is sold in probate court when someone dies without bequeathing their property to one of their heirs

Short Sale - When the seller owes more than the home is worth.

Tie downs - Questions of agreement

Traditional Coaching – It is a repetitive accountability program where you focus on scripts and repetition more than anything else. It also teaches discipline, and progress is measured and recorded.

Training - It is not specific to an individual or a team but it is usually topic specific.

ABOUT CLUB WEALTH

CLUBWEALTH

ABOUT THE AUTHORS

Michael Hellickson - As a real estate agent, Michael consistently listed and sold over 100 homes per month, and at one point had over 750 listings in active and pending status. He is the founder and President of Club Wealth® Coaching and Consulting. Unique in the industry, EVERY Club Wealth Coach has sold MORE real estate than the agents and/or brokers they coach. The only Real Estate Coaching Company that offers a "Double your income, money back guarantee", Club Wealth is the #1 Coaching Company in the World in the Team space! Michael served a 2-year mission for the Church of Jesus Christ of Latter Day Saints. He and his wife, Tara, and their two children, Austin and Madison, make their home in Bonney Lake, Washington with their 2 English Pointers, Ginger and Ruby.

Ron Anderson was a licensed Real Estate agent for nine years. Throughout that time he was consistently doing $150,000 yearly. Although he loved selling real estate, he found his true passion when he began developing and training teams. Anderson recruited and developed a team of over 40 producers. He created a coaching program to improve sales and increase revenue and found great success from those he coached. Ron is a Club Wealth® Tier 2 Coach and the Director of Coaching.

Brian Curtis has been a lifelong learner and teacher and he has a strong passion for it. He started teaching and training when he was an officer in the United States Air Force. Brian started his real estate career in 2005 and has seen the ups and downs of the real estate market from many angles including being a joint owner broker of both a franchise and a small individual shop, and today as a team leader to large team. Brian's team has grown to 22 agents and he's on track to have over 300 closed transactions in 2018. He also started his first expansion team in Chicago, IL and has now successfully launched 4 expansion teams. Brian is a Club Wealth Tier 5 Client and a Tier 4 Coach.

Cheri Benjamin is an USAF Vet, and a wife, and mom of 5 boys. She started a mortgage business in 2000, and began her real estate career in September 2013. In 2016, she joined Club Wealth as a solo agent, searching for the right coach for over a year. Now, she's the founder of the Benjamin Group, a real estate team of over 40 agents, and she is out of production. Cheri is the CEO of Expansion Services at Club Wealth and has expanded into 4 other markets, not including Atlanta. Cheri is also a founder of a national mortgage company.

Misti Bruton found her passion for real estate early in life. After many years in the real estate industry as a solo agent, Misti was working long hours with no real direction on how to grow her business. To avoid burnout, she searched for a coach for answers. After joining Club Wealth, she quickly learned the value of leverage in her business. Her best year as a solo agent was 42 closed transactions at $180,000 GCI (gross commission income), with no assistant. Now, she's a team leader with 5 expansion offices across central Texas, with over 40 agents and counting. In less than 2 years of coaching, Misti's production soared to over 1.5 million and 250 units sold. Misti is now a Club Wealth Coach and has a new work life balance and passion for helping others. She coaches other agents to do the same!

Jesse Zagorsky was born and raised in San Diego to parents who were "fixing and flipping" homes in the 1970's, before any one knew flipping houses was cool. He devours different sales techniques with a nerdy fascination, mixing them into his own style allowing him to connect with clients quickly and effortlessly. He is a creative, solution oriented, problem solving machine (and has repeated that affirmation to himself 1000's of times over his 15 years in real estate!).

CONTACT US:

Club Wealth®
P.O. Box 7617 Bonney Lake, WA 98391
206-300-1000

ClientCare@ClubWealth.com

Find Us On Social Media

Facebook: https://www.facebook.com/ClubWealth/?pnref=lhc

Twitter: https://twitter.com/clubwealth_

LinkedIn: https://www.linkedin.com/company/clubwealth/

Made in the USA
San Bernardino, CA
12 January 2020